HOR[S]

Town & Country

'WHEN THE SIREN SOUNDED'

HORSHAM, The War Years

For Barbara
Happy Birthday.

CLIFF WHITE

All my Love.
Robert xx.

Cliff White Publications
5 Mendip Crescent
Worthing, West Sussex BN13 2LT

13 MAY 1996

No reproduction without express permission
of author/publisher

Copyright © Cliff White 1995

First published in Great Britain 1995

ISBN 0 9525545 1 8

Published by
Cliff White Publications
5 Mendip Crescent, Worthing, West Sussex BN13 2LT

Typeset by
MusicPrint
228 Oving Road, Chichester West Sussex PO19 4EJ
(01243 528936)

Printed by
RPM Reprographics
2-3 Spur Road, Quarry Lane, Chichester West Sussex PO19 2PR
(01243 787077)

FOREWORD

by Dr. Frank Newby, OBE, JP, PhD, M.Ed

former Headmaster, Forest Community School

The story told in this book is not a dramatic one. It is a story which provides windows into the life of an old Sussex town and its neighbouring villages and hamlets during one of the most critical, dangerous and demanding periods in our country's history.

Those who lived through this period were conscious of a remarkable sense of community, common purpose and dogged self confidence which pervaded the nation and was reflected in the daily lives of its citizens.

When their successors learn about the great events of the Second World War and appreciate the scale of its consequences, it is important that they are also helped to appreciate the experiences of the ordinary people whose unsung contribution underpinned our national effort.

Our warm thanks are due to those who have shared their memories with us in this book.

Cliff White has earned our gratitude for drawing them together and undertaking the research out of affection for his adopted community.

For......

*Jill, for putting up with me
through six years of research,
Jane, Simon, David, Sarah and
Thomas for encouraging me to
finish the book......*

*To all my Horsham friends, just a
little token of my esteem and
affection for the town and the
area......*

*My Air Force friends, "PER
ARDUA AD ASTRA", or as we
used to say, "Forget the work,
let's go to the pictures!......*

CONTENTS

THE HOME FRONT

The Ritz, before the lights went out.

HORSHAM'S FIRST WAR CASUALTY

*Young Harry Jones from Southwater, a victim of the torpedo which
sank HMS Royal Oak at Scapa Flow. (Photo courtesy of May Jones)*

Horsham 1939/45

The Horsham of 1939 consisted of 14,900 inhabitants, a town much smaller than the one we now recognise. The shops were more diverse, there seemed to be a much greater choice and a wider variety of shops than we now enjoy. There were more cinemas, more dance halls and for the local lads... more pubs!

Bands played regularly both on The Carfax, in the Park and in the theatres. Transport was better, even during the wartime period public transport was frequent and reliable, often, due to enemy action rather later than advertised !

Traffic was otherwise light, children were able to play quite happily in the Crawley Road.

The first effect of the war on the town's the introduction of the "blackout" which, because of the towns strategic position was strictly imposed.

Life in the early days of 1939 seems to have gone on very much as normal, but the introduction of the evacuees made an impression on the local schools and community. Many schools accommodated children from the London area, together with the staff from the schools. The arrangement was for the local children to be taught in school in the morning and then being taken out in the afternoon for nature study or games. The evacuated children then reversed the timetable. Oxford Road then had the added disadvantage that they also had to find room for children from Victory Road School, after that school burnt down... not an act of war this one, but an over zealous central heating system!

The winter of 1940 was a very severe one, boys from Collyers Grammar School skated on Warnham Mill Pond, the Arun was frozen over and children skated to school. Photographs showing the winter scenes, taken by the West Sussex County at the time were banned by The Censor, for fear that the Germans would find out about the conditions. This little story was related to me by John Buchanan, then a young cub reporter on the paper, he found this attitude strange seeing that German aircraft were flying over every day and also taking photos! John

---

recalled that they were rationed to ten photographic plates per week, and because of the strict censorship rules then in force it was pointless taking pictures of any military action. Very few pictures appeared in the press of the damage from air raids or crashed British aircraft, some photographs did appear of the German casualties.

The war came in earnest to the town with the onset of what we now know as The Battle of Britain. Many of the aerial activities taking place over and around the town, Spitfire, Hurricane. Me 109, Heinkel being as common to the young aircraft spotter as the DC 10 or Jumbo is to the young lad of today.

The town had its Spitfire Fund and raised over £5,000, but few remember that we also had the only Hurricane Fund in the country, organised by Mrs Doll at Slinfold, her son Christopher then flying the said type, from Tangmere.

The Observer Corps, not yet Royal, played a major role during this period, The Horsham Centre being placed in the thick of the action, with its plot table and its accompanying posts reporting directly to Fighter Command Headquarters. What of the men and machines who fought over our heads, those who gave their lives, on both sides and those who survived, did we ever know them?

The end of 1940 saw the first major incident in the town when bombs were dropped and a large portion of Orchard Road was destroyed and a number of lives were lost, including sadly a young evacuee. This action had followed one in the small village of Colgate when a raider dropped a stick of bombs on the unsuspecting village but apparently returned and deposited a second for good measure, killing amongst others The Village Nurse and a young sixteen year old boy, out fire fighting - the ugly and unfair face of war.

Then to liven up the town the Canadian Army arrived!!!!! These young men, looking to the young girls of the town like Hollywood film stars, made an impression that lingers to this day. Many, one supposes, lost their lives or were captured on the Dieppe operation – memories of walking wounded, blue uniforms and The Base Hospital are still vivid. Depending on whom one talks to, they were either "rough" hard drinking fighting men or very kind hearted and generous, giving well remembered parties at Christmas for the children.

Taken all round, one gets the impression that these mainly French Canadian troops were looked upon very kindly and taken to the hearts of the people of Horsham. They were certainly well liked by the local firemen, it was the Canadians who donated the tea wagon to them. Up to that point the firemen had to scrounge tea and 'a wad' from whoever happened to be around at the time.

The evacuees began to drift home, raids became more spasmodic the occasional raider shooting up the town or dropping stray bombs from time to time and the build up to "D.Day" began. The area was once again alive with troops, tanks, equipment and more Canadians! Denne Park was used for training purposes, the ponds in the forest used to test equipment, Warnham Park full of vehicles of every type.

An advanced airfield was built at Coolham, quiet little Coolham! Spitfires, Mustangs racing off a metalized strip to support the landings in Normandy – things seemed to be looking up, – then came The Doodle Bugs! These were the pilotless aircraft, which had been expected, Hitler's secret weapon which would turn the tide in his favour.

Controversy still exists whether Horsham ROC or the Centre at Maidstone plotted the first Vl, but both in the end had more than their fair share of these missiles. Many more than one imagines fell in and around the area.

"D Day" is still remembered, the sky full of aircraft, as one eye witness said "a carpet in the sky" of aircraft, but still there were accidents. Four days after "D Day" two Dutch aircraft from Dunsfold collided over the town eight men lost their lives, fortunately for the town the two aircraft crashed on the outskirts of the town, one in Kerves Lane the other in the Worthing Road.

The toll of aircraft continued, a Halifax bomber burst into flames and plunged into the golf course at Mannings Heath, a variety of German aircraft crashed in the area, many of their crews being buried in the local cemetery.

Horsham had made its contribution to the war effort in many ways,

Lintotts Foundry being heavily involved, Warnham Brickyard working 24 hours a day, Thomas Keatings of Billingshurst not only working to capacity but finding time together with Horsham Rotary Club to set up a Volunteers Engineering Factory, called Horsham Patriot Engineers in which local people gave up their spare time to produce difficult and quite complex high quality components, some for Spitfires.

Eventually, the war in Europe came to an end, the troops came home, the Carfax was a sea of faces the bands played, they danced all night the lights came on again, not just in London but in Horsham as well – the flags flew, church bells rang out – but we still had rationing – children saw bananas, some for the first time – but for most, they had come through and for many people life could not be the same again, too many friends had been lost, too many battles had been fought and for the men returning from near and far the momentous events had taken their toll, many would not realise until fifty years later how great the toll on their emotions had been. Many of these I now have the pleasure of calling my friends and the stories that are to unfold are their stories told in the peace and tranquillity of their homes fifty years later.

FOOTBALL IN THE THIRTIES

EAST END RAMBLERS 1935/36
The lady in the centre is Mrs. Nellie Laughton, JP.

BLAKE HOUSE STOOLBALL TEAM, 1939
Back row:- Doreen Feist, Nora Holmes, Gwen Munday, Joy Loveridge
Middle row:- Peggy Moore, Iris Slaughter, Daphne ?
Front row:- Jean West, Daphne Bruford, Joyce Redman
(Photograph, Mrs. Joy Taylor)

THE WEEK WAR WAS DECLARED – SEPT. 1939.

The local newspaper of the day, was as today The West Sussex County Times, subtitled, The Horsham Advertiser and Sussex Standard, priced then at 2d. The 1st of September edition of 1939 ran a headline proclaiming, "Horsham is ready for national emergency".

It then went on, "Arrangements for Evacuees". Within the period of three hours today four train loads of evacuees from London are expected to arrive at Horsham Station, where they will be met by a fleet of specially chartered buses to carry them to distribution centres in the surrounding villages".

"Altogether, 10,000 evacuees will arrive at Horsham, Crawley and Billingshurst, of these 3,000 will be billeted on Horsham".

"Emergency Notice Boards" on which will be pinned up notices to provide residents with as much information as possible have been erected in three positions in Horsham".

"These are outside the U.D.C. Offices in North Street, in North Parade opposite Rushams Road and in The Carfax near the Bandstand".

"Volunteers are urgently required to fill sand bags and should report to the Council Depot in Stanley Street".

Together with these notices the newspaper still carried little items such as "Sunday evening drives from The Carfax. Cost one shilling, return. (5p) ... COMFY COACHES".

What could people see in the way of entertainment that September week fifty years ago? At the cinemas, The Ritz, now The Arts Centre, was showing from Sunday 3rd Sept. the film Fast and Loose, starring Robert Montgomery and the beautiful Rosalind Russell, with "Sword of Honour"; the supporting feature. At The Capital, for a four day run was a film called "Sargeant Madden", with Tom Brown and Alan Curtis, also on the same bill you could see George O'Brien in "Lawless Valley".

At the newly opened "Odeon" for four days only, you could see "Jesse James" in Technicolor! The "Stars" of this were Tyrone Power and a young Henry Fonda.

The Odeon Cinema carried a "Temporary Closed" notice in The County Times of September 15th, but reopened during the second week of the blackout, cinemas being allowed to open again in 80, so called "soft areas"!

The sad events carried by The County Times during this period included a fatal train crash at Horsham in which a shunter collided with stationary coaches in which Hugh John Tullett, aged 47 of Horsham was fatally injured. The other, which may have been Horsham's first military casualty of the war whilst on active service. The newspaper announced that October that 'Boy' Harry Jones the 17 year old son of Mr and Mrs. H. Jones of "Lorna Doone" at Southwater had been killed on The Royal Oak, a British Battleship which the Germans claimed to have torpedoed at anchor whilst in the supposed safety of Scapa Flow in Scotland.

Sport went on, although with great difficulty. On the 2nd of September Horsham Football Club played away to Newhaven in the Sussex County League and won 6-0. "Horsham 6-0 Victory"! the paper announced, "All the forwards score at Newhaven." "Cox and Broadley absent." The Horsham team on that Saturday, one of the last they would field in competition for nearly six years was, H.L. HEWITT; F. MEYER and H.G. CHARMER at full back, R. GRINSTEAD, J. WHENHAM, F. CARTER at half back and "up front", R. QUASNITSCHKA, N. TUCK, A.V. BROWNING, J. RIPLEY AND E.S. ELLIS. The scorers on that day were Browning (2), Tuck, Ripley, Ellis and Quasnischka. The report goes on to say that Horsham had great difficulty fielding a team, it included Fred Carter from the "A"s and Norman Tuck from East End Ramblers.

Cricket fared even worse, Horsham were due to play but no game took place. At the moment war had not yet been declared but the demands on the team members on military duties meant that most clubs found it difficult to field teams, and in the tense period secretaries thought it best to call off any games. On the 2nd, Horsham were due to play Worthing. The last recorded match before the war was between Horsham Thursday XI and a team called Mendicants, this took place on Thursday, August 31st. For the record the score and the Horsham Scorers were:-

HORSHAM THURSDAY.

L.T. WADDAMS	b. HALL	62.
S.P. BARNARD	b. HALL	68.
A.A. SHEPPARD	c. WHITE , b. HAWKES	0.
S. HORSCROFT	RUN OUT	6.
W.S. PARSONS	NOT OUT	9.
A.W. BUCK	NOT OUT	10.
	EXTRAS	14.
	TOTAL FOR 4 WICKETS	169.

T.C. CRIPPS, N. HUNT, H. MITCHELL, G.W. BRADLEY, S. HOBBS did not bat. Horsham Thursday won the game by 5 wickets.

On August 24th, Horsham Men beat Homefield Park of Worthing by 96 Shots to 84 Shots at Bowls, and the Ladies Section were beating Kingsway of Hove by 43 Shots to 39.

During the course of the next six years local sport was to continue in the face of serious difficulties, football was played, cricket continued, tennis and bowls flourished at one time even baseball was played.

Horsham F.C. continued to play local opposition, a few Cup games were played, many of the matches were against Army and R.A.F. teams. One of the first local teams to make an appearance towards the end of the war was one from the Evening Institute.

Cricket did its best to survive and did so quite well throughout the war, Horsham C.C. played a number of local sides and teams from Dorking and Worthing. Leather Hunters being one of the local sides. The first "County" game south of the Thames was played at Horsham towards the end of hostilities, when Sussex took on Northants. Even then the weather interfered, and the game was curtailed! Would you believe that it rained?

Bowls continued and seemed to grow in popularity and the Horsham Tennis Club opened its doors.

Golf at Mannings Heath continued unaffected, the Canadians making good use of the facilities, and a new professional, Mr Brooks was appointed, and endeared himself to the youngsters of the village by distributing some spare golf clubs.

CAPTAIN J. PUGH

The town's first Chief Warden and Chief of Civil Defence, Jos. Pugh.

A contemporary advertisement for Keatings Insectiside

August 1939   **44**

Sept. 1st. Owing to the fact that H.M. Government
considers it safer to evacuate the L.C.C.
Children before war is declared, 93
Children from Jessop Rd. School, Herne
Hill and the following Staff have been
received into Colgate.   Staff 8.
    Miss House H.T.   Reg No. $\frac{12}{1971}$.   Infants.
    Mr. Gould. C.   "   1899   "
    Miss Hames. C   " $\frac{877}{03}$ "
    Mrs. Holliday C   " $\frac{03}{1171}$ "
    Miss Hughes. C   "   ?   "
    Miss Haynes C   "   ? ⎫
    Mr. Hughes. C   "   ? ⎬ J.M. School.
                                  ⎭
Sept. 4. Miss House and her staff came to school
to discuss plans.
    6. Miss House and her staff came to
school to discuss plans.
    11. Miss House + staff + Children came to
school today and an informal
meeting was held to enable both
schools to plan a scheme + group the
children into classes.
    Mrs. M. V. Thomas The correspondent came
                                        also.

The Early Months: Rationing and the Blackout.

Horsham folk in common with the rest of the population were prepared, up to a point for the onset of the war.

Gas warfare was expected and gas masks had been issued as early as 1938, every one was instructed to carry them, mostly in the cardboard box that had been provided, with a string attached looking something like a ladies handbag.

Special gas masks for babies were issued, Disney characters being used to make them less frightening. Schools carried out gas mask drills.

Cigarette cards of the time issued "sets" devoted to "Air Raid Precautions" which included instructions in the use of gas masks and respirators. Card No.27 issued by Wills showed how to fit a civilian respirator explaining how to adjust the face mask, and stating that "This respirator will be issued to the public."

Immediately following The Prime Ministers broadcast on BBC Radio, no television, not for the general public at this time, there followed a whole series of "Important Government Announcements" one of which concerned gas warfare and ran, "If poison gas has been used you will be warned by means of hand rattles. If you hear hand rattles do not leave your shelters until the poisoned gas has been cleared away. Hand bells will be used to tell you when there is no longer any danger from poisoned gas". The broadcast then went on to give general instructions to the public.

"Keep off the streets as much as possible, to expose yourself unnecessarily adds to the danger" Carry your gas mask with you always".

One memory that stays with me still today is of going to Woolworths and having an Identity Disc engraved and having to wear it on my wrist. Quite recently I mentioned to my mother that I could still remember the disc, she proceeded to produce, from an old drawer a scratched silver bracelet, with a very faint inscription C.H.White TMDEl90/5!

One of the announcements concerned children, there must have been great anxiety for their welfare. "Make sure that you and every member of your household, especially children able to run about, have on them, their names and addresses, clearly written, do this either on an envelope or something like a luggage label, not on an odd piece of paper which might get lost. Sew the label on to your children's clothes where they cannot pull it off".

The announcement went on and stated "That places of entertainment would close forthwith, but some in quieter areas would be allowed to reopen". This appears to have been the case in Horsham, the cinemas may have closed but it seems now that most reopened very shortly. Indeed reading reports in the local press, the places of entertainment flourished.

"Black Out" came into force immediately and locally was very strictly enforced— "Put that light out" soon became a household phrase. Wardens patrolled the streets and checked on windows in factories, offices, shops and houses, it became a criminal offence and people were fined. The local village policeman at Mannings Heath was P/C Joe Lemm, he recalled that the only problems that he had seemed to be at The Vicarage and in the end had to summons the vicar!

Don Bateman was a young schoolboy in those days, Don and his family still live in the village. Don remembers that "We experienced for the first time, what they called "Black Out".

"Black Out consisted of no street lights, every window in the house had to be covered so there was no visible light outside and all cars had to wear special headlight hoods, so that there was only a small amount of light emitted. This caused problems because there were many accidents, pedestrians in collision with vehicles, people walked into objects like lamp posts, and my own brother on one occasion ended up in a ditch". The problem of the immovable object was helped somewhat when the local councils painted white lines and stripes on kerbs, trees, lamp posts and walls, in some cases the remains can still be seen today.

Mrs Vincent from Horsham, observed "That the blackout was very strictly observed, no street lights of course, all cycle lights had to have the top half of the glass obscured. I remember returning home one afternoon in winter when I was stopped by the warden Mr Piggot, because the lamp fixed to the pram I was pushing was not shaded!"

Mrs Vincent went on to say that "Even babies were issued with gas masks, unlike those of adults, theirs were very large and covered most of the baby, they were much too large to carry around, so if you went out with the baby you were advised to carry a blanket and a bottle of water as a sort of temporary aid".

For the local shopkeepers the blackout was an additional burden, somehow they had to rig up a double door, so that when customers entered as little light as possible escaped.

Mr and Mrs Leslie Laker had an outfitters shop in West Street and Mrs Laker recalled to me evening drives in the dark to suppliers in London, returning in the pitch black and without the aid of either street lights or sign posts, they also having been taken away. Queues formed outside the shop whenever "black out" material was in stock, many of the local girls using it for other purposes than that which it was designed! The price, 3/11 pence a yard, today's money, about twenty new pence!

To the Lakers these trips to London became an adventure, not knowing when you set out if your supplier was still in business, had they survived The Blitz? If so, where were they trading? Leslie Laker was at that time doubling as a "Special Constable" at Langhurst the Defence Establishment working in shifts either in the shop when he had time off, or at Langhurst where many of the "funnies" as Monty called them were being developed, flame throwing tanks and the pipe line FIDO being among them. Many people will recall that this establishment went on long after the war, I remember it for being the place to take my children on Bonfire Night!

Food rationing did not begin on the declaration of war but in January 1940, but for many, oranges, bananas had already disappeared, Don Bateman remembers "that we were also experiencing for the first time, what they called food rationing. Rationing meant that each family was allocated so many Ration Books with coupons in these books enabling our families and parents to buy food. Food was difficult to get hold of, I cannot relate exactly what the rations were but I think it was something like 2oz of butter per person per week, but I may be wrong. But for a little boy at the start of the war, I was six years of age in 1939, one can imagine at times we were rather hungry!"

"We never got to the state of starvation, as many people dug up their gardens and well tended lawns and planted vegetables. These vegetables were always in great demand.

My father, in our rear garden always kept chickens, so we were never short of eggs".

The "rations" to which Don referred were, per person,

> 2oz of Butter.
>
> 2oz of Fat.
>
> 2oz of Cheese.
>
> 4oz of Meat.
>
> 4oz of Sugar.

Sweets were on D and E Coupons. Jam was at times rationed.

NO Grapefruits, Lemons, Oranges or Bananas. Eggs were available sometimes dried. Offal from the butchers could be obtained. Everyone had to register with a Butcher or a Grocer. Clothing went on to rationing later in the war.

Shopkeepers today spend much time working on VAT returns, Leslie Laker remembers spending hours sorting out clothing coupons, things haven't changed much!

Everywhere the housewife was being asked to make sacrifices The Ministry of Food was constantly invoking her to greater efforts "coupons" later became "points".

Sainsburys advertised "That you can obtain all rationed, registered and free provisions groceries and meats under one roof. No rushing about in black outs and winter weather".

Shelters were being built or delivered, for many residents this would mean an indoor "Morrison" shelter, quite a large metal construction that in most cases filled the room or for others an outdoor "Anderson" shelter dug into the back garden. The problem in the winter was keeping them dry, most seemed to fill very quickly with water.

The Schools had to do the best they could, it would be some time before the brick shelters were built, indeed Colgate Village School was still waiting long after the village was bombed, some parents refused to send their children to school until these had been installed. The local Headteacher entered into a long dialogue with the County Council imploring them to start the work. At Mannings Heath things were no better, so the parents took things into their own hands and dug an outdoor shelter. At Denne Road the pupils went into the Church or hid under the desks! In most of the local Schools temporary shelters were provided by reinforcing the cloakrooms and placing sand bags around windows and doors. One well remembered custom and one enjoyed by the children was during an air raid they were given free biscuits by the teachers! Many of the outdoor brick shelters survived in school playgrounds long after war finished, I remember that in my days at Oxford Road we used the shelters to store furniture, that must have been in the early sixties.

Public shelters were provided in strategic places in the town, much of my generations early courting took place in them!

My own memory of them is of a different nature. They seemed to be the breeding ground for lice and fleas, most evenings on return from school my mother combed my hair with the dreaded "nit comb".

Shelter at Climping C. of E. School

PUT THAT LIGHT OUT!

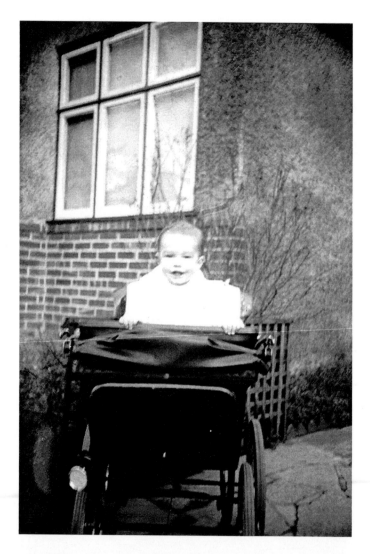

*This wartime picture is one of Mrs. Vincent's pram with the unshaded
lamp. The lamp can clearly be seen low down on the left of the pram and
clearly shows why Mr. Piggot, the Warden, was concerned! The negative
was kindly loaned to me by Mrs. Vincent of Highlands Avenue.*

The Home Front. What were they doing??

It may now seem very strange to recount that for most people that I have interviewed over the past four years, the declaration of war came as no surprise, unlike some of the more recent conflicts in The Falklands and The Gulf. It would seem that even by today's media coverage that the Government propaganda machine had gone into overdrive. Gasmasks, Identity Cards and Numbers had all been issued, indeed if you ask anyone who lived through those times to quote their Identity No. like any ex-service man it will be given without a moments hesitation....mine?...TMDE 190/5! Air raid sirens were in position and had been tested as had the "Blackout", evacuees and evacuation had been organised. Although the announcement was eventually broadcast on the Sunday most people had expected it on the Saturday.

So what were the good folk of Horsham doing on that fateful Sunday in September 1939? Mr Ron Taylor and Mr Peter Wilkins were Choir Boys at The Parish Church and Ron remembered on "That particular Sunday I was at the 11 o'clock Service and because of the imminence of some sort of conflict the T.A. and all sorts of people were at the Service. It was announced by Canon Lee that war had been declared and all those in uniform were marched out, then we were sent home, the whole of the congregation was told to file out." Peter remembers being sent home and in the afternoon going into the Park with his mother.

On a lighter note Mr Ken Lane recalls being in the bathroom at the time, the siren going and his mother crying out that "WE shall all be killed in our beds!". Mr and Mrs Laker, went with their daughter to the coast for the day. Syd Weller went with a pal to Haywards Heath.

One young man from Slinfold, Christopher Doll listened to the news and by a quarter past eleven he and his father left by car so that he could report for training with the R.A.F. at Reading. Christopher reported on the 3rd of September instead of the 11th and went on to fly throughout the war on Hurricanes and Spitfires mainly from various airfields in Sussex, having a number of "kills" to his credit and a D.F.C. by the end of hostilities.

Another family on holiday was Mr and Mrs Percy Spriggs, on the Norfolk Broads and had to return home. Mr. Ron Woolven was at Roffey Institute rehearsing with a band, his future wife, to be, Margaret, twelve at the time was at home with her mother and grandmother, they all began to cry and her mother got the gas-masks out, and forgot all about an apple-pie in the oven! Mr Stan Parsons recalled, "I remember that day very well, my mother lived in a flat over the shop at that time, I was out in the front when the siren went off, my mother called out in a state of great alarm. I didn't know what it was all about and I said. Oh don't worry it's only a practise, I didn't know if it was and I still don't know!".

Frank Holmes was on duty in his Signal Cabin, Arthur Merritt was with his ship in Scapa Flo, with young Harry Jones keeping him company on another famous battleship HMS Royal Oak. John Buchanan listened to the news on the wireless in his parents home at Southwater.

Mrs Joy Taylor, then young Joy Loveridge recalled "I had taken my two year old cousin out in a pram, we lived then in Forest Road and I'd walked down to the houses opposite Roffey Church, the pram I remember, was probably my own doll's pram!

"My aunt hadn't been married long and her husband was in the Territorials' and had been called up straight away, and she was sitting weeping listening to the wireless, then my aunt said "You'd better get that little boy home." I started walking and had got half way up Forest Road when along comes my brother on his bike. He said "You'd better get home quick the war has been declared". We were hurrying along the road when the siren went and he shouted "Hurry up or they will bomb you!"

Most people have a clear recollection of the siren sounding that morning, shortly after Mr Chamberlain's broadcast and most now believe that it was a false alarm, or a practise. In fact it is now thought to have been a French aircraft which had not filed a flight plan and was therefore considered to be "hostile" when detected. The offending aircraft had passed over No.1 Observer Post at Maidstone but as no one could recognise it, the sirens sounded, not just in Horsham but over a great deal of the South of England, it was a sound the people of the town would soon be familiar with!

A strange footnote to this story concerns Collyers Grammar School and a party of Masters and boys who were on the Continent that August. Mr Ken Lane, then a young Collyerian, was with this party and recalled that they had gone to the Continent via France and Switzerland and because of the imminence of war had to be ushered home rather quickly. He also thought that they had been to Germany. A member of staff at Collyers at the time was Mr Austin Willson, who later kindly related the events for me.

"The Collyers School Journey on The Continent was led by my late dear friend Andrew Henderson. It hurried home in August 1939 and was certainly **not** from Germany, but was from Switzerland. "Hendy", as we called him, would not have ventured into Germany as he was in bad odour with the authorities there. A few years previously there had been an "exchange" system under which we took boys one year and then were guests of The Hitler Youth and they sent a similar party the next year to us. In about 1937, when "Hendy" received the names of the German party it turned out that they were sending adults and so we refused to accept them of course. Afterwards Hendy always maintained that if the Germans had invaded in 1940, he would have been high on their list of "Wanted Persons"!

Tony Wales recalls coming back from the 10 o'clock Mass at St Johns' and hearing the broadcast, my mother practically had hysterics and I remember saying with all the wisdom of a 14 year old, "It'll soon be over, it won't last long!" We had been expecting it, there had been manoeuvres in Horsham the year before, and thinking in my stupidity "I hope there's a war it could be rather fun". Of course, I didn't think that later on. My father took it all terribly seriously and completely sealed off our front room to make it gas proof, or he thought he had! The first few raids, which were probably false alarms we would solemnly go into this room, sit down and close everything up. Of course this didn't last long, just the first few weeks of the war."

Although we can smile now, when that first siren sounded a great many people all over the country donned their gas masks, even my own grandmother in Cleethorpes, something the family never allowed her to forget!

And so it was that on a sunny warm September Sunday war came to Horsham, people walking and like Bill Sampson on his bike going to report to his place of work looked up to the sky for the first sign of the aircraft which were to play such a major part in their lives in the coming years.

THE TOWN'S DEFENCES

The Dragon's Teeth

Still visible in 1993 in the Causeway near the Museum, the positions where the Tank Barricades were to be placed in the event of an invasion – happily never needed!

Tank Traps, or "Dragon's Teeth" made an appearance, and the remains can still be seen today near the Museum in The Causeway. The Arun was widened and strengthened for defence against tanks and large stretches of the town had barbed wire entanglements installed. The Local Defence Volunteers was formed, together with The Auxiliary Fire Brigade and a professional Observer Corps with full time staff came in to being.

Movement for the individual became more difficult, after the fall of France, trips to the coast being out of the question, various areas became 'no go areas', particularly when the threat of invasion became real. To visit Brighton as late as 1943 special passes were being issued. Nellie Jackson, then a young 'plotter' with The Observer Corps had to have one of these passes to visit Brighton, and fifty years later was able to produce it for me!

Holidays were out of the question, unless you had a relative who lived in the country or if you were really lucky on a farm! Generally, for the average family holidays were spent at home, indeed one of the most famous wartime posters asked the question, "Is Your Journey Really Necessary?"

The local councils did their bit by organising events during the holiday periods, one such was a large event in the Park in which the Fire Brigade took part, displaying their prowess and equipment. The Horsham Hospital ran a number of very well attended Fetes, one with the help of the Fire Brigade raised over a thousand pounds in a day!

Evenings were spent at home listening to the 'wireless' to such programmes as 'ITMA", Bandwagon, and one surprisingly popular programme, 'The Brains Trust'. The children had "Uncle Mac" and Childrens' Hour, but no television, although a television transmission was shown in the pavilion of the Horsham Football Club to the ARP Wardens. The cinema was of course very popular, it became for most people an escape from the dreary day to day existence they faced.

The 'Phoney War' arrived and the good people of Horsham waited, they didn't have long to wait, the 'Sitzcrieg' as the Germans called it would soon be over, the winter of that year was one of the coldest on record, 1940 had come in with a chilling threat. The children skated on

Warnham Mill Pond and the County Times photographers took beautiful pictures that the censor would not allow to be printed!

I asked a number of people if they could recall a typical weeks menu during this period and Mrs Shirley Glaysher gave me an insight. On Sunday it was probably a joint, Monday was cold meat, also washday! Tuesday 6 pence of scrag end, stew. Wednesday would be either mince, sausages or rissoles then liver or steak on Thursday. Friday was usually fish day in most homes and Saturday would be corned beef or sausages. Fish and chips were from Pizers' in Elm Grove. In many households if you were lucky you might acquire a rabbit. 'Dig For Victory' became a slogan and parks and gardens all over the town were dug up for allotments, although as Don Bateman said things were difficult but we did not starve.

In the villages many people kept livestock, most were used to growing their own vegetables so were perhaps better suited than many 'townies'.

I do recall that after a visit to the Doctor he wrote a note to my parents which stated the word malnutrition, and we all thought that it was some kind of disease!

"Dragon's Teeth" return, Chesworth Farm 1993.

The Look outs!

A "JIM CROW" AT HORSHAM

Looking over Horsham from the Crow's Nest which has been recently constructed on the roof of Messrs. Tanner and Chart's premises, Middle-street, at the instigation of Mr. Don Chart. A triangle of stone at each corner makes it possible for the "look-out" to hide his head, should there be any flying shrapnel.—"W.S.C.T." photo.

The Observer Corps constructed a number of Posts in and around the town, this is one of the early models! They were open to the elements and were linked to the Centre in Denne Road at the Drill Hall, this one did not have the equipment that became common later in the war. This one perched above the town, another was in Depot Road, where the allotments now are, opposite the girls school.

The visiting pass that was required.

From :—   Headquarters, No. 2 Group, Form 348 (Medium)
                Royal Observer Corps.

To :—   Head Observer 2/M.1.
                Copy to Group Officer, No. 5 Section.
Date :—   W/Obs. N.A. Jackson.
                19th June, 1944.
Ref.:—   G2/706/1/ORC.

Subject:-   Visits to Posts.

         It is requested that the undermentioned member of No. 2 Group Centre may visit your Satellite Post, 2/W.2. on Wednesday, 21st June, 1944.

         W/Obs. N.A. Jackson. D.R.12. No. 082750.
         W/Obs. J. Warland. D.R.12. No. 100682.

           O.T. Jurek
           Obs/Lieut.
         for Group Commandant.

(32585) Wt. 32373—O.1971 500m 11/42 D.L. G. 51

The Visiting Pass that Nellie Jackson required to visit Hove as late as Wednesday, 21st June 1944, two weeks after 'D.Day'.

The Horsham Defences in 1940

This remarkable photograph was taken by a young Tony Wales with the camera that had been purchased by his aunt from Woolworths. The camera cost the princely sum of two shillings and sixpence (12½p), but because of Woolworths policy of "Nix over Six", or nothing over sixpence, it had to be purchases in five separate pieces!

The photograph shows some of the concrete road blocks which were constructed around Horsham. Tony cannot be certain but believes that he took it in the Guildford Road, but most certainly in early 1940. The original photographs were very small in size, about one inch by one and a half inches. Having shown the photographs to Frank Holmes he was inclined to agree with Tony Wales. Frank thought that it was taken near Farthings Hill, in the Guildford Road, near to where a new roundabout has been constructed.

> ## LORRY CRASHES INTO CONCRETE BLOCK
> ---
> ### Safety First Medallist Fined for Careless Driving

HORSHAM URBAN DISTRICT COUNCIL.

Urgent Appeal to all Horsham Residents!

FOR IMMEDIATE AND EARNEST ATTENTION!

How to Protect your Home, your Business, your Town.

An Appeal for Personal Service.

This is an urgent call to National Service.

Under any heavy air attack, your home, business premises, and city or town are seriously threatened by fire. The enemy generally begins his raids by dropping great numbers of incendiary bombs. The fire brigade want your help to deal with them.

Every one of those bombs, if it starts a fire that takes hold, not only destroys a house or building, but makes a target for high explosives.

The incendiaries must be watched for, "spotted" as soon as they land, and dealt with before they can start a fire that takes hold. In this work every household, every shop, store, office, institution and factory must play its part

Householders.

Every group of houses should have its fire party, every party keeping watch over its own group of houses, their gardens, and the roadway, the members making their own arrangements to watch in turn during alerts.

If you are the head of a household, call your family together and make up your minds which of you will volunteer for membership of the fire party, and will take training. One at least should serve. If two or three can do so, all the better. It lessens the burden on others, and helps to make up for empty houses and for households where all the members are elderly or infirm, or are night workers.

Women, as well as men, are members of the Civil Defence Force. Women should consider whether they can become members of fire parties. Many thousands will no doubt do so. We are all of us in this fight for liberty and decency.

Businessmen, Shopkeepers, Employers.

If yours is a business subject to the Fire Watchers Order, you are bound to have someone on watch, but in addition you should have on your premises each night fire parties proportionate to their size ready to deal with incendiaries as they fall. You must be sure that no part of your premises could catch fire without it being known at once, and without someone being there to deal with the fire.

Even though your staff may be smaller than the minimum of 30 covered by the Fire Watchers Order, you still need a fire party to take turns going on watch, and all to be there at call to deal with incendiaries.

If your staff is too small to provide a fire party alone, and if yours is a one or two-man business, you should combine with your neighbours making arrangements to keep watch in turn. Those who are not on watch being on their own premises, ready for a call.

To all Householders, Businessmen, Shopkeepers, Other Employers.

See that your house, shop or office building:—

(1) is easy to enter quickly if a fire breaks out.

(2) has a rake, to drag a bomb off the roof or away from anything inflammable.

(3) has a supply of sand and water handy, and where they are easily seen.

(4) has a ladder available or nearby.

(5) has its attic or top floor cleared of inflammable material.

Your Warden or the Fire Brigade will tell you how to set about getting stirrup pump and sandbags, and anything else you want to know.

ALL FIRE PARTIES.

Get a stirrup pump if you can.

Get two or three sandbags, three parts filled, which are very useful for smothering bombs, or use any receptacle which will contain earth or sand.

This is URGENT work for the Defence of your home or your business, and the community in which you live.

ACT AT ONCE!

FORM YOUR FIRE PARTY IMMEDIATELY and consult if necessary the Chief Officer of the Fire Brigade, Mr. Denny, who has been appointed to co-ordinate the various measures to ensure efficiency of the Town's Fire Fighting arrangements.

FALL IN, THE FIRE PARTIES!

THE TOWN'S DEFENCES

Mr. Paul Lansberry stands outside one of the Pillboxes which were constructed along the banks of the River Arun to deter tanks. The top picture gives some idea of the strength of these structures and in the lower he is holding one of the oak piles which were driven into the bank of the river; some of these can still be seen today.

Horsham Urban District Council Civil Defence.   Rescue, First-aid and Decontamination Parties.

October 1944.

THE DEFENDERS – THE ARMY MOVE IN!

The town became once again an Army Garrison, as it had during other periods, camps sprang up all over the place, most of the large country houses were requisitioned, either by the Canadians or the British.

The Bomb Disposal Unit were still in Broadbridge Heath until well after the war, but during the wartime period it had been home to a Searchlight Unit, the girls remember going along to dances held at the camp. Roffey Hospital became The Base Hospital for the Canadians, but it also handled the lads from Faygate and it was to here that the injured were taken after the Orchard Road bombing. A number of injured pilots and aircrew, including Bob Heseltine spent time in the wards after baling out or being rescued.

Many local people recall the 'boys in blue', not R.A.F. but Canadian Blue, walking around the town. These were the lads who had been wounded at Dieppe, and they wore a distinctive blue uniform whilst convalescing.

Tony Wales 'snapped' these troops on the march, in the Bishopric in 1940. Where they are from or to where they are marching is a mystery.

I have it on good authority that they are British and could be Royal Engineers. It was obviously warm as they are 'shirt sleeve order'. As an ex-airman, I'm not well up on 'brown jobs' so perhaps the reader can help.

EVACUATION.

Who'll give a promise to keep this child safe?

This child's home is in the city. Up to the present his home has been safe. But let us face it : one of these days his home may be a ruin. There is no excuse for feeling falsely secure because nothing has happened yet. The danger of air-raids is as great now as it has ever been.

The Government is arranging to send this child, and some hundred thousands of others, to safety if raiders come. Each will need a home. Only one household in five is caring for these children now. Volunteers are urgently needed. Plans must be made well ahead. There must be no hitch, no delay, in settling the children in safety. Here is your chance to help.

You can if you wish make an immediate contribution to this safety scheme. Many households have been looking after evacuated children for six months now. They will be grateful for a rest. If you can take over one of these children, you will be doing a very neighbourly deed and helping greatly in the nation's defence.

To enrol as a host of a child now or in the future, or to ask any questions about the scheme, please get in touch with your local Authority.

The Minister of Health, who has been entrusted by the Government with the conduct of evacuation, asks you urgently to join the Roll of those who are willing to receive children Please apply to your local Council.

THEY CALL IT EVACUATION !

"They call it 'vacuation", or so one of the songs from Lionel Bart's "Blitz" proclaims. The West Sussex County Times reported on September 1st, 1939 that up to 3,000 evacuees were to be expected and that special trains and coaches had been organised and billets were to be found. The Headmaster at Oxford Road Boys' School wrote in the School Log Book on the first of Sept. "School opened as Evacuation Centre No.1. First Evacuees received, all the Staff employed at The Centre. As instructed the School closed for a week and reopened again on 12th September." At Colgate School, Miss Storr, The Headteacher, entered in the Log Book, "Owing to the fact that H.M. Government consider it safer to evacuate L.C.C. children before the War is declared, 93 children from Jessops Road School, Herne Hill, together with their Staff have been received in Colgate." Miss Storr then goes on to give the names of the Staff evacuated with the children. By the 18th of September, Miss Storr and Miss House, the Headteacher from Jessops Road, had worked out a temporary timetable:-

(A). School Session. 9 to 12 or 12.45 to 3.45pm.
(B). Recreational Session. 9 to 11 or 1.45 to 3.45pm.

"Lunch time is 11am to 1.45pm and is to be taken in The Village Hall. Colgate School and Jessop Road are working alternate sessions in Colgate School." By the beginning of November the schools had combined with Miss Storr as Headteacher, the School being organised into six classes.

Oxford Road had absorbed two schools, The Tavistock School, (Boys), Croydon and Wimbledon Central Boys School and like Colgate had introduced a two tier system of education. In October the Log Book records "a system of work to be done at home (when the weather prevents outdoor work) has been started."

Collyers Grammar School had accepted pupils from Mercers' School, and this was quite an amicable arrangement. Roffey had its share. All Saints as it was in those days took in children from Effra School, Brixton, and these were thought by the locals to be very rough! The girls were housed in Roffey Institute and the boys in the Working Mens' Club.

The teaching staff kept to their own pupils, but eventually, as the children filtered back to London the schools combined in the Working Mens' Club, half the Staff moving back to Effra Road with the children.

'Trish Chanter went to school with these children and has the feeling that they were not very welcome in Roffey. "Their background was poor and some were very badly dressed. They, in turn didn't like the country very much, some had never seen a cow , sheep or pigs, and the fact that there was little traffic about didn't help!"

Broadbridge Heath School also had evacuees, these were from Streatham High School and the Village Hall was utilised by evacuees and so was the Cricket Club Pavillion.

Sheila Comper remembers waking up to find lines of people in the street, mothers and children all waiting for a foster home. These she recalled were all Jewish children. One young boy with bright red hair, a German Jew, David Meidner stayed with them, whilst his mother remained in Golders Green.

There was another side to the evacuee story, the local children often got their own back, Mrs and Mr Ron Taylor remember "That at school when the evacuees were absorbed into the school, they tended to get blamed for everything. If things went wrong they blamed the evacuees, because they were different and they spoke differently."

"There were always jokes about them, they used to say that if they found a milk bottle or two they had found a cows nest! All sorts of silly things like that, rather cruel really."

It must have been a difficult situation for all concerned, the sudden transformation from city to agricultural environment, all for most within one day.

What did the evacuees think of Sussex and the inhabitants of Horsham?

Mr Terry Briscoe came as an evacuee after surviving being bombed out twice by the Luftwaffe, the family moving from Brixton to the peace of Rusper village.

Terry recalled "We came in October, 1940. It had been a good summer and a long one, but we were not one of the original evacuees, and to my knowledge myself and my brother were the only evacuees at Rusper

School. Dad moved us in a baker's lorry, it was a flat top and you could put up a canvas, something like a stage coach with canvas covers to it. I sat on an arm chair facing backwards, and as it was open they put some iron hoops stuck into the floor on either side then dragged a canvas top over in case it rained over the furniture. I suppose it seemed a long way, but when you are only seven years old it's exciting and the time passes very quickly. We didn't know where we were going, we knew we were going to the country and we actually landed up in a farmhouse with these weird looking animals with things on their heads! Some idiot told us that that was where the milk came out, we didn't believe them of course!"

"I'd never been to the country, I was a Cockney boy really used to playing in the streets of London. I was scared of the animals, I've just about got over it, but I still can't face a bull. They had these geese on the farm, they were frightening because they put their heads low to the ground and hissed like a snake and they chased you, at least the gander did!"

In 1994 I had the pleasure of visiting Rusper school and was given an opportunity to read the School Log Book. Terry wasn't the only evacuee at the School, they took in over 30 children from London.

At Oxford Road School for Boys teaching at the time was the late Harold Champion. I think it is fair to say that all those who taught with him, myself included, and all the children that he taught over the years will always remember him and his Sherlock Holmes stories with great affection. Harold began his education at Oxford Road School, won a Scholarship on to Collyers Grammar School and then went on to Teacher Training at Oxford and by one of those twists of fate returned to teach at Oxford Road just before the war .... English and Gardening! Harold was one of those teachers who had to cope the best they could with part-time schooling. What, I asked did you do with the children when the school was occupied?

"Gardening, P.E., Swimming when the weather permitted and lots of nature walks in the countryside or up Denne Hill."

I wonder what the modern educational administrator would make of all this?

Joy Loveridge, now Mrs Joy Taylor, enjoyed her forays into the countryside, she recalled "another part of the time when there wasn't any room for you to have lessons you went on nature walks, you gathered various plants. The Teachers always had a list of what was useful for the "war effort". "You gathered Coltsfoot and you gathered Sphagnum Moss which they told you was used for wadding, for bullets or shells." "On other occasions when there wasn't room for you in the classrooms you spent the time taking out the twigs from the moss, cleaning it to send away."

Even in those early years of the war the children were contributing to the war effort and for most of these children it has to be remembered the war brought a normal education to a full stop.

The young men, such as Ronnie Rivaz at Collyers and Les Hebden at Oxford Road and Frank Cordell at All Saints' at Roffey would soon be in uniform and their places taken, in the main by female supply teachers, many being brought back out of retirement, who strove to maintain some sort of standard of education against appalling shortages, and it must be said before "Equal Pay".

Summer holidays for the schools were at this time staggered, some staff taking their holidays in shifts.

Air Raids during normal school periods were also very trying, all are recorded minutely in the Oxford Road School Log Book by the new Headmaster, Mr Clfford Hawkins. During severe air raids the children and staff remained in the shelters long after the end of school. The staff having to wait either for the "All Clear" or for the parents to collect the children.

An interesting entry in the Oxford Road Log Book on 2nd April 1940 states "I Clifford James Hawkins, Trained Certificated Teacher, commenced duties as Headmaster this day. On Roll..........136 Present.........113.

Schooling for the children was not only disrupted, but, unless you were lucky enough to be at a grammar school you left at fourteen. No examinations for those at Oxford Road.

Later towards the end of the war a Junior Technical School was opened, teaching the skills that would be needed after the war was over. In this period the children left the school normally at the end of the week in which they were fourteen, no specialised careers service for them!

EVACUATION: THE TEACHER'S STORY.

I had over the years met and interviewed a number of the youngsters who were evacuated to the town's schools and some had enjoyed the experience and stayed in the town. But what of the teachers who came with them, did they also enjoy the experience?

To find out I visited an old friend whom I had known in my years as a teacher in Horsham, Mrs Una Penny. Many people will recall not only Una, but also her late husband Ralph. Ralph Penny also came to Horsham to teach the evacuees, but unlike his wife he did not come with the original group, but came at a later period. He later joined the Royal Air Force and after the war returned to the town and became Deputy Headmaster at Forest School. I asked Una what was it like to be sent to this sleepy little market town in Sussex from the hustle and bustle of London?

"We had little choice as a teacher, you were sent. They said "You are going" there was no choice. Of course you wondered where you were going. When we arrived Miss Lyon, who lived off Kings Road, was in charge of putting people here, there and everywhere. She was the Billeting Officer I suppose?

I don't know how many children we brought out, there must have been three or four hundred of us I should think. They didn't all stay for very long, but most of those that stayed actually stayed the whole time and some are still in the town."

"I started off teaching at Victory Road, before the fire, then after it burnt down we went to The High School and Hurst Road, now The Art School. When we first arrived I and two others of the Staff were out at Coolham, at the farm there, we were only there for a few weeks then we managed to get into the town. The children were all over the shop, quite a few were at Shipley, Hilaire Belloc had one out at Kings Farm, he was very good. She was a girl and she was out there quite a while."

"After Hurst Road I went to Roffey School, but I didn't get on with the Headmaster, he was the only one that I quarrelled with! He didn't like evacuees and he didn't like me! He didn't approve of it, I think part of the trouble was the salary?"

"In those days there were 'scales', and as a Londoner I earned more than the locals did, and this was a great source of irritation. There were four scales, 'London, Kent and Middlesex' were the two top scales, and I think the locals were on Scale Two?

While I was at Roffey they were going to take the Seniors away and Mr Hawkins offered me a job. I had always taught boys and as they would be taken to Oxford Road Boys' I was rather pleased. After a while we were integrated, as far as the boys were concerned, but 'Joe Soap' still had her 'London Allowance'! I was paid by The London County Council until after the war stopped."

"I liked Horsham, I was intrigued with it, mind we were not accepted. Ralph and I had bicycles and we used to take the boys out for cycle rides at the weekends, but some of the people who they were billeted with got quite crusty about it. They said you shouldn't take these children out cycling you don't know your way around here! No we were 'outsiders' we made friends with people, but I was aware we were outsiders. But now it's cosmopolitan. It was definitely 'Them and Us!' but I will say that I was very fortunate in the people that I met and adopted me when Ralph was away during the war. There wasn't a lot of half time schooling, not as far as I was concerned, we managed , we coped, but it was only for the first few months, because when Ralph came over and was at the Cricket Pavilion, they used to take the boys up Denne Hill, there was far more bracken then than now, and Ralph used to come back and say "You know you can't find the little buggers there's so much camouflage"

"In those days there was discipline and you had a timetable and you kept to it. We weren't too disrupted by air raids during the day, but I remember at night on Fire Duty at the High School we were often disrupted. I remember the Science Mistress had a goat and that we had to go and get this goat in!"

THE HEADMASTER

Mr. Clifford Hawkins, The Headmaster at Oxford Road School for Boys throughout most of the wartime period. He developed the School and saw its transfer in 1954 to Comptons Lane. He will be remembered for his love of sport, he introduced rugby to the boys and was himself a keen golfer, and it was on the golf course that he collapsed and died.

(Photo, Forest Comm. School)

THE VICAR

Canon Lee, who was in charge at the Parish Church during the war. It was Canon Lee who announced to the congregation on that Sunday in September that war had been declared.

(Photo, courtesy of Mrs. E. Farley)

In my own travels while researching the story a number of people can remember a very smart Mrs Penny and her racing bicycle, Don Bateman recalled how chic she was, so I put the question to her.

"Talking about a smart Mrs Penny one former colleague moaned that when Mrs Penny comes into Assembly the girls all turn round to see what she is wearing, she said that upset the whole Assembly!"

"In those days I would call Horsham a proper little market town, everybody knew you, even the shopkeepers."

"When we first came I had a wealthy aunt and she let us have a flat in Brighton, the flat was in The Steine, but after a short while we gave it up, because we couldn't get out after dark because of all the barricades along the front. Before 'D.Day' there was a certain amount of restriction near and around Coolham Airfield, but apart from that I don't ever remember being stopped anywhere."

"By and large, I don't remember much bother with the children, much depended on where they where and who they were living with whether or not they felt isolated. I think some of them did for a bit. I was the bigger nuisance at times, because I found the kids I'd brought were so much quicker and faster on the uptake, I was always rubbing it in! I was most unkind! Of course I realised after I'd been here awhile that they weren't all 'Country Bumpkins' although there is a lot in that saying "I'm Sussex and I won't be druv!" That was very apparent, but I think that most of the children enjoyed themselves, and of course some of them stayed and are here today."

"We didn't of course get a full Summer Holiday, you had to be 'available', as they put it! We didn't go in, but just available, but I seem to remember that the Easter and Christmas Holidays were foreshortened, to help the people who had the evacuees."

"Occasionally I went to church, I'd go to The Parish Church. At that time Canon Lee was there, he was a funny sort of man, he didn't smile very much, he didn't have a good reputation, people said that he was 'soulless'. Well on the face of it he probably was, but on the other hand I know a lot of people who he really helped, he was a good man, but I know that he wasn't popular, but the church was always well attended."

"I liked Horsham. it was a lovely town, where ever you went people wanted to serve you."

CRIME AND PUNISHMENT.

In the course of my conversations I would ask the question, "What was the town like during the war?". Invariably the reply would be that Horsham was a lovely safe town where it was possible to walk the streets at night without fear of being molested, certainly all the girls felt that they were in no danger.

I suppose that compared to a modern city now at night, the town was quite safe, but if you care to take the time to read the local paper of the period you could be forgiven for believing quite the opposite! Every week the paper carried stories of various crimes, some even by today's standards very frightening. Cases of assault were quite common, mostly, but not always involving the troops, fights after the pubs had closed; the Canadians according to P/c Joe Lemm were fine until they had consumed the local ale, which compared to their own beer they found quite strong. Joe would let them fight until they had knocked each other about a bit, then with the help of the Provost Sergeant from Monks Gate they would load them onto the transport and send them back to camp. They were also involved with pilfering, especially poultry, and this caused a number of problems for Joe.

People were appearing every week for various wartime offences such as having lights showing in 'The Black Out'. Joe Lemm found the vicar at Mannings Heath to be a constant offender, until he 'knicked' him. Petrol coupon abuses were also quite common, but there was only one serious "Black Market" case in the town.

It may come as a surprise to read that there were a number of very serious crimes perpetrated, involving the loss of life.

The County Times recorded one of a local woman who attempted to axe her husband to death whilst he slept and of another case where an R.A.F. Officer shot his wife several times. In this case the Officer was found not guilty of murder but was sentenced to 15 years Penal Servitude.

There were a number of shooting incidents involving the troops in the district, and we even had a number of armed 'hold ups', one at the Ritz Cinema where the Staff were held at gun point. Another, this time foiled attempt was at The Lorna Doone Cafe at Southwater, where the gunman was demanding £5, but the female proprietor fought him off!

A number of young women were molested, none seriously injured but never the less frightening during the war, but all these stories only made the local press in those days. One other incident worthy of note happened at Broadbridge Heath, when an intruder was found trying to climb into the bed of an 18 year old girl, who happened to be the daughter of the local police superintendent!

Even the gentry didn't escape, Lord and Lady Hawke were subject to a robbery, this time the thief was chased away.

Those are just some of the stories and events from the period which has often been referred to "As the good old days"!!

The overall impression of the town being safe is very strong amongst the older generation but a stroll through the Police Occurrence Books that are held at The County Records Office at Chichester is very illuminating.

The Occurrence Books are now 'open' to the general public. Each Division and each Police Station kept them, Horsham Division being no exception.

The great majority of the incidents relate to every day events, and I was very surprised that any major incident such as the air raids, bombing of the town was not recorded. I did expect to find the aircraft that had crashed and at which the Police attended would have been recorded, but none of these seem to appear, perhaps I was looking in the wrong place!

What was recorded on a regular basis was the large number of road accidents. Motor vehicle offences, even in those days seemed to figure very highly in the work of the Police. They had of course to keep a check on vehicle lighting, all lights had to be shaded in some way, including cycle lamps. Quite a few people were summonsed for failing to immobilise their vehicles, you were supposed to take off the rocker-arm if you left the vehicle for any length of time. This offence figures quite prominently in the Occurrence Book. Parking, especially in The

Carfax was a problem. The Police were concerned about blocking exits and access to premises for The Fire Brigade.

There was an Act of Parliament prohibiting 'Lights in Roofed Buildings', this was the reason the ARP Warden would be heard shouting "Put That Light Out!". It was in fact an offence and in Horsham was strictly enforced. One lady was prosecuted for lighting a bonfire after dark.

Larceny was also a problem, 'simple larceny' seemed to be the most common charge, and there was a lot of it! Larceny from unattended vehicles also seemed popular; we now see it as a modern day crime, not so if you read the Occurrence Books!

One item that took my eye ran for two pages, 23 people on one day were caught without a Dog Licence (Dog Licence Act). It seemed as though there had been a directive to the man on the beat to check up on strays, also, rather strange quite a few of those fined 7/6d were landlords of various hostelries in and around the town!

Although I couldn't find any mention of air -raids or crashes, I did come across one related item. On the 13th August 1940, a man was reported for photographing the wreckage of an enemy aircraft, contrary to the Control of Photography Order(No.l), 1939 at Romans Gate at 6.30pm on Monday, 9th September, and a caution was issued. This was the Me.109 which had crashed.

From time to time various members of the Armed Forces were arrested for fighting and drunkenness and also for being Absent Without Leave. German aircrew members were brought into The Station from time to time and this is recorded.

Joe Lemm recounted a serious fire at Bourne Hill Farm, and this was suspected at the time of being arson, as petrol was strewn over bales of straw and a man was shot in the arm. It was a serious fire and incident but was I believe not proved.

The girls did not go around in complete safety, although many now look back on those times as a time of freedom and safety. There were a number of young women attacked and a number of rapes even in quiet little Horsham.

All in all, it was the number of road accidents that I found surprising, the Occurrence Book seems to be full of them, not all by any means were minor, many involved fatalities, perhaps with our crowded roads of today we are better drivers than we are given credit for!!

Sergeant Trott.

One of those involved in keeping crime off the streets of the town during the war.

WHAT THE PAPER SAID!

It might be of interest I thought to look at the weekly output of The West Sussex County Times for the wartime period and look at what was making the headlines. Some items led me to the conclusion that in some areas not a lot had changed!

One or two interesting items appeared before September but were connected to the events later in the year.

1939.

June 16th Edition.

BLACK OUT.

over

Urban and Rural Districts.

From July 8th (Sat.) 10pm to 2am (Sun).

> The PUBLIC are requested to assist the Police and A.R.P. Authorities by:- Obscuring Lights: Reducing Traffic and Remaining Indoors.

July 14th.

> Umpires report favourably on Horsham Black Out!

August 4th.

> Black Out plans for next week.

> Wednesday. Midnight 'til 4am Thursday.

> 1,300 planes exercising.

Sept 15th.

> Emergency Committee to carry on work of Urban and District Councils.

> Double shifts for schools.

> "Air Raid Warnings in Rural Areas not needed" (Capt J.E.Pugh MBE)

October 6th.

House for sale or auction (advert) £375 - Within easy walking distance of Horsham Station and shops, - pre-war house, 4 beds, 1 rec. kitchen etc. Rackham and Smith. Horsham Rural District Council.

Notice of General Rate in Horsham 4/9d

Roffey Infirmary to become Horsham Base Hospital.

October 13th.

First Black out cases at Horsham, 3 offenders fined ten shillings each and warned by Magistrates.

October 20th.

A.F.S. Keep Watch. Day and night 3 members of the A.F.S. are on duty at Horsham Fire Station.

HORSHAM'S FIRST WAR CASUALTY.

17 year old Boy victim of Royal Oak disaster. Rev. Lee, Vicar of Horsham declares at Speech Day "Old Educational methods a dismal failure!. The speech day in question was at Herons Ghyll.

November 10th.

Remembrance Day Parade as usual at Horsham. 105 Rotarians confer at Horsham. Rotarians from 30 Clubs agreed to carry on as usual and work for various charities. Notice from The Horsham Gas Company to customers.

GAS PRICES IN HORSHAM HAVE NOT BEEN INCREASED.

November 17th.

Odeon Cinema applied for a varience to their licence - so that more variety shows could be put on - Forces entertainment, which was granted.

Horsham Urban District Executive Food Officer Mr E. Howarth explains his task.

November 24th.

Urban Council resumes monthly meetings, "No elections until 1941".

December 1st.

"More evacuees arrive at Horsham".

December 8th.

Horsham fight for freedom and MAYOR!

December 15th.

"All Star Charity Matinee" Odeon, Sun 7th Jan. at 2.30 in aid of British Red Cross and Hospital. Starring—JESSIE MATTHEWS AND SONNIE HALE. Others including Basil Radford and the Horsham Borough Silver Band.

December 22nd.

First Military Concert at Odeon. Military Night No.1. given by members of Royal Engineers.

Christmas Postal Traffic heavier than ever!

77,779 Food consumers register at Horsham.

December 29th.

Coroner urges need for more care by drivers and pedestrians. This was after a number of fatal accidents. (See below)

The year ended on a brighter note, the Horsham Gas Company announced: "FUEL RESTRICTIONS ENDED"

GAS and COKE rationing is off!

Road accidents and deaths were a major cause for concern even in those days, and Ministers were issuing stern warnings in Parliament. The Transport Minister made an appeal in The House for all drivers to recognise the need for a reduction in speed in black out conditions, after announcing that 1,130 people had been killed in September compared to 554 the previous September. The Government viewed this increase in road deaths, said Capt Wallace, with deep concern.

Nationally the most heartening news during the month of December was the scuttling of The Graf Spee in the River Plate. The news that was to have an effect on the town appeared in The Daily Telegraph on December 16th 1939 and read. " The first contingent of Canadian active service force arrived in Britain this week".

Income Tax had been raised in the War Budget to 7/6d in the pound, spirits rose from 12s 6d to 13s 9d a bottle, wines were increased by 2s per gallon and a penny on a packet of 20 cigarettes. Never mind, in The County Times, Southern Railway had been advertising "Cheap fares from Horsham" Littlehampton for 2/1, Bognor for 2/8d, London (Vic) 4/-.

CARS. Used cars were on offer at Jackson Bros.

1938 .... Austin 7 de luxe saloon .... £90.

1938 .... Morris 8 saloon .... £95.

1938 .... Ford 10. Tourer .... £100.

1932 .... Humber Sixteen saloon .... £35.

"PAGE'S for Cooked Meats."

PAGE'S Perfect Pork Sausages 1/2 and 1/4d per pound!

Charles Page and Son. Carfax.

ENTERTAINMENT

The subject of entertainment figures prominently in the thoughts of those that I have interviewed. It was important to be able to get away from the everyday cares of the world.

For many it was home entertainment, music and singing around the piano or listening to the wireless and of course the cinema.

During that period there were five cinemas to choose from, The Ritz, which is now the Arts Centre, The Odeon which has disappeared under the new centre town development, also available The Capitol, The Carfax and The Central.

The selection of public houses was greater than it now seems to be, long since disappeared but open then, include The Swan, The Prince of Wales, The Gardeners Arms and various others which no doubt I shall be told about! King and Barnes were busy, but had trouble acquiring material for brewing, the beer I suspect being less alcoholic due to wartime restrictions.

Radios in those days were quite often battery operated, but not the small compact unit that we are familiar with today. The radio was then run by an accumulator, a large heavy battery that had to be taken to be recharged when it had run down, many remember having to take these down to Quicks in East Street to be recharged and rows of them sitting on a bench in the back of the workshop.

The BBC was of course the source of news for many, most seem to recall the Broadcast by Mr Chamberlain and the fun of hearing "Lord Haw Haw". Childrens Hour and Uncle Mac were popular and with the older generation The Brains Trust and of course ITMA.

Whist Drives were very popular in Horsham, and were often run before dances. Childrens parties, especially at Christmas were organised, those run by the Canadians being especially well remembered. The local firemen ran parties for the kids and in their off duty periods made hundreds of toys for the local children; Mr K. Parfitt recalled that these started for the children of the firemen and for the evacuees, each child receiving 2 toys, and that the parties became annual events,

Dances were held throughout the war, in the Drill Hall, The Black Horse and various other venues in the town. Out at Broadbridge Heath Camp they were called Searchlight Dances, the camp being occupied by a search light unit. It may be a surprise to some, but The Bomb Disposal Unit did not arrive until well after the war.

There were a number of dance bands in the town and of course at times supplemented by Service Bands one of these being at Faygate. The one that most seem to remember is the band organised by Mrs Layton. Mr Layton was at the time The Station Master at Horsham and his wife taught from their home piano and accordion. The Accordion Band played at fetes and concerts and was made up mainly of Mrs Layton's students.

On many of the photographs which I have seen of childrens' parties it was this band that provided the entertainment.

Dances were held on a Saturday for the general public in The Drill

Hall, and seem to have been organised and run by the Army. These were the days of black out, so one has to visualise the problems of getting about in the dark. To those who have not experienced the effects of a blackout, try to picture a street totally in darkness, no street lighting no shop lights or house lights to guide you, car lights dimmed and only a small hand torch to help you on your way! Even so the local ladies went out, and I am told were not worried even going on duty, either to The Observer Corps or the A.R.P.; perhaps that in itself says a great deal for the town.

What of life in one of the cinemas in those war torn days? To find out I visited Mr and Mrs Jack Scrase who both worked at The Ritz during the war. I asked Jack what was he doing the day war broke out? "I was down at The Ritz getting the Sunday programme ready, Head Office phoned up saying "Don't open". They stopped us opening, but we opened again, I think next day, or Tuesday, could have been a day that's all. We were looking forward to a long holiday, I'd only come back that same day from the Isle of Wight, Reg Quested and myself had been down there on holiday."

"Of the cinemas, there was The Ritz, but all five were open then, The Carfax, The Central, Odeon, Capitol and The Ritz".

"The Central was down North Street near where The Odeon was, near Linden Road. (The land marks have long gone, and were where the new road and underpass are now situated.)"

"The Ritz opened in 1936 and The Odeon a year later in 1937, I had been at The Capitol before that. The Manager at The Ritz was Mr Charles Ellison, not a local man he came from the north".

"The Manager at The Capitol was old George Napper he also owned The Lamb in The Carfax; he was never in his own pub, always in someone else's drinking. Always had a button hole, rose or something, he was a character, he could drink too!!"

"In 1937 The Chief at The Ritz put on the wrong part so they transferred him to Dover and me from Wokingham to Horsham.

"I was Chief Projectionist at Wokingham, I had been also Chief at The Carfax first and when I came back I was Chief at all three places, Carfax,

Capitol and The Ritz. I was Chief at The Ritz until it closed down in 1982."

~We used to work from 1 until 11 o'clock six days a week, only had one day off, early night from nine o'clock then it gradually got better. We usually ran four complete programmes depending on the length of film, if they were short sometimes five. We had an organist all through the war. We had different organists, we did have some fun sometimes. We had one who used to like a drink and come in just before he was due to go on; we knew he was there when we could see the small lights on his console. We knew he was there one afternoon but he didn't put the lights on, so we didn't think he was ready so we put on a Ministry of Information Film, just at the moment he began to play his signature tune "Sussex by the Sea", he kept playing, we kept showing!"

"We were also responsible for putting on the slides to tell the audience that an air raid was in progress, these were normally bought, but in an emergency we made our own. The old Fire Station was just across the road so there was no difficulty hearing, there was no question you heard it alright! As soon as the siren sounded you put this slide on, 'Nearest Shelter, Air Raid in Progress!' and in big letters across the bottom the words "The Show Will Continue"!"

"We never turned anyone out, never turned the cinema out during an air raid, any A.R.P. personnel or a few troops or women might leave but otherwise nobody shifted, we never shut!

"The pay was three pounds, fifteen shillings a week in those days, we put in for a pay rise so we got four pounds. I got my Call Up Papers but my job as Chief was what they called a 'Reserved Occupation', so I stayed."

"We had a couple of women and a boy and myself, and I was also responsible for The Capitol, they had a woman there in those days so I had to jump on my bike, biking to and fro' if they had trouble down there. We were lucky with equipment; we kept running, we had good equipment, it was good stuff and lasted, no doubt about that!"

"The biggest film that I remember was 'Gone with the Wind' we did a trade. We also had charity concerts, I think in one Savings Week the Duchess of Kent came down?"

"During the war the troops came down in the mornings, we showed films on VD and that sort of thing, they all came from Denne Park, mainly Canadians, but they never caused any trouble."

Early in the war the Manager of The Odeon applied to the Magistrates for permission to stage variety shows at the cinema. Up to that point they were only allowed by licence to stage one 'turn' per week, but requested permission to be able to put on a 'Military Night'. This was granted and the first one, "Military Night No.1" was staged late in December 1939 given by members of The Royal Engineers and included the Bulldog Mascot!

The Odeon then put on a Charity Matinee early in January 1940, starring the popular singer and actress Jessie Matthews supported by Sonnie Hale.

Dances continued at The Drill Hall, at The Nelson Arms and at The Black Horse, both formal and informal affairs going on throughout the war. Many of the young ladies of the town also went along to the 'Searchlight Dances' held at the camp at Broadbridge Heath.

Although organised sport came to a standstill some football appears to have been played by a Horsham team, a number of cup games were played, and a County competition of sorts seems to have been organised. A number of ad hoc teams played against service sides, the lads from Faygate being the opponents on one occasion, but little local football appears in the paper. Cricket did not resume, the cricket club pavillion being used for a variety of functions including a classroom for the evacuees. Like the football club cricket teams were formed, these were usually drawn from the likes of The Observer Corps or service teams, but the normal fixtures went by the wayside.

I was surprised and delighted to learn that the first First Class Cricket south of the Thames was indeed played at Horsham towards the end of the war, and would you believe it – it was brought to an early close ... by rain!!! Northamptonshire were the visitors and many of the old pre war players played.

The visiting service men tried to introduce sport into the area. Baseball was played by the Canadians and a Gymkhana was held on the Horsham Football Ground and golf continued to be played at Mannings Heath. This was one local amenity that was much appreciated, especially by the Canadians.

CINEMA DAYS IN HORSHAM

The Ritz, Organ and Stage from Jack Scrase's Projection Box.

Looking back to the Auditorium and the Projection Box

THE JOHNNY OSCAR BAND

MUSIC AND JOURNALISM PLAY TOGETHER!

John Oscar Carter was one of the three young apprentice journalists employed by the County Times during the wartime period. He also found time to run a band which played for local dances and parties and was from all accounts very popular. It was made up mainly from ex-Collyers Grammar School Boys. Included in the band was another young reporter John Buchanan, who very kindly provided this photograph.

THE BAND (from left to right):

Johnny Oscar, Derek Dinnage, Bruce, a Canadian soldier, John Buchanan, Frank Swabey (Bass), Kevin Anderson (Violin), Godfrey Matthews (Piano), Reg Renshaw and Eric Howard on the drums

ENTERTAINMENT... Mrs Layton's Accordion Band

The band pictured outside at a Garden Party at Padwick House in North Street. The young blond lad? Alan Woolven!
BELOW: some of Mrs. Layton's pupils about to board the ENSA bus to give a show for the troops. The two lads? In uniform Ron Woolven, the other his brother Alan. Shouldn't he have been at school?

OXFORD ROAD SCHOOL FOR BOYS SOCCER XI.

Y.M.C.A. GROUND 1943

TEAM:

Back Row: D. Laker, A. Rose, R. North

Middle Row, sitting on the roller:
D. Linfield, P. Wilkins, S. Hunt, P. Paige

Front Row: P. Standing, C. Grant, K. Knott

Photograph courtesy of Peter Wilkins

ENTERTAINMENT 1940 STYLE.

The Canadians held parties for the children from time to time, but the town also did its bit. Childrens' Day was held in the Park, and over 1000 children took part. The two photographs show the children dressed up for a Fancy Dress Party, whether this was during Childrens' Day I know not, but I do know that the young man in the Bell Boy uniform is young John Sampson!

In the Park?

REPORT OF THE HORSHAM MUSIC CIRCLE

An audience of 170 attended the second concert held by Horsham Music Circle on Friday, when the artists were Margaret Harmsworth, who played piano solos by Debussy and Brahms, Jean McCartney who contributed violin solos by Bloch and the Mozart Sonata in E minor, and Donald Munro, who sang among other items the prologue to Pagliacci.

An open discussion followed, and it was decided to hold concerts at the Friends' Meeting House, Worthing Road every second Friday in each month at 3pm and 7.30.

There will be no subscriptions and collections will be taken to help various good causes. Mr. F.L. Hammond was elected treasurer and Miss Grace Humphrey organising secretary.

CELEBRITY CONCERTS.

There were a number of celebrity Concerts during the period and The Ritz and The Odeon organised them. In December of 1939 there was an "All Star Charity Matinee" in aid of the British Red Cross and the local Hospital and starred the popular Jessie Matthews and Sonnie Hale, supported by Basil Radford and The Borough Silver Band. In January 1942 for a full week The Odeon presented Henry Hall and His Broadcasting Orchestra. On Thursday night, 15th January the band broadcast 'live' the show 'Henry Hall's Guest Night to the nation.

One young man who remembered seeing one of the shows was this chap, on the right, better known in later years in the green and yellow of the town football team, John Elphick. John recalled for me that the singer with the band that week was none other than Betty Driver, now seen regularly in the popular 'Coronation Street'. I thought that I would try to confirm this and wrote to the lady in question, who very kindly confirmed and said that they had a very pleasant week in Horsham with great audiences.

THE GAME GOES ON!

It took more than a war to stop the local lads playing football. This 1941 photograph was taken at the YMCA ground and shows a team dressed in whatever they could find, even boot laces were a scarce commodity.

The team; Back Row, left to right:-

Don Corbett, Abe Grant, Roy Lindfield, Gordon Head, Goalkeeper from Broadbridge Heath, Eric Rycroft.

Front Row; Harold Griffin, Fred Woolven, Joe Dixon, Bill North, and Ron Allingham.

The photograph was taken by Ken Head, Gordon Head's brother. Gordon kindly supplied the picture and thinks that at the time he would have been about 15 or 16 years old. He does not remember who the opposition were!

"The town doesn't smell the same".

A strange title for a chapter you say? It came from a chance remark made by John Buchanan when I was talking to him about working as a young journalist on the West Sussex County Times during the war. I misunderstood the meaning. I had many years before heard the late Mr Harry Knight, the groundsman at Forest School use the same expression in a talk to the boys. To give the boys some idea of the changes that had taken place in the town we would invite Mr Knight, then in his late seventies to give a little talk. He could remember when he was a lad the horse drawn transport, fire engine and carriages, horses from the "Taxi Rank" at the Station being used to pull the fire engine and that in general, the town closed down around four o'clock in the afternoon. It was about this time in the day when the horses returned to the stables. The town became very quiet and the "left overs" were cleaned away!

Far from John's comment. He could remember those smells that came to the nostrils as he walked through the town on his way to Market Square, the saddlers, the brewery the fresh fish shops, alas no longer with us.

The comment intrigued me; I had met and interviewed a number of former shopkeepers and business men and began to look at the provision of shops and shopping and was very surprised at the variety of shops in the town during that period.

I started in the Library, with the Kelly's Directory for 1939/41. The choice was quite wide for the Horsham shopper, although later in the war rationing would reduce the choice considerably. Everyone had to register with a local grocer, but it was possible to grow your own produce and keep at least one pig.

It is not possible to list all the establishments, but as I walk round the town today I do look out for those that are still in existence and trading, not many but if you are observant there are perhaps more than you think, and I'm sure others will be pointed out to me which I have missed!

A quick look round, start with the banks, most are still in the same place, the Midland, Barclays, Lloyds were all well established. A walk down East Street reveals a number of old well established firms that survive today, Agates, the corn merchants, Scott and Sargents, Wakefields, Trelfer the jewellers and on into Queen Street you could find Brewers and David Bryce.

Although some of the shops retain the old names, it does not follow that they are still in the hands of the same families. Many of the old businesses did survive until quite recently.

One of the first casualties of Horsham redevelopment was The Black Horse Hotel, standing on the corner of West Street and the Worthing Road, it was here that many of the special events and dances took place. Working along West Street we could find Apedailes, hosiers and out-fitters and next to them Currys Ltd., almost in the same place that you would find them today. On the opposite side of the street was Stephens, the ironmongers and another well known old local firm E.T.Lane & Sons furnishers and upholsterers, and also in the same line of business Fromes, The Sussex Furnishers.

Hairdressers seemed to like West Street, there was Rhoda Hull for the ladies, Thomas Sharp for the men, The West End Ladies Hairdressers, J.W. Josephs, ladies and gentlemens hair stylist. F.V.Slade-Symes was at number 43a and of course there was Wickershams in The Carfax.

There were a number of Public Houses along the street, I remember The Swan but do not remember the Prince of Wales, a small pub quite close to where Woolworth once stood.

Woolworths had a store in Horsham in West Street, so did Boots, The Chemists, then called The Cash Chemists!

Although we did not have the large superstores of today, the town centre seemed to be well served by various high quality grocery chains. In West Street alone you had the choice between David Greigs, Walk-ers Stores. International, Home and Colonial The Maypole Dairy and Liptons, this in West Street!!!

The Wakefield family were well represented, there was the bakers and above, the restaurant, the watchmakers and on the other side of West

Street, the tailors and outfitters, and they are one of the few family businesses still in the town today in their original places. On into East Street, Wakefields china shop and Wakefields pastry cooks were to be found.

Other well known names to be found in the area included such stores as Foster Bros., Dolcis Shoes, Hepworths, Timothy Whites, Dewhursts, the butchers, Freeman, Hardy and Willis.

Building Societies and Estate Agents seemed to be in short supply in those days ! At least one appears in the Carfax, Rackham & Smith, auctioneers, surveyors and land agents, but there must have been more, perhaps someone will tell me.

One or two of the wartime shops survived in different forms. Who will forget the smells of the saddlers William Albery and at least although the smells have drifted away visitors to the Horsham Museum can see for themselves the tools and the impedimenta of the saddlers shop. One of the most interesting shops for me was Glayshers the ironmongers in Middle Street. It was like an Aladins Cave, full of tools, hardware and machines required in a small market town. Little boxes and drawers hiding thousands of screws, nails and the oddments for the local building trade. It was one of those long lost shops where the tradesman would go for the unusual or out of stock item, although Horsham is lucky to have one shop in Queens Street carrying on this tradition. When Glayshers was modernised and a new shop front fitted, the original shop front was discovered under the façade; this was carefully removed and rebuilt at the Open Air Museum at Singleton.

Another local name that will be long remembered is that of Quicks. The East Street premises sold cycles, prams and toys, if they were available. Many local childrens Christmas presents came from the shop. It was also the place that you took the family radio battery to be recharged, not the modern day mini battery but a large accumulator type, heavy old things for a young lad to cart about. According to Mr Ron Taylor, who worked in the shop there was a large bench at the back of the workshop with rows of these batteries on constant charge. The reason of course, was that many houses were not on electricity so that power had to be supplied by battery and of course these wirelesses were the main source of news and entertainment.

Horsham then had its own electricity station providing its own power, some of this coming from local refuse. The Power Station finally closing down when the new stations came on stream. Mr Ron Woolven, a former engineer at Stanley Street remembers Sundays in particular, and that some Sundays they had problems providing the power for cooking Sunday lunch. He recalled that if you lived up on Tower Hill, Sunday lunch would often be served quite late! By the time the power got to them it would be so weak that cooking became difficult!

There was a selection of local outfitters, Lakers, Hunt Bros., Dolands, Arthur Lyle and Hawkins the ladies outfitters. As the war progressed clothing coupons were introduced and many of the clothes disappeared from the shelves. Mrs Leslie Laker remembers queues forming for blackout material when people knew it was in stock, but being used for making dresses and clothing. Even obtaining stock was a time consuming operation, visits having to be made to suppliers in London, often during The Blitz and not knowing whether the suppliers were still in business and this at night in the blackout. Counting the clothing coupons became a chore, nowadays it is VAT returns, but at this time coupon returns were time consuming, often delegated to the younger members of the family!

Art materials could be acquired from Goughs, there was a number of chemists, Camplins and Trevor Cale in the Carfax. Fresh fish, poultry and game from Humphreys', spectacles from Dixeys or Horstmanns, flowers from Jupps and the newspapers from Prices' or on the Carfax from a certain Stan Parsons!

I asked Stan whether newspapers were hard to come by or in short supply and was surprised to find that they were not; as paper became short the papers reduced the number of pages or the size of the page. There seemed to me to be a large variety of papers to choose from considering the events and the problems of the time. Let's have a look at what was available from the shop. The daily papers then cost 1penny in the old money. The West Sussex County Times cost 2d, and was printed all through the war. You could have any of these delivered to your door depending on your taste, The News Chronicle, The Times,

Telegraph, Manchester Guardian, Express, Mail, Herald, Sketch, the pink Financial Times and of course The Daily Mirror. On Sundays the choice was either the Sunday Times, Observer, News of the World, Telegraph, Dispatch, Graphic, Express, Pictorial, People, and my own favourite because of its' sports coverage Reynolds News. Evening papers consisted of The Standard, the Star, Argus, Brighton and Hove Herald and Sussex Daily News.

The shop had its early closing day but Stan had to open in the afternoon for the papers, likewise on Sundays staying open until lunchtime. Sally Wickersham was one of the girls who worked for Stan and gave me much of the information about the papers and the prices. She could also recall that they sold Woodbines loose, they were in boxes of 200/500, any packets were 5 for 2d or 10 for 4d, Players were 10 for 6d or you could purchase a box of 50 for 2/5d. I well remember my own brothers buying single cigarettes or very flimsy packets of 5. One of the reasons for the inclusion of the cigarette card was to strengthen the flimsy packet. Although these were dropped soon after war was declared they were expected to restart again after the war, but with few exceptions have never reappeared. For the tobacco smoker Stan sold Black Beauty at 8d an ounce, Digger Flake at the same price and the Best St Julien at 1/6d an ounce.

Prewetts Mill was operating in the Worthing Road and selling its products, the smell no doubt wafting over the town.

I hope the reader will now have some idea of the diverse character of the town and the variety of the shopping then available to the people of Horsham and forgive me for omitting their favourite shop.

I tried to ascertain who were the largest employers in the town during the period but it would appear that there were few by today's standard of Sun Alliance. Farming was by far the largest and shops had not developed the self service ethos.

Many of the local girls went into the local shops or took the Civil Service Examinations and went into places such as the Post Office. CIBA had only just moved into the town, indeed they were still moving on the day war was declared and it would be some time before they were really under way.

One company that I could not omit is of course our local brewery of King and Barnes; if John Buchanan could remember one smell it must have been from the brewery! The company continued to brew throughout the war with the obvious difficulty of trying to obtain ingredients, even after the brewery had been machined gunned or at least the mineral works had!

Lintott Engineering and the foundry would have been fully engaged on war work, some of the engineers would have been in a reserved occupation but as the war progressed many did indeed volunteer and their places being taken by female labour. The girls were employed on turret lathes or capstan lathes, rows of them turning out machined parts for the aircraft industry.

Out of the town the brickyards at Warnham, Southwater, Capel and Ockley were working twenty four hours a day in full production, although building had stopped on private housing the war effort required millions of bricks. This in the days before Motorways meant goods being moved by rail, consequently the railways employed large numbers of men and a great many were employed at Horsham.

The old editions of the wartime County Times make fascinating reading and especially the advertisements. I was absolutely amazed at the diversity in the newspaper and these adverts on their own would make an interesting study and perhaps warrant a book of their own!

What of the man who began my interest in this part of the story? I decided it was time once again to pay him a visit. John Buchanan was at Collyers Grammar School when war broke out, living in Southwater. In 1940/41 he left school and began as an Indentured Apprentice with the West Sussex County 'Times in Market Square. He used to cycle in to Horsham each morning and told how later " I ascended to the heights of taking the bus from Southwater and got off at The Black Horse. I don't know when it became apparent but I could find my way by smell from the Black Horse to Market Square".

"Rice's had the garage at the Black Horse and that smelled of oil and petrol. You got from the Black Horse Hotel each morning the smell of coffee and a faint cooking smell and the sort of stale smell of tobacco and beer that used to come from out of the Public Bar when they opened

THE COUNTRYSIDE IN TOWN!

John Buchanan, who said "the town doesn't smell the same", searches for inspiration amongst the animals in the field at the top of New Street. A country scene which was still to be seen in the sixties when the boys from Oxford Road still used "The Twitten" as a short cut to the Louisa Churchman Canteen, where lunch was served.

the door in the morning and that would waft over. Then from the other side there was Stevens, a sort of general store and it was the smell of candle wax, rope and tin, it was distinctive. You walked up the street a bit and there was Woolworths; I don't know what it was about Woolworths, it could have been an extraordinary mixture of smells but it became a melange which was instantly recognisable as Woolworths, a sort of warm smell.

Then on the left hand side the very distinctive smell of Albery's leather, then a little way up the street on the right was Fosters, which had that smell of clothes; I don't know why Fosters in particular but I always thought- yes Fosters! Further up was Timothy Whites, that smelt very much like Stevens but it sounds odd to say - but a bit more up to date. Stevens was an old fashioned candle smell, but Timothy Whites had a more modern smell. Then there was Evershed & Cripps on the corner of Middle Street; they smelt of a sort of mustiness of wine, seed and groceries."

"In Middle Street there was the tobacconists, a lovely clean distinctive smell, unsmoked tobacco always smells great. Glayshers had a nice smell, then there was Rowlands Cafe, it was probably a very clean cafe but I thought it was the sleaziest place under the sun, because you went down to get into it. It had oil cloths on the tables and when you went by there was always the smell of something awful frying!"

"Then there was the Bear and there was a sports shop, no matter how good a sports shop, there's always the smell of socks - worn socks! Finally you came to The County Times which smelled of ink. You can go to a newspaper office now and it does not have this distinctive smell, but I had never been, until new technology, in any newspaper office where the smell was different. It didn't matter where you went, even to the Chairman's Office in Fleet Street, it still had about it a smell which comes from ink, oil and hot metal - so vivid and evocative!"

"Horsham today has lost its smells, you could be anywhere and you wouldn't know it, except perhaps the fish and chip shop in Colletts Alley, that always smelled appetizing. The Carfax, I wasn't conscious of it, perhaps it was too wide".

WAR AND THE COUNTY TIMES.

I think that one of the real surprises for me was to find anyone around who had worked on the paper during the war time period, and I have to thank the Staff at the paper for putting me in touch with John Buchanan, who himself put me in touch with Tony Smith, both having worked as young men on the County Times.

I met John at his home in Cricketfield Road on more than one occasion and we discussed the problems of wartime reporting. "The bombing was not talked about", John told me, "We didn't know it all happened, as if it was a different world, as if, somehow, we weren't connected with it. The casualties were not talked about, you'd have thought that it would have been the subject of intense schoolboy gossip, but it wasn't!"

"From the first day of the war, it stands out so clearly still, I know where I was sitting and I know where the radio was - I can remember where every piece of furniture was. There was John Mumford, a church warden from Southwater, my father, a Bush Radio and my mother, sitting on an upright chair and we listened to Chamberlain; I can almost remember every word!"

"I was immensely excited. I was excited because for a year I had been saying there was going to be a war and I was sick of adults telling me there wasn't going to be one."

"We pinned up maps, but nothing happened, and I remember when I heard the first German aeroplane, I was terrified, I really thought that it was going to drop its bombs on me!. I left Collyers, and joined the County Times in 1941, in Market Square, it was very ancient and crummy in those days."

"We hand folded the papers. The papers were so small that the machine couldn't do it - the reporters and the printers used to spend most of Friday morning folding as they came off the flat bed; the paper was 6 pages. The print started on Thursday night when a certain number were run off, some were folded on Thursday night, the rest on Friday morning. They used to be delivered in an old Austin 7 van, some were also delivered by bicycle. I joined them when it was a big "broadsheet" paper, and then when paper rationing got severe, and there was paper available but at a different size, we altered the paper to the new size, which was smaller."

"All that we managed to do was just to cover what was going on locally in the town. At that point there was 3 reporters, Katie Wain, who was very, very old, she was about 22! Me, Johnny Oscar Carter, Tony Smith taking photographs. It was as if there were two lives going on at the same time; there was the purely civilian and there was the war, which seemed quite separate. This was basically to do with censorship, because we simply couldn't mention anything in connection with the war. We covered weddings, Tony taking the pictures, flower shows, fetes, and the Magistrates Court and Council Meetings. I remember the pompous debates the council had over Sunday Cinema opening."

"We had hundreds of troops in the town and nowhere for them to go on a Sunday, and it always seemed to be raining! There were a number of court cases about "black marketeering" which at the time sent shock waves through the town! You will find no pictures of the defences being prepared, tank traps or the river widening. We had 10 plates a week and it was a waste of time bothering to take any military work!".

"The class divisions in the town were very sharp in those days, the golf club had a County Section, a Town Section and an Artisans, who couldn't use the Club House. Very often the Artisan members were the best golfers! It was in the town itself that the divisions were very sharp, between the professions and between the tradespeople and between them and the shopworker and the farmers who came in, and didn't they protect those divisions closely."

"I was very offended on one occasion when I was sent to cover a funeral. It was in Kings Road, a big house. I knocked at the front door and said I was from the WSCT's, the lady of the house said "Oh you're the reporter, will you please go round to the back of the house!" I didn't bother. It's changed now somewhat, more cosmopolitan."

"I remember Horsham as being dark, a lovely warm glow on a Saturday night, but you see, I was working in the period of the blackout, and only saw Horsham lit up when I returned to the town after the war."

Tony Smith remembers starting, with John the paper's first dark room, down stairs in what had been a coal cellar. The paper was modelled on the London Times and they did not run photographs on the front page.

"I think I'm the chap who really got photography moving at The County Times" said Tony when I visited him at his home in Horsham. "We had this great big box camera, a Thornton-Pickard, like a square conker box. A blind shutter went "clunk" down as you took the picture. One of the best photographs taken of me was with this camera by John Buchanan, I still have it!"

"I remember Lord Woolton, The Food Minister came to the town, and I took the pictures and had to rush them through and I was drying them in front of the fire and saw the gelatine disappear before my very eyes! Of course what they used to do was to have the old blocks made, we used to have to send them to Brighton to have them made and screened, you couldn't have quick pictures like they have today. You had to put them on the bus and wait for them to come back, it was a slow process in those days. I didn't join as a photographer, but as I had been taking pictures and developing them with my father it just happened. I was there before Jack Marren."

"It was a happy band of people in those days, Mr A.R. Hodges was The Editor, there was Mr Rowlands and Mr Goatcher, the compositors and Ted Hellier. It was all type set, it was "flat bed" stuff and as it came out of the press, we folded it!. I think the circulation was about 11,000. The owner was Miss Gooding and it was her niece, Mrs Green who eventually took over; it was a family newspaper. We rarely saw Miss Gooding but the Editor always took her a bunch of flowers on a Friday, she was someone you never saw!"

"We used to go round the hospital, police, the courts, the churches, St John's to find out who had died, been born, and who was getting married, it was our morning round. Besides myself there was John, a Miss Jones and John Carter, it was very enjoyable but hard work."

One story that John Buchanan related was so visual that I asked John if he would be kind enough to tell it in his own words, I felt that my attempts to retell it would be quite inadequate. The following is his story in his own words:-

It must have been the autumn of 1941 or early in 1942. Nellie Vesta Laughton, then Horsham's only woman councillor, was wearing black and she dressed all in black in the winter and all-white in the summer.

Nellie helped policemen and although traffic was minimal by today's standards there was always a policeman on point duty at what was then the crossroads of Middle Street-East Street/Market Square-Carfax.

A convoy of Canadian tanks was coming through the town. A dozen maybe. They came up West Street and somehow three got into Middle Street. The Canadians' own military police saw there was a problem with the narrowness of Middle Street and diverted the rest round the Carfax.

This was Nellie's big moment. The three tanks in Middle Street could have got through - just. But while they stopped to measure clearances the other tanks rounded the Carfax and the policeman was busy ushering them into East Street.

Nellie went down Middle Street ordering the three tanks to back. She waved her arms and shouted, all black hat, scarf and handbag, a sort of oversize bat that would have frightened anyone, even a man in a big tank.

The men in the first tank's turret made the mistake of turning the turret round. The gun was not all that big, but it went through a draper's plate glass window. The man in the turret reversed it and the gun went through a chemist's shop window on the other side.

After that all the tank turrets swung as the soldiers followed Nellie's instructions. There seemed to be glass, curtains and underwear all over Middle Street and draped on the guns.

I watched as Nellie was shooed away and the tanks were driven forward into East Street and then away.

What happened next was like a speeded-up video. An army truck carrying plate glass on its sides drove into Middle Street. A swarm of men with brushes got out and cleared out what was left of the glass in the broken windows and swept it all up. Another swarm measured and cut glass and puttied it into windows. Within a couple of hours it was as if nothing had ever happened.

No crowd gathered. There seemed to be no shopkeepers making a fuss. And the only policeman on the scene was the one who had been on point duty. Years later it struck me that crowds usually gather because police with loud hailers cordon places off and tell people to stay away.

There were traces of what had happened. It was a few days before the putty on the windows was painted and for months you could see the scars in Middle Street and the Carfax where the tank tracks had scraped roads, pavements and kerbs.

Did we report it? No. Censorship was such a part of life we never even thought of it. I once took a very pretty photograph of North Street under a blanket of snow and the censor held that up for weeks."

WHAT THE PAPER SAID. 1940.

Christmas 1939 seemed to pass off without incident and the local paper reported the usual round of Yuletide events. Boxing Day 1939, Horsham F.C. 8 Haywards Heath. 1. "Cox scores four ".

Jan.12th.

> Horsham School destroyed in a blaze, Wet uniforms freeze on firemen during 6 hour vigil.
>
> Victory Road School fire caused by faulty central heating system.
>
> Space reserved for 200 war graves in local cemetery.
>
> Enemy casualties not to be interred with British.

Jan. 19th.

> More "blackout' offenders fined, including cyclists motorists, and shop manager.

Jan 28th.

> Hunt may face difficult times!.

Feb 9th.

Less drunkenness reported at Licensing Sessions.

Feb 16th.

Triumphant return after 4 weeks matchless for Horsham F.C. Bognor beaten 6-1 in Sussex Senior Cup.

Horsham Council pass vote of confidence in Fire Brigade, unfounded allegations withdrawn. Problems with water supplies.

Over 1,000 see Darts Final played on Odeon Stage. Mr T Freeman of Coolham beats Mr R.Fowler of Kinsfold.

Feb 23rd.

Public meeting urges need for attested Policewomen. In tragic cases women should have skilled service of their own.

March 1st.

Winter of 1939/40 will be recalled for generations to come. Skating on Warnham Mill Pond.

Horsham Headmaster leaving Oxford Road School.

Mr E.G.C.Bolwell accepts Salisbury appointment. G r o w i n g need for Maternity Centre at Hospital

Mar.15th.

Horsham family's unique Military History!

Seven members 54 years service.

Mr H. George - 6 sons serving in the Royal Sussex Regiment in which he had served 18 years.

"Are school subjects too attractive?" Inspectors views on modern tendency!

Mar 22nd.   Football. Horsham win 9-1 in loose kicking league game against Chichester,'

Council reduce Urban Rate from 11/2d to 10/5d in the pound.

Horsham A.R.P. Rehearsal a success.

Mar.29th.

Bonus for dustmen on all waste paper they collect.

April 5th.

200 eager boys arrive from Tom Hood Central School Leytonstone to their new camp at Itchingfield, Coopers Camp, built by James Longley & Co Crawley.

April 12th.

Working horse in unfit condition!

Soldiers steal car to go joy riding!

May 3rd.

Younger Councillors want more work to do!

May 10th.

Modern Sundays have been turned into Bank Hoildays

Evangelist condemns Sabbath sports, cinemas, hiking!

May 17th.

Over 500 Horsham men rush to join new defence corps. Police Station "Besieged" soon after Ministers broadcast.

Jack Broadley retires at 34, well known local footballer announced his retirement from the game, over 500 goals to his credit.

May 24th.

L.D.V. Officials appointed, Col. Alan Binny, Capt. G. Hornung c/o and Mr C. Gardner

Binoculars wanted by L.D.V.!

1,000 men have enrolled in Horsham Division. On patrol on Sunday!

May 31st

Playground facilities wanted for new Victory Road School.

June 14th.

Air Raid Warning was received at Horsham, but Roffey slept through it! Sirens not heard!

June 28th.

Portable A.R.P. Siren for Roffey.

July 26th.

Troops welcomed to new "Luxury" YMCA Canteen in Sterling Building.

Wounded soldiers entertained in Wakefields Cafe by Old Contemptibles.

August 9th.

Home Guard on Parade at Horsham. First Inspection' by Col. Pyke C/O West Sussex Home Guard in The Cricket Field. Gala occasion.

August 23rd.

Horsham opens £5,000 Fund to "buy" a Spitfire.

More sugar for all jam making says Food Officer.

August 30th.

FIRST photograph of bombing. Filling in crater. The only "casualty' was a haystack!

September 6th.

Spitfire Fund tops the £1,000 mark. Photo. Guarding a fallen raider. British Tommies guard a wrecked Heinkel. The machine fell apart in three pieces.

Slinfold inaugurate a Hurricane Fund. Mrs H. Doll raises over £300.

Sept 20th. (13th)

Home Guard give up beer and cigarettes for Spitfire Fund!

Sept 20th.

American ambulance given to Horsham and District by Mr Stuart Duncan of New York City.

COLGATE. Colleagues pay tribute to victims of German raiders

Civil Defence Workers killed in bombed village.

Three enemy planes down.

Miss Heather Barnes buried.

Triple funeral, Mrs G.A. Hocken; Mr W. Doick and Mr R. Constable.

Advertisement for Spitfire Fund.

12 pence = 1 shilling.

20 shillings = 1 pound.

5,000 pounds = 1 Spitfire.

1 Spitfire = 30 Messerschmitts.

NOW COME ON HORSHAM — FLY TO IT!!!!

(I wonder if our Spitfire Pilots would have agreed?)

Sept 27th.

Traffic problem in East and West Street.
Unattended vehicles would hinder A.R.P. services in an Air Raid.
Spitfire Fund now at £2.783.

Oct.4th.

Heinkel on display in aid of Spitfire Fund.

Oct.11th.

Train wrecked, but no casualties.

Horsham Legion knit 1,200 garments.

Nov. lst.

German Pilot rescued from blazing plane, after machine gunning workers at Plummers Plain.

Nov.16th.

Bones of Prehistoric Iguanadon discovered at Southwater!.

Dec. 6th.

Two year old girl rescued from wreçked building.

7 killed when Germans bomb South East town.

Dec. 20th.

45,000 gallons of water went to waste when main burst, Orchard Road supply restored in 24 hours.

Rural Councillors criticise "Red Tape", "Various Government Departments don't know there's a War on!"

Dec. 27th.

Trades Union Speaker describes Earl Winterton as a "reactionary!", but pays tribute to his "Selfless Devotion to Public Service!"

And so the second year of the war came to an end for the people of Horsham. We had survived Dunkirk, The Battle of Britain, and were living through the Blitz. The town had had it's share of bombing, the villages had suffered and the first casualties of the war had been recorded.

POLITICS, POLITICIANS, "ARSENIC AND OLD LACE".

Local politics were to all intents and purposes abandoned during the war; those already in office at the outbreak stayed in office unless 'called up'. No elections were held during those six years.

The County Times of 15th September announced that "Emergency Committees are to be set up to carry out the work of both Councils."

Sir Oswald Mosley's Black Shirts made an appearance prior to the war, the local branch having a room in Denne Road, over The CO-OP. Mr Ron Woolven remembers them marching round the Carfax, much to the amusement of the populace, whilst others remember and attended a meeting that Mosley himself addressed in The Drill Hall, and had a beer bottle thrown at him for his pains!

The local Member of Parliament for the constituency, which was I believe then Horsham and Worthing, was The Right Hon. Earl Winterton, P.C. Lord Winterton first entered Parliament in February 1905, and retired at the Dissolution in 1951, having completed an unbroken period of parliamentary service lasting nearly 47 years. Although never holding the highest offices of State, towards the end of his career he was Father of The House.

His autobiography "Orders of the Day" (Cassell) gives an account of events in The House of Commons during the whole course of his membership.

During the mid thirties he became alarmed at Britain's lack of preparation to combat the rising tide of Hitler's Germany and together with other like minded individuals, including Mr Winston Churchill, began to harass and harangue the Government of the day, albeit on his own side! One weekend party at his home at Shillingly Park near Plaistow, now a golf course, almost put the 'cat among the pigeons' when a group of journalists camped outside the door, suggesting that it was a meeting of the 'unofficial opposition'!

Strangely, in 1940, after Neville Chamberlain's resignation and the subsequent rise to power of his friend to Prime Minister, he did still not see eye to eye with the Government. He felt very strongly that Churchill's conduct, not of the war, but of Parliament, was to say the least 'unparliamentary'!

He believed strongly that there were far too many 'secret' parliamentary sessions, Churchill having more of these meetings in his first six months in office than Lloyd George held throughout the entire First World War.

Enter then 'stage left' a very strange bedfellow indeed! The entrant was none other than a certain Manny Shinwell, both ardent loyalists, but neither enthusiasts of Churchill's conduct.

Harold MacMillan, in his book, "Blasts of War" states, when writing of Earl Winterton, "an organised opposition, especially concentrating on production problems began to appear from the very first months of the Churchill administration. Emmanuel Shinwell made his first appearance in a role which he was to fill throughout the war. His speeches were always critical, even acid, but generally well informed and always interesting."

One of the leaders of this group was Clement Davies, together with Dick Stokes, Austin Hopkinson, George Garro-Jones, Thomas Horobin and an incongruous member of such a group Lord Winterton.

In one episode, whilst attacking this group it was Churchill who rounded on the Lord and suggested that if he did not improve his arguments "He', the Noble Lord, "was in danger of reaching senility before the onset of old age!"

"Winterton and Shinwell began to hunt in a group, closely together and became inseparable companions in the chase. Winterton, gaunt, awkward, angular who combined a long undistinguished administration in minor positions with a curious almost childish egotism was never the less something of a favourite; there was an endearing quality about him!

As these two strolled through the lobbies with Shinwell running at Winterton's feet, one was inevitably reminded of "Don Quixote" and "Sancho Panza"! At this time "Arsenic and Old Lace", a popular play, was running in the West End and these two Characters, the agitator and the aristocrat were quickly dubbed by this appropriate nickname".

In his own autobiography, Lord Winterton describes his recollections of the period, "The relationship between Mr Shinwell and myself was described by Mr Kingsley Martin of The New Statesman as "Arsenic and Old Lace" the title of a celebrated play of the time. The name stuck. I found it easy to work with Mr Shinwell, despite our differences on domestic policy. I liked his intelligence and integrity."

"The House on the whole treated us well and did not regard our efforts as ignoble or self righteous."

Reading the local papers of the time, there does not appear to be a great deal of friction between political opponents; the events surrounding them and day to day living were the main preoccupations. The work normally undertaken by the men was gradually taken over by the women as their menfolk were called up. Bus drivers, land girls, were soon to be common sights in our streets.

The Emergency Committee.

Who were these people who were given these wartime powers and did not for some time have to be answerable at the ballot box?

On the Horsham Urban District Council were the following:-

Chairman: H.W. Bowen Esq. JP. Vice Chairman, E.E. Lawrence, JP.

Councillors: Messrs. S. Agate, D. Bryce, JP. D.P. Chart, E.R. Dinnage, A.H. Eyles, Mrs N.V. Laughton, JP., A.F. Lower, A.V. Murrell, R.H. Redford, A.H. Saunders, Lieut.Col. H.A. Vernon, MC. R.A. West, A.G. Wheeler.

Clerk to the Council: Mr A.Slyfield.

Treasurer: H.N.F. Arnold and Dr K.N. Mawson was The Medical Officer of Health.

Horsham Rural District Council, Chairman: Mr. S.D. Secretan, Vice Chairman: Mr.W.R. Burrell.

Councillors: Southwater Ward: Messrs. J. Champion, A.Deacon S.Gardener, C.Hodson, A.C.Pemberton, H.Stoner, D.Wickersham.

Roffey Ward: Messrs. R.Etherton, G.E.Naldrett, A.Standen, W.E.Whiting.

Broadbridge Heath Ward: Messrs E.G.Apedaile, N.C.Harris, (Chair) J.Packham, G.H.Swann.

Amongst other Public Officials were: A.R.P. Officer Captain J.E. Pugh, MBE. Supt. Police Mr G.H. Heritage. Coroner, F.W. Butler Esq. and Electrical Engineer, Mr F. Ffrench.

In August 1992, I had the pleasure of meeting one of those Councillors on the 1940 list, Mr Alf Murrell and spent some time talking about the work of the Council in the early days of the war.

"I was a Councillor from April 1939 and then the war came in September. They had started preparing the Council for war, things like the A.R.P. and the Civil Defence, but I left after 12 months to go into the Forces."

"I had been in the Observer Corps before the war, I was at Denne Road. We didn't have any uniforms, just an arm band, we were classified as Special Constables. We didn't go on any recognition courses, you just joined. They said to me "you can use a telephone, can't you?" So I just sat there and got the training at The Centre".

"As a Councillor we weren't given any specific job to do. When war broke out there was an Emergency Committee formed, some of the senior members ran it."

In one edition of The County Times there was a complaint from the younger councillors to the effect that they hadn't been given enough work to do, indeed one Council Meeting lasted for only eighteen minutes on one occasion! In May of 1942 the Chairman was accused of 'wanting to Rule the Roost' by the younger members and they also criticised The Emergency Committee. There was an outcry from the same quarter when it was found that certain Council Officers were being paid for 'doing' two jobs!

The Council were also critical of the expenditure on the A.R.P., refusing to award pay rises to their employees and seemed to be dragging their feet over a new Maternity Hospital. The latter is a running story in The County Times over a three year period and came to a head when a new born baby was found abandoned at the Station.

Alf Murrell did refute Ken Parfitt's story about the Firemen's' uniforms being only provided with single breasted rather than double breasted coats because of the cost, but he thought it was a good story!

The Council Meetings according to Alf were two in the afternoons and the rest in the evenings. There were two separate Councils, Urban and Rural but they didn't mix, they ran separately.

"In those days we were responsible for the town's electricity and the Station was in Stanley Street. The dust carts used to come up to Stanley Street and shovel the refuse into the incinerator and it would come out as clinker; this was then sold to a contractor. We were busy saving as much as possible even in those days. We were also responsible for sewage and also for burials, but there was a separate gas company."

When Alf returned after the war he was told that he was the first serving councillor to leave for war and to return to take his seat after serving his Country.

In 1945 in The General Election, Earl Winterton was again elected to serve the area, with a majority of over 10,000.

I felt that I could not neglect the other side of the political coin, the local political situation in the thirties and the rise of Fascism, even in quiet little Horsham! I had heard from a number of people about the 'Blackshirts' in the town and the visit of Sir Oswald Mosley in the late thirties. One branch of the Mosleys lived just outside the town, in Joe Lemm's patch at Mannings Heath, but I subsequently learned from the son of Sir Oswald that the Horsham family had little to do with any political activity.

HORSHAM POWER STATION, STANLEY STREET

Both photos of:

Horsham Power Station Main Engine Room.

Background is a Fullagar 6,600 volt diesel engine for Roffey. Morcom and Bellis Steam Engine at side.

THE MOSLEY CONNECTION.

Frank Holmes remembered the 'Blackshirt' meetings before the war: "Yes I remember Mosley coming, he came at a time when most of our respected gentry didn't know whether to join or not. There was a strong group in the town, I can't remember who was the 'Gauleiter', but four of us, two Communists and two Labour Party members, whenever we were off duty would go together to their meetings, to disrupt them physically!"

"I can't remember who it was, but as soon as we went in he would organise four big heavy guys, "Minders', I suppose you would call them today, who would stand behind our chairs and as soon as we stood up two hands would push us down again!"

"At The Town Hall these meetings were quite frequent; they were very active at one time, but I don't recall any parades. We broke up our arrangements. We sat in four different places in the hall, so that the disturbances would come from four different places rather than one; yes we had a marvellous time! That's a section of my life that I had not thought much about, but it was exciting!'

"They had a place in Denne Road. They were in the town and pretty powerful, and their influence was much greater than people think, because they had got all the background of the monied people who were ready to join, but just sitting on the fence. They were breeding like fleas in the town, 'cos the action in London, in the Jewish quarter was different to what we had here; in Horsham it was just a bit of fisticuffs, but we had it all the same."

There was a Public Meeting at which Sir Oswald Mosley addressed the assembled crowd. The late Bill Sampson went to it: "I went with a friend of mine Syd Dunscombe. At the time we were both energetic and this meeting was in The Drill Hall. So what Happened? Well Syd and me go down there and being a little bit wary at what had happened and what might happen at this meeting Syd said "We'd better sit near the door and if anything happens we can beat a rapid retreat, I thought that was fair comment so we seated ourselves where we could see what was going on. If a 'punch up' started we weren't going to hang about!"

"So all these "Blackshirts" were walking about, all dressed for the occasion; looking back goodness it was open! Anyway there was a platform in the middle of The Drill Hall, and then in comes the 'great man' himself and starts the business with a salute. He gave a great talk on how wonderful a man Hitler was, he went on about how Hitler had no intention of doing this and that or the other, and the business of the Jews. It was all anti Jewish, all this sort of nonsense and it went on and on and it got to the stage where a few local chaps had a gut full and started to ask questions, you know the ones, those that are difficult to answer, but he never really answered any. But what he had done, the crafty so and so, was when it happened he had a record ready; he struck up the National Anthem and as it struck up he was off the stage and disappeared. That was the drill and with all his henchmen around they got him away and out of the place, before a 'punch up' could start!"

"He definitely came to the town that night and afterwards there was a great controversy about him using The Drill Hall because it was a military place. Old Mosley himself was all dressed up in all the gear!"

THE DEFENCES. THE EMERGENCY COMMITTEE.

Before war was declared, the two Councils were preparing themselves for its eventuality. An Emergency War Committee was set up in May 1938, and its activities are recorded in the Minutes which are held at The County Records Office at Chichester.

In March 1993, I spent some time looking through them and noted some of the more noteworthy events they reported.

The first recorded meeting took place at Comewell House, then the home of The Rural District Council, on 23rd May 1938. This was a sub-committee which called itself The Air Raid Precaution Executive Committee and its Chairman was David Bryce. One of the items on the agenda was the appointment of an A.R.P Officer.

There were five candidates on the first short list, but as time went by some of these had already found posts with other councils so a second list was drawn up and an appointment was made. The Minutes note:,

"It was resolved that Capt. J.E. Pugh of Blackheath be, and is hereby appointed A.R.P. Officer to both Councils at a salary of £350 per annum, plus £100 travelling expenses. To commence on 1st June 1938."

Capt. Pugh took up his appointment and began to organise all the civil defence activities, looking for suitable premises and enrolling and training staff. In his first report to the Committee he recorded an interesting item on 12th July, 1938.

"Mr Dalton, of East Street also contributed by giving a demonstration of A.R.P. methods by TELEVISION in the Horsham F.C. pavilion". This was a most novel way of showing the work. It must have been the first time many of the audience had ever seen television, certainly in Horsham! Can anyone remember? He also reported at the same time that "Lectures have been started in The Town Hall on Wednesday evenings at 8pm. 180 Air Raid Wardens will be required." By October of 1938 they had got round to discussing the purchase of a siren and its cost.

"1 'Gent' 4hp Electric Siren A.C. 3 phase	£33.0.0
Automatic Wailer for Siren	£ 7.0.0
Contactor.	£1.17.0.

The first temporary Headquarters were to have been No 10/11 in The Carfax, but this was declined in favour of No 9, Causeway.

In February, 1939, it was reported that the basement of Park House had been inspected and that this would be suitable for a Control Room. After adaptation, strengthening and gas proofing it could accommodate a Report Centre and Message Room, accommodation for Senior Officers and shelter for H.U.D.C. staff.

The same report recorded the strength of the Defence Force.

Personnel.	Male.	Female.
Wardens	172.	35.
Casualty Services.	32.	42.
Rescue/Decontam.	11.	
Communications.	18.	19.
A.F.S.	18.	

On March 20th, they were announcing the first practise "siren" Warning, to take place that day between 9pm and midnight. July saw the announcement that a number of Wardens Posts with telephones had been established.

District

No.1. Car Park in The Bishopric.

No.2. The Common, plus a room at Collyers.

No.3. Roffey Institute.

No.4. In hand.

No.5. Town Hall.

No.6. Odeon Theatre.

No.7. In hand.

A report on the first trial run on the blackout was reported as 'splendid'! These Blackout exercises had been on 8th/9th of July and instructions were issued :-

"A bomb will be exploded and a flame will burn for 8/10 minutes at various sites. All A.R.P. personnel should, if possible carry an electric torch, there will be a complete 'blackout' of the County." The same report reported "that sand will be supplied free to all houses in the H.U.D.C. at 561b per house."

The meetings gradually ran down, and became monthly. In May 1940 it was decided that schools would become shelters and feeding stations in emergencies and that Wakefields Cafe would take on the task of feeding the homeless. An order had only then been placed for uniforms for the wardens, 200 were needed.

Eventually the whole process was wound down and the last entries were in September, 1945. Capt. Pugh and his assistant Mrs B.E.Barnett stayed on until the end of September. The equipment was then put up for tender and sold off. An Austin was sold for £30, a Sunbeam for £36 and a Vauxhall fetched the grand sum of £40.

The Horsham Wartime Emergency Committee was formed in Jan. 1939 with 4 Councillors, Lawrence (Chairman); Lintott; Lower; and Vernon.

Later Cllrs. Bowen and West joined. These also formed the nucleus of the Evacuation Committee.

On 19th June the provision of shelters for the townspeople was discussed and tenders from 6 local firms of builders were on the agenda. After some lengthy discussion it was decided that at least 5 of the tenders were far too high, only one seemed to have been awarded. The sums tendered, by today's prices, some as low as £200, must have been good value! The Committee decided to build them with direct labour. The following positions were agreed upon:-

1.   Carfax, between the Bandstand and Memorial. To hold 50 people.
2.   Next to The Capitol 200 people.
3.   Island in The Causeway, for 50.
4.   East St. Car Park. 150.
5.   South St. Car Park. 50.
6.   Bishopric for 100.

These were all Surface Shelters and were built, like the school shelters to one design, 9 inch brick walls and 9 inch reinforced concrete roofs. They had a blast wall to stop direct blast and some had a metal door.

A number of small but interesting items appeared on the agenda from time to time and I have picked out some that brought a smile to my face, such as this one on 1st July 1940,

"The keeping of pigs, hens, and rabbits now permitted in Council houses." Later in the same month; "Steel helmets for A.R.P. Personnel to be provided at 11 shillings each."

On August 14th, "All lofts to be inspected and cleared of inflammable material and rubbish." They were discussing in September the provision of a shelter for Roffey, to be built at The Star Inn. Later in the war a "Fire Guard Officer" was appointed and a separate Fire Guard Service was formed. The first officer was Mr C.I.L. Percival, but as yet there were no static water tanks in the town, one being built in Queensway sometime later. In November they gave permission for the removal of railings and in March 1943 asked CIBA to camouflage the factory.

The same councillors that were on The Emergency Committee by and large sat on the Evacuation Committee. Indeed it was reported at one stage in The County Times that a number of younger councillors had asked to be given more work to do. They complained in Council about an 'in group' within the Chamber, which of course was strenuously denied. But something that wasn't denied was that a number of Council Officers were indeed doing two jobs and getting paid for more than one job, within the Council!

The afore mentioned Evacuation Committee was formed on the 10th of January, 1939 well before war was declared, so to a degree they were prepared. Six distribution centres were set up at local schools and teachers were to act as clerks.

The evacuees arrived and Billeting Officers, such as the Misses Lyons, sorted out the arrivals.

The town did what it could, the teachers and the children drifted back to London as the war progressed, but throughout the war some children lived in the area. In November '41, it was recorded that "A cheque for £34 had been received to cover Christmas 'treats' for L.C.C. children, this worked out at a shilling a head, 674 children all told." Horsham U.D.C. added another £5 to this sum.

Another item to catch my attention was the use of "Holmwood" house in Forest Road which had been used as a hostel for very difficult boys. After a visit from a Welfare Officer from The Ministry of Health, she informed the Council that Mrs Warren and Mrs Hillman were not being paid enough, so the salaries were raised to £2 and one pound, five shillings, respectively per week, less insurance!!! The Committee met for the last time on 23rd of July, 1945.

The Rt. Hon. Earl Winterton, P.C., M.P.

BEING PREPARED!

The shelters arrive at last

HORSHAM POLICE STATION IS PREPARED

A HORSHAM AIR RAID SHELTER

This pile of sandbags at the junction of King's-road and Station-road is the exterior of one of Horsham's three public air raid shelters. The others are at the Old Malthouse, Worthing-road, and in the North-street subway. Further protection is afforded by a trench near the bandstand in Hurst Park and on the Brighton-road Housing Estate at Elm-grove and Orchard-road. ("West Sussex County Times" photograph).

These photographs were first published by the West Sussex County Times early in the war, and were reprinted fifty years later in a special edition in 1989.

GROUP "B" WARDENS POST No. 7

Top Row:
Mr. F.G. Holmes, Mr. A. White, Miss P. White, Mr. R.G. Harper,
Mr. W.P. Harmsworth.

Middle Row:
Miss M.K. Page, Mr. B.F. Pay, Mr. H.B. Mason, Mr. A.A. Baker (Senior
Warden), Mr. A.C. Shreeve (Deputy), Mrs. M.S. Hutchence,
Mr. A. Walton Jones.

Bottom Row:
Miss D. Rogers, Miss K. Redford, Mrs. M. Costello, Mrs. M. Pierce,
Mrs. E. Houghton, Miss P. Topham, Miss D. Dance.

The Home Guard.

The story of the Home Guard has been well documented, but from all my contacts it appears that Horsham's was no better or no worse than most. All those that had joined had a story of sorts to tell, and I have selected a few.

John Christian was not a good soldier and was not impressed until they gave him a motor bike! Frank Holmes was in the Railway Platoon; he remembers going on patrol with three other chaps, but only one rifle between them, and taking it in turns to carry it!

Ken Lane was in the platoon at Holbrook. He seems to think that all their exercises and parades always finished up at The Fountain public house in Littlehaven Lane.

Percy Spriggs was also in the same platoon, 3rd Sussex, and remembers doing duty at Ferring Beach which was not at that time defended and was used to practise "D.Day" landings. Being able to bathe in the sea was a real luxury.

Austin Willson, who taught at Collyers and was a L/Cpl in the Home Guard, recalled guarding White's Bridge Pumping Station, Colgate Reservoir, the Gasworks and Council Depot, Horsham Park House but they were asked to leave the latter when someone put a "round" through the ceiling and the bed of the Chief Warden who slept there at times! "I was used as a Drill Instructor, my despair was trying to get a ploughman to march in step!".

Syd Weller was in the Post Office Platoon. They met in the P.O. Garage in Glanford Road if it was wet but would on a Sunday do field work outside. "We were quite well kitted out, we had greatcoats and gasmasks the same as the Army. I was involved with the signals, we used to wear a blue and white flash on our shoulders."

He went on "The P/O H. Guard was unique in its own way, it was almost a private army, the postmen and the engineers" and of course the Head Postman was the Q.M.Sgt and the inspectors were officers, we were just "privates!". The Co. C/O was Major Hoad."

"We met twice a week, Tuesday evening and Sunday. In the town I think we were treated more or less as a bit of a joke, but my attitude was, if I could kill one of them and then get killed I had done my job!".

"We had no light tanks; the "Tommy Gun" at the start and then the Bren and later a spigot mortar, which fired a rocket sort of thing, but very accurate. The forest was a good area for exercises. We did an exercise one night against the Railway Home Guard, and the Canadians."

Jack Scrase was in the platoon at Agates Yard with Harold Champion from Oxford Road School, but later was transferred down to The Drill Hall. He laughed when he told me that they had gone on one exercise into the forest to throw some live hand grenades. One of the lads pulled out the pin, panicked, threw the grenade straight up into the air, "Cor" said Jack "did we scatter!" Agates was No.7 Platoon, Reg Wakefield was in charge.

John Buchanan was 16 when he joined the Southwater platoon, who paraded in the old school, under Major Latilla Campbell.

"One day, it was terribly cold, we were out firing our Ross Rifles; it was the first time I had fired a live round. Anyway I fired my five rounds and a couple of days later I was in hospital with pneumonia, it was that cold!"

John remembers that, "We had one exercise in which we were supposed to be invaded. Our H/Q, was Southwater railway station. We went without sleep for a night and drank lots of tea and absolutely nothing happened; my memory is that the telephone or messenger system didn't work and we weren't sure whether the exercise had ended. We never knew, but they always told you that it had been a success!"

Should anyone be under the impression that it was always fun, there was a tragic accident at Steyning in May 1944, when a practice shell killed one man and injured two others. Private Leslie Wiley of Maplehurst was the unfortunate victim.

Everyone seemed to think that the success of the B.B.C's series "Dad's Army" was because it was true to the way the whole business was run. Although John Christian said he was a shocking soldier, I feel sure that if he had been needed, he would like the rest of them, John Buchanan, Frank Holmes, Jack Scrase, Syd Weller have risen to the occasion.

"D" Company 11 Sussex Home Guard. G.P.O. and Telephone Engineers specialising in communications. Part of 3rd Sussex Home Guard. Photograph courtesy of Mr Syd. Weller.

THE BASE HOSPITAL.

One of the everlasting memories of the wartime period for many of my friends and acquaintances was the "boys in blue" as they strolled in the town. These were the walking wounded from the Base Hospital at Roffey.

On the outbreak of war, the Infirmary and Workhouse in the Crawley Road was converted into a hospital. One of the young nurses working at the hospital was Marjorie Bowyer, or Nurse Marjorie Coste as she was then. She recalled that as a St John's Ambulance Nurse she was on duty at Horsham Station meeting the evacuees on the day war was declared. She had to take up some sort of war work and as she had always wanted to go into nursing she chose to go to the Base Hospital. Things were very quiet at first but life became very hectic after Dunkirk. She was on duty the night that the bomb dropped on Orchard Road. She recalled that together with another nurse she was washing up in the kitchen when they heard the whistle of the bomb. When she turned round her friend had dived under the sink! It wasn't long after when the ambulances began to bring in the injured, including Harold Rose and his pal Mr Weedon.

The hospital treated civilians as well as the military, and was on the 'Outer Ring' of hospitals to take in those injured in 'The Blitz'. Amongst those that came in from London were wardens and firemen. At that time anti German feeling was as you might imagine very strong, and Marjorie didn't care for them very much until two young German airmen were brought in and she felt very sorry for them. They were only about 18 and looked absolutely terrified. They thought that they would be killed.

After about eighteen months the Army moved in and at about the same time the huts were built, twelve huts with forty beds in each hut. The shift lasted twelve hours and Marjorie stayed for two and a half years until the Canadians took over.

After her stint at the hospital Marjorie moved to Crawley Tools working nights as a nurse.

Amongst the 'boys in blue" later in the war was Bob Heseltine, one of the survivors from the Mannings Heath Halifax crash.

THE BASE HOSPITAL, ROFFEY

One group of Staff taken in Autumn 1940, with at the front in the centre Miss Belton, the Matron, Dr. Thompson and Sister Thompson, Assistant Matron (no relation!). On the back row, sixth from the left is Marjorie Bowyer, (Nurse Coste). Also in the group are members of the Red Cross.

BELOW: Nurse Coste with some of the "Boys in Blue".
All the walking wounded wore a blue suit to go out into town.

Is there a reply?

One of the sights which was commonplace at that time, was the G.P.O. Messenger Boy or the Telegram Boy. These young men at first on cycles and later on small motor bikes were often seen round town delivering their messages, both welcome and unwelcome. One such young man in Horsham was Syd. Weller.

The job was a much sought after position and was difficult to come by.

"The full time Messenger Boy worked 6 days a week, 8 hours a day and every other Sunday taking telegrams. Some of the telegrams were of course quite sad. I've often thought that they ought to have warned us what was in them before we took them to the door. I remember one lady at a house in the Bishopric who almost collapsed because her husband had been killed, and of course you had to wait and ask if there was a reply? Some of the telegrams were to tell a man his leave had been extended by a week or so, in which case you often got a tip!"

"There were 4 boys in 4 shifts and a temporary on Saturday; I started as a "temporary". It was a sought after job, it was a sort of apprenticeship, a "Youth in Training" we were called. They called us "YITS"! You had to do 2 years and attend night school as part of the scheme."

"At night it was very dark in the winter, because of the "blackout". We had very small lights, about 18 inches off the ground, the bottom half of the reflector was done over with black boot polish to stop reflection, the top half was blacked out. One evening out at Southwater it was so black that I cycled along the white line. I thought it was the curb until I met a car coming straight at me! We had to work in those days until we had finished. One regular job was to cycle out to Coolham and deliver some messages to an Army gentleman. I think they were from The War Office, but it was every week."

"I don't think communications improved in the town during the war. If anyone wanted a "line" it had to be priority, such as a doctor. If so we just ran an overhead line."

"The Telephone Exchange was behind the Carfax, near to the present Post Office. All operators during the day were girls, but at night all men. At Christmas we were busy, perhaps more so than today. They used to take the oldest boys to move the mail at the Station. They put on a big show, they used to hire vans, often removal vans; it was a time when people sent cards and messages, perhaps because of the war."

"We earned 10 shillings (50p) a week, less 2d for National Insurance and 2d for health! In those days you didn't go on holiday. I did go to my uncles at Chailey on the farm, to help with the harvest and the milking, but there was an area shut off at Poynings where there was a "check point". From Poynings to the coast was shut off. If you wanted to go further, you had to get a permit from the police. I had to attend a funeral at Lewes, and I had to get a permit. If you were a workman, they issued you with a pass."

I well remember myself the day the Messenger Boy came with a telegram to say that my eldest brother "was missing in action, believed killed" but there would be a further telegram to confirm. It was the waiting for the next telegram which had a profound effect. When it arrived my mother sent me to my neighbours to ask the lady of the house to come round while she opened it. For us it was good news, my brother had been captured at Tobruk, but for many the second telegram did not bring such good news. I can't help but think that it was rather a cruel way to break the news.

On the opposite page is one of the pleasanter Telegrams, this one sent by my mother to my brother Roy, a Flight Sergeant in the Royal Air Force, to inform him that his elder brother had arrived home from a P.O.W. camp in Germany. The camp from which he had been released was in the east German town of Dresden. My brother was in the camp on the night and the day that it was raided in 1945. At the time he was being forced to work in a factory producing chemicals, and by so doing was able to supplement his ration of food. There were to my knowledge at least three P.O.W. camps around the city. The prisoners were also employed to help clear the debris and restore some kind of order. After the collapse of the German Army the local people encouraged the P.O.W's to go west to meet the British and Americans, and this my brother was able to do.

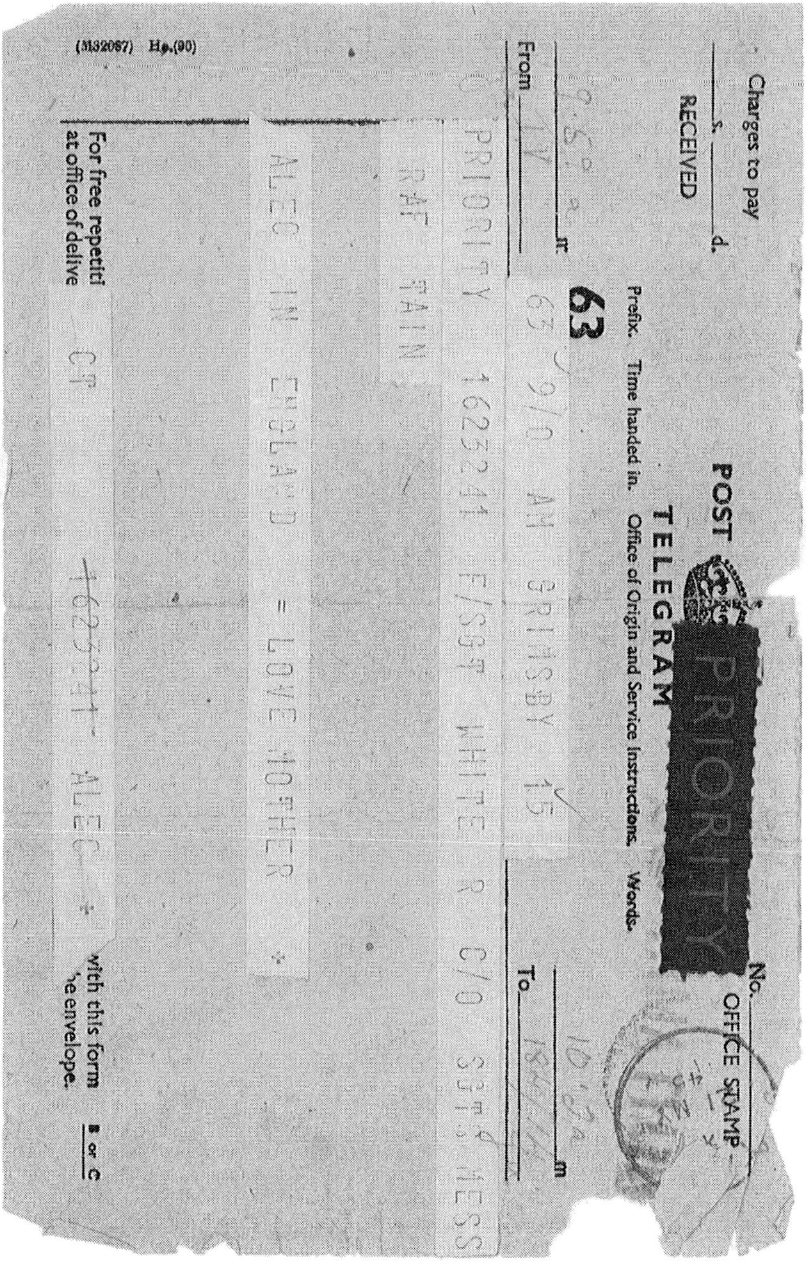

POST OFFICE TELEGRAM

PRIORITY

Charges to pay s. d.
RECEIVED

Prefix. Time handed in. Office of Origin and Service Instructions. Words.

No. OFFICE STAMP

From

To

63

63 9/0 AM GRIMSBY 15

PRIORITY 1623241 F/SGT WHITE R C/O SGTS MESS

RAF TAIN

ALEC IN ENGLAND = LOVE MOTHER +

For free repetiti... with this form
at office of delive... ...he envelope.

CT 1623241 ALEC +

B or C

(M32087) Hq.(90)

GET THE FIRE BRIGADE!

One of the most interesting stories that I was told came from Mr Ken Parfitt. Before the war he had worked at David Grieg's in the cooked meats department, second in charge. He had joined the Fire Brigade, first as a part time fireman and then as full time after the outbreak of war. In those days it was The Auxiliary Fire Service run by the Urban District Council. In the photograph it can be seen that he is wearing a single breasted uniform; this was because he felt the Council were too mean to provide the double breasted type. The single breasted uniform was found to be extremely dangerous when they were attending the huge fires in the large cities. It gave very little protection from sparks and heat.

The Horsham men not only covered the town but covered and attended major bombings in larger cities. Ken recalled that this included, Portsmouth, 3 times, Southampton, 2, London, Biggin Hill. They were on "Stand By" at camps for Folkestone, Dover, Tonbridge and for anywhere between Tunbridge Wells and London.

Ken went on to relate:- " Our first call to Portsmouth meant we were there for three days and nights with no food or drink provided. After this experience our crew carried our own supplies, as the Service had no catering organisation at that time. Later the Canadians gave us a mobile kitchen. I was put in charge of catering and provided meals from this caravan, but was not excused fire fighting duties! I was often returned to the Station by motor cycle to stock up and tow the kitchen to the scene of the action. They paid us £3.00 a week - no over time; if you were out on a job, you stayed until it was complete. I remember once when we were on 12 and 12, we were just about to go off duty, when we had to go out to this fire. By the time we got back again it was our time to go back on duty again - we did three duties in a row! "

"At this time we had three machines, No 1 was a Bedford, a Dennis Pump and the old Urban machine. The pump in the photograph is a Pyrene Pulsometer, and the idea was that it was a trailer pump and you could slide it off the trailer and carry it, - providing you were strong enough. Remember you had a water pump and a 10hp engine and the petrol of course! On the trailer there was 50ft of rubber lined hose and

75ft of canvas hose. The difference was that the rubber lined hose allowed more water to pass through quicker, because there wasn't the drag. With a canvas although it was smaller, the rough canvas caused a drag on the water, so you didn't get as much water through. The machine was kept in the Park House. We were provided with a waterproof, leggings, a coat, and of course a tin hat and Wellington boots. The Rural District had no machines so we looked after that as well. When the N.F.S. took over early in the war there were pumps in all the villages, Crawley, Cowfold, Mannings Heath and Broadbridge Heath. I would go out every week with another fellow and service all these Sub-Stations. I used to go out as Catering Officer, and I had to make sure these sub stations had certain rations. If I deemed that a certain ration had been in the Station too long I would replace it, and then bring all this stuff back to Horsham Canteen, where it was used up. Nothing was wasted!"

"We would get our water anywhere, but this particular motor was years later, put on the back of a Ford lorry, which had a water tank on it. The idea was, I would drive to anywhere, start this pump, fill up the tank and take it to wherever the fire was. We took our own water with us; we took the water out of stream, hydrant, whatever! Even the odd pond. There were surface tanks in Horsham, one on The Carfax, which was a surface tank, 10,000 gallons I believe. There was another near the Iron Bridge, there's a row of shops there now, this held about 5,000 gallons. This lorry I used to drive took 1,000 gallons at a time. I can tell you a funny story; we had a fire at Billingshurst, couldn't get any water, so I came back to Horsham Fire Station on the back of a motor bike. I got this tank out, which was kept full up - it was an open topped tank, and I was driving around the Carfax. I had the bell going and some old lady stepped out in front of me. Naturally, I dropped my "anchors'" - the motor stopped, but the water didn't - it came right over the top and she got soaked!"

"The engines were originally painted red, but later we had to paint them grey. Later we were split into three "watches", red, white and blue. We did watches of 48 hours on and 24 off. The girls were Watchroom Attendants, cooks and secretaries; before we had girls we had to man the Watch Room ourselves, which could be rather awkward! All that finished when the NFS took over. When the Urban was running it we had to man the Watch Room; when you got a fire call the Watch Room was left unmanned!"

"I didn't attend the Orchard Road incident. It was funny, I was off duty and we heard the bomb drop and I pushed my wife and daughter under the table and stacked stuff around them. I went and had a look round outside. I walked up the road, about halfway, I still couldn't see anything, so I went back and said, you can come out there's nothing here, it's up in the forest. If I had gone another 20 yards I would have seen it!"

"I attended on one occasion to a Spitfire at Shipley; the pilot was a Canadian. I rendered first aid, for a broken back. The crash was near a pub. We brought the pilot back to the Base Hospital on our tender. I attended the lot in Kerves Lane and we attended another at Nuthurst, a German aircraft. We went past The Black Horse and up a lane. We had to find the plane and we were searching this field and were cautioned that there was one more bomb on it, which hadn't exploded."

"We were spread out across this field and I found it, at least I found a bloody great crater! I was looking into this crater when this bomb went up! I can see it now, and the only thing I can think is, this crater was so deep down that when it exploded it went right up and over the top of me. I shall always remember because I shall never see a colour like it - a blue flash coming up out of the hole - I couldn't describe it, all I can tell you it was a luminous blue. Cor we were lucky!"

"We also attended the fire at the Rubber Factory. It was a big fire, but it needn't have been; there was no water. It was the same at Victory Road School, no water pressure!"

"Just in front of the Station, in those days there was a place where you lifted up the lid and inside there was a kind of a scale there with a weight on it and to allow more water through you took more weights off. At the rubber factory I was standing there waiting for the water to come through and it did! It wasn't water, it was mud! Then someone opened up the valve and the water came through, but of course it was far too late."

"One of the activities I organised was toy making. I started the whole thing off; we made 200 toys for the evacuees that were billeted with firemen's families. I started off the toy making and the other fellows took it up more or less as a hobby. We had Christmas parties at St. Leonards Hall for the evacuees and the firemen's children and these became a regular event throughout the duration. There was an allotment in the Park, where the bowling green is now, which was worked by two firemen to demonstrate food production in small areas. We also organised a fete in the Park; this consisted of Flower and Vegetable show, toys made by us and other items. It was a big success, it was the first time that £1,000 had been raised in one day in Horsham. Half the proceeds went to the Hospital, the other half to comforts for the troops."

" Our quarters at first were the Fire Station floor between the fire engines, the hayloft near Park House and then a hut by the tennis courts, built with wooden grocery boxes, plaster board and roofing felt."

In January 1943, the former Brigade Chief Mr J.G. Gadd died, after 35 years service to the Brigade. The N.F.S. paid tribute and the coffin was borne on a fire engine.

To help those who are a little mystified by the terms I have used. A.F.S. was the Auxiliary Fire Service and N.F.S. was the National Fire Service.

The Horsham Auxiliary Fire Service outside Park House.
From left to right: Bill Saul, Jasper Ward, Bob Hamilton, George Gravitt, Tim Booker and Ken Parfitt. Photo provided by Ken Parfitt.

HORSHAM FIRE BRIGADE AT WORK

Attending one of the incidents, but where?

Bill Dimmock on motor bike, Ron Lampard behind the wheel.
Note the shaded lamps.

WHAT THE PAPER SAID – 1941.

Looking through the weekly editions there seemed to be a great deal of petty crime. People were still being prosecuted for 'black out' offences and injuries and deaths on the road were still a major cause for concern. During the year there were two murder cases for the police to solve and the good people of Horsham were once again asked to put their hands into their pockets for a number of worthy causes.

January 1941.

3.1.41.   "URGENT APPEAL TO ALL RESIDENTS." "How to protect your home, business, your town." This was an appeal for personal services, and continued..."FALL IN THE FIRE PARTIES." "Black Out lamp that was too bright." Nurse among cyclists fined at Horsham. New Years Eve Spitfire Dance raises £'s

10.1.41.   Fire Watch plans explained to Traders. "Have everything ready if Blitz comes!"

17.1.41.   Horsham wants more Home Guard. Butchers to close on Mondays and Thursdays.

24.1.41.   Slinfold "Hurricane Fund" closes, Mrs Doll collects £500. Inoculations against Diptheria.

31.1.41.   "One man, Two jobs criticised" This was at Horsham Urban D.C. meeting when it was learnt that some Council Executives were being paid for doubling up on certain jobs. In future Officials were not allowed to be paid for two jobs.

February 1941.

7.2.41.   First published pictures of Orchard Road bombing. Horsham to have its first ATC Squadron, but Collyers to maintain own existence. PUBLIC NOTICE...DIG FOR VICTORY. (Public Meeting)

14.2.41.   Y.M.C.A. asks for £1000 towards £700,000 commitment. Carfax Canteen sets standard.

21.2.41.	Horsham area to raise £200.000 for "War Weapons Week." "MONEY FIGHTS AS WELL AS TALKS!"
28.2.41.	Car parking in East and West Street may be banned?

March 1941.

7.3.41.	No increase in the County Rate, still 6s 3p in £1.
14.3.41.	Bomber brought down in flames, German found in field with parachute unopened. (Pondtail Road)
21.3.41.	Photograph of cottage damaged by enemy action. (This was most unusual, normally no photographs were published.)
28.3.41.	Bomb detonator went off in their hands! Two local schoolboys injured by souvenirs. The two boys concerned were treated in hospital for facial and hand injuries. This was not as rare as you might think, most of the young lads were able to hunt for pieces left around crash sites. Although it was illegal we all popped bits into our pockets and hid them in our bedrooms.

April 1941.

4.4.41.	Horsham A.T.C. is now fully established, the C/O was Dr Braybrooke.
11.4.41.	1000 take part in mile long War Weapons Week Parade in Horsham.
	"Rescued German Pilot from blazing plane". Three Sussex men awarded commendations." This was the MelO9 which came down in flames at Plummers Plain.
	The Pilot Unteroffizier Alfred Lenz died the day after in Horsham Hospital from his burns. "£5,000 cheque sent to Lord Beaverbrook. 5000 contributors to Spitfire Fund."
18.4.41.	AFS amongst Bonfire offenders in court!
25.4.41.	War Weapons Week realises £418,500, with more to come! "Cricket spirit must be kept alive", President's appeal to Horsham C. Club's AGM. Bowling Club loses £2 - but gives £59 to local charities!

May 1941.

2.5.41. Cricket and Tennis open tomorrow! Chief ARP Officer to combine office of Chief Warden! Two jobs again?

9.5.41. Weapons Week total £425.644. Kitchen Front Campaign opens with 3 Course Lunch for 9d (4p in today's values)

16.5.41. RAF Officer charged with murder of his wife. Doctor tells of numerous bullet wounds found in body.

30.5.41. King and Queen pass through Horsham.

June 1941.

6.6.41. Cricket... Horsham beat Dorking. "Home Guard in hand to hand fighting", but only a combined defence exercise!

13.5.41. Americans send guns to Home Guard, handed over at The Odeon Cinema. "White Weddings will be fewer after clothes rationing".

June 1941.

20.6.41. The King decorates 'Nanny' White. Congratulated on bravery that won her the George Medal.

27.6.41. Alarming shortage of water in Horsham U.D. Fears that rationing would have to be introduced.

July. 1941.

11.7.41. Wife charged with attempt to murder husband while he slept, said to have hit him with a chopper!

18.7.41. Judge's sympathy for wife on attempted murder charge. Sentence of one years imprisonment reduced to six months.

25.7.41. Air Force Officer found Not Guilty of Murder, but sentenced to 15 years Penal Servitude for Manslaughter.

August 1941.

1.8.41. Bread to be delivered only three days a week. "V".. Your Country Needs Scrap". Campaign begins. Junkers 88 crashes on village.

18.7.41.   18 tons of scrap collected in Urban District. Most of this month was devoted to Flower Shows and Village Fetes. Life was conducted as near to normal as possible.

September 1941.

5.9.41.   Registration for Civil Defence under the Emergency Powers Act. Public Announcement. "German children must be given chance to be pure and Clean", Rotary speaker on "Task to be faced when victory is won".

19.9.41.   Magistrate fined five pounds at Horsham; he failed to carry out order for land cultivation. Mr A. Mitchell was photographed with a 19½lb. Pike caught in pond at Mannings Heath. 40 inches long.

October 1941.

3.10.41.   "HORSHAM EXPERIENCE FIRST GAS ATTACK!!! Shoppers caught without respirators, women with prams warned to leave the streets." This was of course a mock attack! Evening Institute Club formed and opened at Oxford Road School.

17.10.41.   80 gallons of Military Petrol stolen in Horsham. Memorial dedicated at Colgate. The Bishop of Lewes dedicated a seat in memory of those who lost their lives. Is it still there I ask?

24.10.41.   Queen honours Colgate Heroines at Buckingham Palace. Posthumously to Heather Barnes. November 1941.

7.11.41.   Posthumous award of Guides' V.C. to Miss Heather Barnes.

14.11.41.   Mrs Muriel Brown of Station Road claims to be the first woman taxi driver in Sussex! Three local men lost amongst crew of HMS Cossack. HMS. Cossack was a Destroyer and it was torpedoed in the North Atlantic while on convoy duty and foundered under tow on 27th October.

28.11.41.   Rural councillors question A.R.P. Expenditure? Do things ever change I ask?

December 1941.

5.12.41.   "War effort has reduced Psychological disorders." So says Dr Bradbrooke addressing Horsham Rotary Club.

12.12.41. Horsham shops to have three days holiday at Christmas this year.

19.12.41. Fire Watchers among "Black Out" offenders.

26.12.41. Evacuees entertained at Warnham and Horsham. Police Raid Bookmakers Office. Sequel to four day watch kept on premises. £20 fine and '14 Visitors' bound over!

And so on that 'fine' note the year ended, one in which life had continued, people were even then talking about victory and the rebuilding of Orchard Road was being discussed. Evening Institute had restarted and a number of fund raising campaigns had been undertaken, and, like The Spitfire Fund had raised huge sums of money.

Unbeknown to the good folks of Horsham their Spitfire had not only joined a squadron but had been in action, shot down a number of enemy aircraft and had itself been shot down in October by one of the Luftwaffe's top "Aces" and was with its pilot lying on the bottom of the English Channel.

"Why do mothers do it – they keep all those embarrassing photographs?"

NATIONAL REGISTRATION

TMDE	190	5

WHITE   CLIFFORD. H.

1. This Identity Card must be carefully preserved. You may need it under conditions of national emergency for important purposes. You must not lose it or allow it to be stolen. If, nevertheless, it is stolen or completely lost, you must report the fact in person at any local National Registration Office.

2. You may have to show your Identity Card to persons who are authorised by law to ask you to produce it.

3. You must not allow your Identity Card to pass into the hands of unauthorised persons or strangers. Every grown up person should be responsible for the keeping of his or her Identity Card. The Identity Card of a child should be kept by the parent or guardian or person in charge of the child for the time being.

4. Anyone finding this Card must hand it in at a Police Station or National Registration Office.

NATIONAL INSURANCE.
ZL. 20 34 87 D

S1-33120 I

NATIONAL REGISTRATION

TMDE	190	5

WHITE   CLIFFORD. H.

DO NOTHING WITH THIS PART UNTIL YOU ARE TOLD

Full Postal Address of Above Person:—

99 Brenton Road
Clethorpes

(Signed) Clifford H White

Date 23/5/40

THE HORSHAM SCHEME OF PATRIOT ENGINEERS

150 VOLUNTEERS WHO GAVE 4 HOURS EACH FOR 3½ YEARS FOR FREE - 1942-45.

Certainly one of the most unusual stories to come to light in my research was that of The Patriot Engineers, and is perhaps typical of the people of the Horsham area. The story is well documented in a booklet which can be seen in The Library of Horsham Museum. Having read the booklet, I began to search for those who had been involved, but where were they? Many, sadly are no longer with us.

The project had been set up and run mainly under the inspiration of a Mr Tom Greenhough. I made strenuous efforts to trace him, but was told that he had emigrated to Canada shortly after the war. Thanks to my friends at Thomas Keatings at Billinghurst, I obtained an address, so I duly wrote, more in hope than expectation!

In due course a reply dropped through my letter box, and what a reply. It contained much new information and many of the original photographs used in the booklet. Tom and I then carried on a regular correspondence until in 1993 we met when he made a trip to this country, and we were able to sit and chat.

Tom told me that during the crisis years of 1940, 1941 and 1942, there used to be a slot after the 9 o'clock news on Sunday evening called 'Postscript'. On one Sunday in February 1942, Sir Stafford Cripps made an appeal for us to make a greater effort to help our Russian Allies to survive. This was after he had just returned from a trip to that country.

Tom went on, "I was running as Works Manager, Thomas Keatings, making precision tools. I met my old friend Jos Pugh, the Chief Warden, who was concerned that now the air raids had tailed off he had a problem occupying his regulars, and asked if I could use them at Keatings?"

"I told Jos that this was not a practical proposition, but the thought struck me that there must be thousands of jobs in factories being done by unskilled labour. The question was, could this be transferred if volunteer organisations could be formed throughout the country?"

"I had occasion that day to visit a Mr Phillips at the Ministry of Aircraft Production and asked him if he had any unskilled jobs to place out? Yes he said, the tapping of three million nuts. Mr Phillips asked what machinery, shop size and men we had got? He didn't actually say "run away and play", but closed our meeting with ~When and if you can put it together come and see me", then perhaps thinking "here is another nut", the three millionth and one nut!'

"A few weeks later, with a capital of Four Pounds and some nut tapping equipment we put it together".

"Jos Pugh quickly recruited 50 volunteers working four hours per week."

The Scheme had been sponsored by the Horsham Rotary Club and started life in a converted motor car showroom, given to them by Rice Brothers, with benches and machinery loaned by various local firms. Most of the volunteer work force did four hours a week but eventually so many people came forward that an afternoon shift had to be introduced and a full time supervisor appointed. The gentleman appointed was Mr Charles Portwine, 'Charlie' to all those who worked with him and he is remembered with great affection by Tom Greenhough. Mrs Portwine, his widow, recalled in the County Times in 1994, " that her husband was responsible for the day to day running of the little factory and the training of those good people. He used to cycle in from Coolham, seven miles each way, always returning after dark. The cycle lamp restrictions made lighting ineffective as all cyclists of those days will remember."

By this time considerable interest was being shown by the press, both local, national and international. The New York Times sent over their Chief Reporter to cover the story and in March 1943 a Canadian film crew descended on them to film a 'short', showing the volunteer workers contribution to the war effort. The film had its premier at The Ritz and Tom and I have spent a great deal of time trying to find a copy!

In March 1943 they were approached by The Ministry of Aircraft Production to help with the production and manufacture aero engine parts. These Tom related were called 'Banjo Bolts'. Although the bolts were no problem there was a hold up with the drilling; a small hole could not be drilled in two opposing corners. Because of the angle that the drill approached the bolt it caused the drill to shear off and break. Both Tom Greenhough and the late Tommy Holt drew sketches for me and it was with the help of Thomas Keatings Toolroom that a 'sleeve' was made which allowed the drill to be supported as it was brought into contact with this hardened bolt. When the job was first suggested Tom was told that they would need one drill per bolt but with this 'sleeve' a great quantity were produced per drill; indeed it is recorded that the record was held by Rear Admiral Bruton who, aged over 70, drilled 246 bolts in a four hour spell without a breakage!

This record was held for some time but was bettered later by Mrs Gilroy, who achieved the amazing total of 374 in a four hour shift.

There were periods when the work dried up. Tom had to keep badgering away to keep the workforce employed but in the Spring of 1944 The Patriots took on a large contract from Vickers Armstrong for the drilling of two million components for aircraft parts. This job demanded great skill by the machine operators because the size of the drill being used was about the same thickness as a sewing needle. Apparently one Horsham lady, a Mrs Pyke, completed 192,000 pinholes in a ten month period, while the factory completed 1,500.000 by the time the war had come to an end!

In October, 1944, they received public recognition when Sir Stafford and Lady Cripps visited Horsham to view the factory and to see the volunteers at work. At the end of the visit Tom was able to hand a cheque for £3,000 to Sir Stafford, the profits so far accrued.

The successful conclusion of the Scheme was celebrated in a 'Victory Party' held in St. Leonard's Hall on September 16th, 1945, and a further cheque for £1,500 was handed over. In summing up Tom said that in all £4,500 had been handed over to the Exchequer and that over 3½ million components had been made, of which none had been rejected. Tom expressed to me his appreciation of the help that he received from the Wylde family and the Staff at Thomas Keatings. They never complained about the amount of time he spent on The Patriots and especially to his Secretary Mr Alfred Ellis who acted as Honorary Secretary to The Patriots and wrote something like three thousand letters.

I think those who were responsible deserved to be recorded, they were:-

The sponsors .... Horsham Rotary Club.

Hon. Chairman .... Mr Tom Greenhough.

Hon. Vice Chairman .... Capt. J.E. Pugh. MBE.

Hon. Secretary .... Mr Alfred B. Ellis.

The Directors .... Mr E.R. Hayward.

Mr W. R. Holmes.

Mr L.W. Mace.

Mr J.Y. Miller.

Mr H. Jackson.

After the close down of the factory all those who took part received a certificate and a copy of the booklet, which also includes the names of all those who took part. In all Tom told me that over two hundred actually gave of their time. The only full time employee was the Shop Supervisor, Mr Charles Portwine.

The W.S.C.T. were involved giving encouragement with articles such as that on April 17th, 1942, "Are You a Patriot Engineer?" and "Volunteers Needed to Drill Munition Parts" and followed this with "Become a Patriot Engineer, Help The War Effort and Set An Example To The Rest Of The Country and finished off by asking volunteers to contact the A.R.P. HQ. at Park House. In June with production under way the headline ran, "Factory Without Wages Or Profits, Horsham Patriot Engineers Begin". The story ran "In a converted shop in the town new high speed drills woke to life for the first time on Tuesday night, though the engineers maybe amateurs, the machines, lighting and equipment are excellent and the job is being turned out to a high standard".

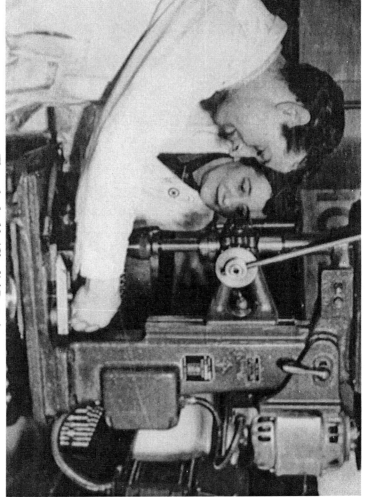

The redoubtable 'Charlie' Portwine.

Patriots Old and Young.

Rear Admiral Bruton, aged over 70 years.

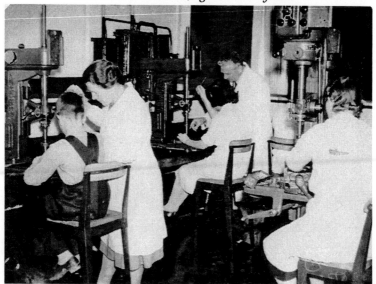

Little Michael Wakefield, aged 9 years

The Horsham Scheme of Patriot Engineers

In October 1944, Sir Stafford and Lady Cripps visited the factory and
accepted a cheque for £3,000.
The face between them is a very young Tom Greenhough.

THE HORSHAM PATRIOT ENGINEERS.

Extract from The New York Times of Monday, October 5th, 1942. Kindly supplied by Mr Tom Greenhough.

SUSSEX VILLAGERS IN WAR FACTORY.

Working Without Pay in Their Spare Time, They Turn Out Bomb and Plane Parts.

ROTARY CLUB IS SPONSOR.

Workers at "Patriot Works" little Schoolboys, Retired Colonels and Minister. (James MacDonald, somewhere in Sussex.)

In a small agricultural village here there is an important war factory. It is the symbol of this country's patriotism at its best. It is a plant - so little, but so large in its implications run by 150 volunteer workers.

In their spare hours from grammar school, business ventures and professional activities the volunteers have turned out in ten short weeks, without asking one penny from anyone in return, 3,000,000 minute but vital parts of bombs used by the R.A.F., 20,000 screw thread fixtures for planes and 20,000 other tiny pieces of metal that help keep planes flying.

Under the leadership of the village Rotary Club, schoolboys who should be home abed, retired octogenarian colonels who do not like the word "retired", business leaders, housewives and engineers - a cross section of the whole community in which there is even one minister- bend over lathes night in and night out, day in and day out, taking what they firmly believe to be "shots for victory" form Britain's industrial front.

In a one storey building that formerly was a Ford Motor Co. showroom men, women, boys and girls can be seen working at top speed under the Rotary Club emblem and examining their handywork by the aid of overhead lights the beams of which are screened from the seemingly deserted streets outside by heavy blackout curtains.

This is the first factory of its kind in Britain and the indications are that many more will come into being in other parts of the country, the Rotary Club is now swamped with enquiries from all over the country.

The scheme was inspired by a greasy young engineer Thomas Greenhough who has an important job in an engineering plant that is turning out armament supplies and therefore must remain where he is rather than don a uniform. He is one of the leading figures in the local Rotary Club.

Last March Mr Greenhough heard a radio speech by Sir Stafford Cripps, who said he believed that there was much idle time being wasted that otherwise could be put to use directly in behalf of the war effort. Mr Greenhough thought of the townspeople he knew and wondered if their idle time could be utilized. He approached fellow Rotarians with a proposition of establishing a voluntary factory. The response he received was as emphatic as an electric shock.

A local business man sent £4 to Mr Greenhough with the 'hearty' injunction "Go To It". Two other business men, not to be outdone, sent £10 apiece. With the £14 in hand, Mr Greenhough approached the Ministry of Aircraft Production and put it to them the idea of running a non profit-making plant. He assured officials that he could find workers.

The village ARP chief, who was connected with a Ford distributor offered the showroom building for factory quarters, without rent or taxes. Word went abroad. Soon commercial firms throughout Britain offered to supply the baby plant, free of charge, with drilling machines, benches, lighting, wiring, woodwork, typewriters and other equipment, including even an electrically controlled factory clock.

The Rotary Club appointed a minister, a druggist, a garage owner, a grocer, a restaurant proprietor, an optician, a tailor and an insurance agent as members of a committee to find out about workers. Knowing everybody in the town, they had no difficulty. Their wives and children and friends signed up quickly as non-paid employees. But the committee itself had been the first to sign on the dotted line.

FACTORY HAS TWO SHIFTS.

Ten weeks after the long period required by the industrious Mr Greenhough for organising, the affairs of the factory got going. It is now putting in about 1,200 man hours weekly on two shifts – from 2pm to 6pm, and 7pm to 10pm.

"We hope," said Mr Greenhough "to increase the man-hours to 3,000 weekly."

Much of the material that comes to the factory is semi-finished. In other words, it needs "unskilled touches." The work done here saves time in raw products factories and frees men for more important jobs. These so called unskilled touches involve teaching housewives, newspaper delivery boys and elderly ladies who ordinarily would be having their afternoon naps how to operate machinery that cuts, drills, and threads within one-thousandth of an inch of specifications.

The volunteers have taken to the work enthusiastically. Conversation with them was difficult because they appeared to think that every moment taken off to turn their heads and answer questions was time wasted. Here was a nine year old schoolboy who said that he did not know what kind of thing he was boring holes in - it was a small cup-shaped piece of brass – but what he hoped was that it would "beat Hitler." There was a sun tanned milkmaid with red hands who said that she could not explain what she was helping to make, but she hoped "it is good."

A high school girl – whose father was bending over a bench – said that she would be serving tea for soldiers at the local army canteen during the forenoon, digging for potatoes "for victory" on a nearby farm in the afternoon and also doing her homework in preparation for Monday lessons.

At another bench was a pale, smiling young man who had been in the Army, but as a result of his experiences at Dunkirk, had been discharged, where he suffered wounds that he would not talk about. He seemed to sum up the spirit of the entire group when he pointed a grimy finger at white-smocked men, women and children – whose upper left pockets, in true Rotary Club fashion, bore their first names – and said "They're a damned good lot."

Tom made a few comments about the article for me, and I quote:-

"The young man was CHARLES PORTWINE, a young ex-soldier invalided out after Dunkirk, affectionately known to everybody as Charlie, he was our only fully paid worker."

"The contents are not exactly right from this august journal, but this lovable bullshit warmed all our hearts at the time!"

FROM FLEA POWDER TO TOOLMAKING.

Interwoven with the story of The Horsham Patriot Engineers has to be the Billingshurst firm of Thomas Keatings. The firm is well known to-day both locally, nationally and internationally as one of the foremost in it's field in high class engineering, but what is less well known is that it started life as a London company producing flea powder.

I had known of Keatings Flea Powder as a lad because one of my ever-lasting memories now is of fleas and lice during the war, especially at school and in neighbours' homes and shelters. One house in our avenue as far as my mother was concerned was a 'no go area', we entered at our peril! I well remember my mother combing my hair every night with the dreaded Nit Comb, and searching the bed at night for any unwelcome visitors.

Happy days, I'm not so sure!

The firm of Thomas Keatings was in Billingshurst at the outbreak of the war and soon after the declaration turned part of the premises near to the station over to War Work. The company grew steadily under the direction of Mr Douglas and John Wylde producing high quality precision work making various 'Tools' for the production of aircraft and tanks.

Tom Greenhough joined the company from Crawley Tools and began to expand the Toolroom and took on apprentices. Tom insisted that the toolmakers should be treated with respect, that each man should have a working area that would be kept clean and tidy, the benches be covered with easily cleaned and washed linoleum and that there should be a rubberised mat at each work station. Toilet facilities were provided and were to be kept clean and tidy, and in return he expected each man to wear a clean white coat whilst at work, a tradition which still applies today. The working conditions were such that they were considered a model for the industry.

One young apprentice who joined the firm in the early war years was Dennis Childs and he recalled that when he joined he had absolutely no idea about toolmaking and found it was tediously boring until he had been there a few weeks. Endless filing filled his days!

Strangely there were no shifts, or shiftwork. The day was from 8 o'clock in the morning until 5.30 and no night work, except of course fire watching. They were mainly producing Press Tools and Gauges for the war effort. There was, I was surprised to find, no fabrication work.

During this period Tom Greenhough was the Works Manager and Mr Douglas Wylde and John Wylde were the Managing Directors.

The Flea Powder Department was run from London but there were 6 mills at Billingshurst crushing the flower from Pyretheum which has no smell, the powder coming from Kenya. The two so different components went on side by side until 1971, when the powder production ceased. Today there is little to show of the original powder plant except a few outbuildings.

Many of the Horsham Patriot Engineers' problems were resolved by the toolmakers at Thomas Keatings; the jigs for boring the "Banjo" bolts were produced in the toolroom. Tom remembers that the company never complained about the amount of time that he spent with The Patriots and never refused a request.

Thomas Keating's Staff 1941

Fourth in centre from left is Mr. Tom Greenhough, seated next to Douglas and John Wylde.

THE JUNIOR TECHNICAL SCHOOL.

In 1989 I had the pleasure of interviewing the late Mr Tom Holt. Tom came to Horsham from Todmorden in Lancashire in 1944 and lived in the town until his death in 1991.

Tom came to assist in the setting up of a junior technical school and told me of the problems that they encountered.

It was realised quite early in 1940 that there would be a shortage of trained craftsmen once the war was over, and that a large re-building programme would be required. During the war all forms of training were curtailed to a great degree. Men were trained quite often in the forces, but young men were poorly or inadequately trained because of the lack of facilities or teachers then available. The need for a future well trained work force was foreseen in Horsham.

Mr Eric White of Longleys and Mr Billy Hoad lobbied County Hall for a Junior Technical School to be set up in the town.

County duly agreed and a School was set up. It opened on 16th of September 1943 in the British Legion Hut with 30 boys under the temporary care of Mr A.Anderson the former Headmaster of Denne Road School. On the 6th January 1944 Mr Ted Crawford took over as Headmaster, with Mr Tommy Holt as his Deputy. They were still occupying The Legion Hut but had some accomodation in The Art School in Hurst Road, with the use of some workshops in Linfields Building yard and buildings.

The problem was of course materials and tools. Tom recalled that they did the best they could, scrounged timber and materials and "raided" the local tool shops! They descended on Bert Glaysher's shop in Middle Street and bought the entire stock!

It was still war time and when the siren sounded they were duty bound to take all the children to the air raid shelters.

They were very unlucky with the weather in the early days and The Log Book makes fascinating reading. It stated on January 23rd, 1944, "Due to extreme temperatures,attempts are being made to run the School in the Legion Hut only, with disastrous results to schemes of work". The first apprentice classes were started in the Art School in July of 1944~and these were to lead to Day Release Classes in later years. The weather had not relented even in 1945.

In January 1945, classes in the workshop were closed when the temperature plunged to 4 degrees of frost, and then a day later on 17th of January the Log States "Workshop temperature showed 13 degrees of frost!".

In August 1946 the contents of the Legion Hut were moved to The Base Hospital at Roffey and this was to be the home of the Technical School until it closed down in 1959.

London City and Guilds Examinations started in May of 1947 and were to continue and many of our present day craftsmen benefiting from these courses.

The staff were involved in a number of out of school activities, Messrs Holt and Dawkins taking the boys to a Summer Camp at Great Hucklow in June 1947 and by 1955 they were confident enough to take 21 boys and 7 adults for a 10 day School Visit to Engelberg in Switzerland at a cost of 19 pounds, four shillings and seven pence per pupil!

In July of 1957 the school lost its Headmaster, Mr Crawford, when he left the town to take up an appointment in Bermuda.

Gradually, with the change in education the school began to run down. There was talk of a new College for either Horsham or Crawley, new schools were being built in Horsham and staff were finding positions in other schools. Tommy Holt went to Crawley to set up The Building Department in the new college, the equipment being distributed throughout various educational establishments in the County. One circular saw bench, American Lease Lend, was still in use in the 1970's at Forest School, by yours truly! The School vacated The Base Hospital and transferred to Robinson Road at Crawley in August 1958 and eventually closed its doors on 17th July 1959. The School Log survived and was delivered to The County Records Office at Chichster on April 22nd, 1991.

That was the history, but what where they teaching? I was given a copy of a report presented by Mr Crawford to the parents in November 1944 which gives a picture of the kind of education being offered to the pupils. I quote from passages in the report.

"The School, the first of its kind in Sussex, was opened in September 1943 with an attendance of 30 pupils who had passed an entrance examination. The aims of the School have been firstly to lay the foundations of good citizenship and to provide some standard of knowledge in English subjects, civics, science, calculations, sketching and the events of the day.

We also introduce the pupils to the six major building trades and to the rudiments of technical drawing.

The actual subjects taught may be divided roughly into two classes,- academic and practical. The first class includes English, Science and Arithmetic. The second class includes Drawing (Geometric), building constuction and workshop practice.

In this two years' course the academic work is bound to be limited, and therefore parts have been omitted which would serve no useful purpose.

In English the work includes spelling, the choice of words, writing letters, letters of application and the practice of writing clear and concise accounts.

In calculations the work includes, a revision of some elementary work to exercises in area and volume with some algebra, trigonometry and logarithms, as may be necessary.

History deals with the development of modern government and the social sevices, together with some basic Goegraphy.

Physics is limited to the study of elementary facts in mechanics, heat, electricity, sound and light, always keeping in mind the usefulness of these facts.

Chemistry includes the study of acids, alkalis, lime, with calculations based upon simple chemical actions.

Art consists of perspective drawing, sketching objects indoor and out, blending of colour, washes and design.

Several visits have been organised, including a brickworks at Southwater, Messrs J. Longley and Co. builders at Crawley, Messrs Agates timber yard the foundry of Messrs Lintotts, the Gas Works, the Electrical Works and the sewage farm.

After the war this course will be of three years' duration and better accommodation will be available.

I would like to thank all the gentlemen who have shown such interest in the progress of the School and who have provided us with materials, wireless sets and given lectures.

It is pleasing to know that in these difficult times there is always someone who will give enthusiastic help.

Finally please remember that the School was a pioneer of its kind in Sussex, that wartime raised conditions in almost everything, accomodation, supply of tools, materials and even heating of rooms. However we have overcome many difficulties and are now developing along what we hope are the correct lines."

The School turned out a string of pupils who later in life became well known in and around the town, many setting up their own businesses. Amongst the first intake on September 16th, 1943 were the likes of Alan Woolven, George Francis, Cyril Atfield, Geoff Burt, Bill Day, Malcolm and Steven Carter, Bob Myson, Pat Weekes, Ken Weedon. Later young lads like Jim Knight, John White, Fred Miller would join the School.

Photographs of the School are difficult to find but some have come to light. The one overleaf was taken some time after the war but it does have some of the Staff who came in the early days. On the extreme right is the late Tommy Holt, next to Tom is Bill Maitland, in the centre is The Headmaster Ted Crawford, who I understand died recently and next to him is Reg Pearmain, with whom I taught for many years.

The Staff at the Technical School (see page 125 for details).

THE OBSERVER CORPS IN HORSHAM

No story of Horsham during the war would be complete without a mention of the part played by The Observer Corps. From their Centre in Denne Road they collected reports from the outlying posts, sifted them and passed them on to Fighter Command Headquarters.

The history of The Centre has been covered by others, more fully than I am able to, but I have chatted to a number of former "Observers", some who spent hours on duty in The Centre others, perhaps less fortunate, who spent their time in very exposed "posts" out in the countryside.

Stan Parsons recalled that they were all given the status of Special Constables. At first they gave their time free, but later they became a paid organisation.

Henry Day very kindly told me of his experiences, "I was in the 1914/18 war, so I was just too old for this one, but in 1939 there seemed to be every chance of another war, so I joined the Observer Corps. That then was run by the Police, we were sort of Special Constables, a sort of voluntary affair. We didn't get any pay or anything, the police were sort of running it! We had training sessions at the old Centre behind the Drill Hall in Denne Road. Then of course as the war got going it came to a more important thing and finally we had uniforms and were attached to the R.A.F. We were now a part of the R.A.F. and we got paid. I can't remember how much it was, but it wasn't very much.

What we were doing was tracking all these planes, either our own or the enemy, where they were going or what they were doing. I think the Air Raid Warning system came through us, 'cos our people were plotting these planes from various posts around. Our post was at Depot Road, at the top end, where the allotment is now. Each post plotted and passed them on to the next post. These fellows were standing out in all weathers with simple instruments. It was quite a simple little thing really; it had a point on it, pointing on to the plane, when they could see it. Then it had another pointer going down onto a map, which corresponded with our big map at The Centre, but of course at night you could not see them, so they went by sound. We had a special way of checking them.

They could detect them by the sound of the engines, they were all different I suppose".

The Observer Corps became according to one young lady, more of a social club. It was, she said, somewhere to go! Unfortunately, she didn't like them at all! She found them very snobby! One other former member confirmed this feeling; she told me that on The Victory Parade through The Carfax they were booed. According to another gentleman, there was a very strong feeling of "trades v professions" in Horsham at that time, even socially!

I had the pleasure of talking to one young lady who had been at The Centre during one of its more interesting periods, just after 'D Day' and at the outset of the 'Flying Bomb' period.

Mrs Nellie Gill, in those days Nellie Jackson, joined The Observer Corps in 1943. She had she told me a choice between factory work or agricultural work and chose to go into the Corps at Horsham.

She had six weeks training at The Centre. They were issued with a uniform which included one skirt only but material to make a second. They worked three shifts a day and were paid for the work. She thought that it was quite good pay, but of course no overtime; the shifts were eight hours a day.

The girls worked at The Centre. The observers on the Posts were part time, all men. The Roffey Post down Depot Road was 'Oboe One' and there were others at Billingshurst and at Cuckfield. Nellie felt that they often felt cut off from reality when they were in the Centre. They just plotted the aircraft and it was only when they went outside and saw the searchlights and flares that they felt frightened.

Mrs Jack Scrase was on duty on 'D.Day' and when they arrived for their shift they were told what this was, that this was 'It'. They were as pleased as punch that it was their crew on duty. They found that it wasn't possible to plot the aircraft there were so many of them! Many of the local people have told me that on that day it was like a 'carpet' over the sky.

The late and well loved Tommy Holt had also been in the Observer Corps, and he recalled to me how they coped with the 'doodle bugs'. It was known about the V1's in January of 1944 and when they eventually started coming over a Royal Air Force van was parked outside the Centre so that they could give instructions to the pilots.

Tom recalled that they also used another method to track them. Rockets would be fired from The Posts as the 'doodle bug' passed over within one mile of the Posts, these rockets then hung on a parachute so that in theory the pilots could follow the path of the machine. Tom, like most of the eye-witnesses that I have spoken to remember vividly how low these wretched things flew! He recalled one Sunday walking through 'the Twitten' near the station when one flew over a about a thousand feet. A man at the station let off some tracer but Tom threw himself down full length half expecting to hear an explosion. When he picked himself up and dusted his uniform, there were two elderly ladies standing over him. They had serenely watched the entire proceedings without batting an eyelid! Tom said in that lovely Lancashire accent, "I did feel a fool and me all in my officer's uniform!"

After the war Richard Dimbleby came to the town to record 'Down Your Way' and one of those he interviewed was Nellie Gill .

The Centre continued to operate long after the war was over, taking on a different role once the plotting of aircraft was no longer feasible manually. A new building was built and with the threat of nuclear war the Royal Observer Corps in Horsham continued to be on the front line, eventually closing down quite recently.

The Observer Corps.

THE OBSERVER CORPS: Horsham Centre: Section 2: 1940

This photograph taken on the steps of The Drill Hall shows No. 2 Section before the arrival of uniforms Note the arm bands are the same as those worn by Special Constables. The photograph was kindly loaned by Mr. Kevin Harris.
Back Row:- E.W. Mitchell, R. Oakley, W.C. Dinnage, E.J. Rowlands, L. Nash, F. Kempshall, D.P. Chart.
Middle Row:- L.J. Ray, W.A. Scott, W. Evans, C.G. Jackson, A.C. Dendy, C.J. Kay, F.W. Bridges.
Front Row:- H.E. Scott, R.L. Fisher, L.C. Robinson, G.B. Lea, C.F. Coben.

THE OBSERVER CORPS CENTRE
Denne Road, Horsham.

The Centre at work, the photographs kindly provided by Mrs. Nellie Gill, formerly Nellie Jackson. Nellie was on duty the night that the code word "Diver" was first used; this was the code for the Flying Bomb.

The Canadian Invasion.

Wherever I went there was always a story about the Canadians and always with a great deal of warmth towards these young men who "invaded" the town from 1941 onwards.

In the Horsham Museum booklet, "The Town That Disappeared", the letters which were sent to the curator show a similar feeling by the boys to the town and the people; some in fact married local girls and stayed over, many never came back from the beaches of France.

Everyone remembers them with affection, the childrens' parties at Christmas, the dances, the pipe bands, and their generosity.

It was through them that the NFS. acquired its first canteen vehicle. They helped the locals to build the town's defences and later take them down.

Many families adopted a Canadian or two, a couple used to come over to The Post Office at Colgate to have a hot bath, Mr and Mrs Bateman had a young man who used to come on a Sunday for tea. Joe Lemm remembers them for a different reason, but still with great affection. John Christian's father used to collect pig swill from the camp at Monks Gate and said that in the swill there was always a tin of bully beef. Which Provost would put his arm in that?

They were all over the area, great camps of them. To give some idea, there were camps at:- Monks Gate, Plummers Plain, Strood Park, Denne Park, Warnham Park, Summers Place, Coolhurst, Barns Green, Knepp Castle, Marlpost Wood. At a number of large houses the officers were quartered and of course they were in Roffey Hospital, which became The Base Hospital.

Many people remember the fleets of ambulances carrying the wounded from Dieppe and seeing the injured in their "Hospital Blues" in and around the town. The hospital catered for the British as well as their own; it was to here that the injured from the Halifax bomber were brought to be treated.

The local girls were in great demand, and enjoyed the dances. The Canadians had better uniforms, were better fed and had more money to spend; it was like Hollywood coming to town!

They took part in local Home Guard exercises; at Mannings Heath they dressed up as Germans to defend the pill boxes. They sang, played their bag pipes, they boozed, they fought not only the locals, but each other. One shot his pal over some bread and cheese, and as John Christian said," They were of course over here, over paid and over sexed!", but we loved 'em for it".

Among the regiments in the district I have found the following :- Cn. Scottish; R.C. Engineers; 13th & 14th Field Rgt; 9th Cn. General Hospital; North Shore Rgt. Princess Pat's Rgt.; 85th Cn. Bridge Co.; R.C.A. Service Corps.; Stormont, Dundas and Glengarry Highlanders (what a lovely title!), Calgary Highlanders; Cn. Seaforth Highlanders; Cameron Highlanders; R.C. Corps of Signals; R.C. Anti Tank Rgt.; R.C. Artillery; Cn. Nova Scotia Highlanders; Royal Winnipeg Rifles.

Eventually they were presented with their own Y.M.C.A and Canteen by the town, where they held parties and dances. By and large it was a time that is remembered with great affection. One of my former colleagues who had been at Collyers, moaned to me that you couldn't get anywhere near the girls from the VIth Form at the High School, the Canadians were queuing at the gate! That reminds me — I must have a look at the birth rate for Horsham during the war!

THE AIR WAR.

The story of the men and machines, the bombings, the survivors and the flying bombs in and around the town.

THE AIR RAID INCIDENTS.

The following is a list compiled from the Police Records which are held at The County Records Office at Chichester and gives some idea of how the villages also suffered.

HORSHAM RURAL DISTRICT.

> 15 incidents. 28.08.40 to 25.03.44.
>
> 55 H.E's. 200 UXB's.
>
> No deaths or injuries recorded.

HORSHAM URBAN DISTRICT.

> 12 incidents. 01.10.40. to 24.03.44.
>
> 25 H.E's, 3 UXB's.
>
> 6 Killed, 26 Injured.

COWFOLD.

> 7 incidents. 29.05.40 to 21.12.44.
>
> 9 H.E's. 5 UXB's,
>
> No injuries or fatalities.

BILLINGSHURST.

> 13 incidents. 09.05.40 to 09.02.43.
>
> 27 H.E's 2 UXB's.
>
> No fatalities, 3 injured.

(facing page) KERVES LANE
On a sunny August morning in 1992, John Elphick and Alec Francis recount the day in 1944 when one of the two Mitchell bombers collided over the town and plunged to earth on the spot.

CRAWLEY.

    23 incidents. 25.08.40, to 24.03.44.

    30.H.E's. 7 UXB's.

    2 Killed. 11 injured.

HENFIELD.

    20 incidents.

    1 Killed and 2 injured on 13.10.41.

ITCHINGFIELD.

    7 incidents. 19.07.40 to 16.04.41.

    11 H.E's. Numerous UXB's.

LOWER BEEDING.

    22 incidents. 07.09.40. to 24 03.44.

    5 Killed and 2 injured on 09.09.40.

    The above at Colgate.

    11 H.E's.

NUTHURST.

    5 incidents. 11.09.40 to 23.03.44.

    5 H.E's.

RUDGWICK.

    8 incidents. 09.09.40 onwards ending with a Flying Bomb near the Church.

    31 H.E's

RUSPER.

    9 incidents. 09.09.40. onwards.

    13 H.E's.

SHIPLEY.

    5 incidents.   09.09.40. onwards.

    20 H.E's

WARNHAM.

8 incidents. 29.08.40. onwards.

29 H.E's.

WEST GRINSTEAD.

6 incidents reported.

There may well have been more which have gone unrecorded, and there were thousands of Incendiary Bombs dropped, but the above were those that were recorded at the time. For those with an interest in these things the staff at The West Sussex Records Office are only too willing to help.

Although the County Times reported them, they do not state where the bombs were dropped.

THE AIR RAIDS.

The town did not escape unscathed from the attentions of the Luftwaffe during the war, although considering its strategic position if got off quite lightly, but that is of little consolation to those who suffered from the bombing.

The most serious incidents occurred during the Battle of Britain period, but the town was never a specific target for bombing. I have often wondered what the effects would have been if the town had been targeted? The town centre with its small tight little streets and alleys would have been reduced to rubble in a short space of time. Indeed the problem of East Street was high on the agenda of Council Meetings in 1940. The parking of cars in the town and The Carfax and East Street in particular was a cause of great concern. The Fire Service felt that in the event of a major incident during the daytime the Brigade would have found great difficulty in attending.

The fire which destroyed Victory Road School showed up the weaknesses of the emergency services. The school was not the target of the Luftwaffe but the victim to a faulty central heating system! The local Fire Brigade became the target for a number of Councillors and the competence of the firemen was bought in to question. Mr Ken Parfitt, who attended as an A.F.S. fireman explained to me that it was not the Fire Brigade but the lack of water which was the cause of the problem. When they were called to the blaze there was insufficient pressure and the only stop cock which controlled the supply was situated near the railway station and this was only allowing a trickle through. The Councillors who had been most vociferous withdrew their allegations and apologised in the press. It didn't seem to make much difference, for when the Vulcanising Factory burnt down it was also a lack of water which hindered the fire fighters!

In Horsham and the surrounding area a number of people were killed and injured, including a young sixteen year old lad in the first major incident at Colgate in August, 1940. In November it was Horsham's turn when bombs were dropped on Orchard Road. In this a little baby was found in the rubble but her parents were sadly both killed. The villages suffered attacks, many because enemy aircraft were being pushed further back and in some cases just jettisoned their loads.

Hundreds of unexploded bombs were recorded throughout the area, thousands of incendiary bombs were unloaded, and there was also the added danger of shot down aircraft which seemed to make the villages a target. Mannings Heath had a spate of these and a house at Shipley was partly demolished one night.

As the war progressed the area became a target for 'hit and run' raiders. These were usually single engined fighters flying very fast who would creep in over the coast and look for a likely target such as a railway bridge or a train. One of these raiders dropped a bomb onto the line near the Worthing Road bridge, another did the same on the line at Southwater, others shot up the station at Partridge Green and shot up a train near Bramley. The town had its share of trigger happy pilots, a number of incidents being reported.

The Germans did not always get away. Nineteen airmen were buried at Hill's Cemetery in Horsham, some were also captured and became Prisoners of War. One or two of them had, so I'm told very lucky escapes, being snatched away just in time before irate soldiers could get their hands on them! The raids by aircraft of the Luftwaffe began to diminish and some street lighting was being considered when, just after

'D.Day' the town and villages awoke to the strange sound of the doodle bug or Pilotless Aircraft as it is referred to in the Log Book at Chichester.

Hitler's Revenge Weapon, had arrived. The first crashed in the Cuckfield district, but an early one is recorded to have exploded quite close to Marlands House at Itchingfield. They were so unsure of its origins that the markings are recorded and some of the makers numbers.

The town only received one direct hit, and that was on the fringe of the town, but cottages at Barns Green were hit, so was little Colgate again. Crawley had a nasty incident when some houses and the Post Office were hit. In all 23 of these missiles crashed in the district, but from my conversations with those who remembered the period they were very frightening. I was surprised when I discovered how low they often flew over the town. Fortunately for the people of this part of Sussex they were not visited by the later version the V2. The nearest that I have traced fell in the Guildford area.

In his book, Frank Holmes recorded that "In the area Captain Pugh was responsible for there were: 717 Alerts, 281 Incidents, 349 High explosive bombs, 23,692 Incendiary bombs, 23 Flying bombs, 10 Enemy planes crashed and two of our own. 22 people were Killed. 102 injured, 957 Buildings in the Urban district and a total of 2,676 for the whole area."

One of the saddest bombing incidents, not in our area, was the bombing one morning of The Boys' School at Petworth. It did not involve the greatest loss of life, but 28 boys, two of their teachers and a number of civilians were killed.

Reading the ARP Logs at the County Records Office at Chichester revealed an interesting statistic — many of the villages had more recorded 'incidents' than the town of Horsham. There were 12 recorded incidents for Horsham Urban District Council 15 for the rural District Council, but 22 for Lower Beeding, 20 for Henfield and 13 at Billingshurst.

Air Raid sirens had been provided for the town but many, if not all the villages did without. Roffey residents had to rely on the one from the centre of Horsham in the early days of the war. Many schools were still without shelters. In some village schools the parents either provided or dug their own; at Colgate parents started to keep children away at one stage until one was provided.

The town was defended by searchlights and some anti aircraft batteries, but there are no memories of a balloon barrage over the town.

My own memories of the 'Blitz' are very mixed. My home town in the north of England shared the same dangers. I still can remember being taken out to the shelter and seeing the flares hanging in the sky, and knowing that tonight it would be your turn! One memory is of a 'stick' of bombs dropping and realising that they were getting closer. They missed my parents' house, but demolished a number of shops and houses in the main road. The sound of the masonry and brickwork collapsing seemed to me to go on long after the explosion. The next morning I went up the street to have a look, but as a lad I couldn't help but wish that it had been Barcroft Street School. Why did they have to bomb the chip shop?

THE ORCHARD ROAD INCIDENT.

"Seven Killed When Germans Bomb South-East Town", that was the headline in the County Times on Friday, 6th December 1940. The South East town in question was Horsham and the unfortunate target was Orchard Road.

In the event, it turned out to be the most severe attack that Horsham would suffer, but in 1940 they weren't to know that. Seven people were killed, including a young evacuee from London.

One young child had a miraculous escape, but sadly her parents were killed in the raid. The baby became known as "The Orchard Road Baby" and I heard different stories about her rescue from a number of people, and determined to find her to hear the true story.

A number of the survivors are still living in the town and told of the events on that evening.

One of my former colleagues Andrew Snaddon and his wife lived in the road. Andrew died in 1980, but Laura still lives in the town and very kindly told me her recollections of the night.

"It was in November of 1940, it was only three doors up from us. The grandmother was in the house, it was a wonder anyone survived. We lived at No.26. The bomb went down in the middle of the road and took down the front of the houses. Mrs Dinnage, I think, was in No.8 and she was under the table and survived, but her whole house crumbled about her."

"They weren't Council Houses, they were called Subsidy Houses, and at the opposite end of the road there was always wheat fields and a row of five walnut trees."

"I don't recall the siren going, we weren't sheltering, it was before we got frightened about things. We were living in the front of the house and Andrew said that he would not go to choir practice, which he usually did on a Friday. I was rather pleased and I was very glad that he was at home at the time it happened."

"The first I knew was when the windows were blown in. I had a settee under the window and there was glass all over the place - otherwise I didn't hear a thing – I didn't hear the whistle, I didn't hear a sound as the bomb came down, I don't even recall an explosion, although there must have been. They say when you are close to it you don't hear it coming, but away in the distance they heard the whistle of it coming down - but we didn't hear a thing until the curtains blew in and all the things started to fall about us! We must have had some sort of warning. My daughter Jean was in her pram in the back sitting room and Brenda was on a bed I had made up from two easy chairs. My first reaction was to rush to the girls; I had brought them downstairs thank goodness! Immediately I rushed into them, I had to be careful not to put on a light, there were some Wardens outside patrolling up and down, I think they yelled "Put that light out", so we had to switch the light out in the front sitting room and I couldn't put the light on in the passage to see, but the front door was lying across the passage; it had been blown in. I said to Andrew, we can't stay here, we'll go round to my mother. The girls I think were still asleep! I had then to go upstairs to look for clothes for them and it was horrible. You took a step, and you didn't know whether your feet were safe, the ceiling had come down, half in the bedroom, there was plaster everywhere. Anyway we dressed them and put them in the pram and came out. The Wardens were hurrying up and down and said "You can't go up the road, a bomb has come down", and that was first we knew that it was a bomb that had fallen!".

"But all night long we had planes going over. I thought that it was a long raid, but we did hear afterwards that some of the planes could have been ours, probably from Shoreham. We came back to the house on Saturday morning; it was all cordoned off and we were told that we could not go up, but we said our house was up there, so Andrew and I went to see. The windows were all blown in at the front, plaster from the ceilings all over the floor, the front door was open and we had tiles off the roof; we certainly couldn't go upstairs to sleep. I remember that when we came back we had tarpaulin over the roof for well over a week or maybe longer!"

"As you got further down the road the last three houses weren't badly damaged. Ours wasn't too bad, I suppose, not as bad as two or three doors down. I think the road was repaired very quickly and of course there was the bus at the top of the road; there was a great deal of talk after, was it the bus lights or the lights of one of the houses where a door was opened and the light shone out when the bomb came down!"

"There was a very sad thing; in one of the houses there was a young girl evacuee, a very nice child. Her father had said could his daughter live in Horsham to get away from the air raids in London. The baby which was found in the debris went, I believe, to live with Dr. Williams for some months afterwards until her grandmother came out of hospital."

Another one of Mrs Snaddon's neighbours was Mr Garner, who told me "That I lived next door to them (Charman's) at No.18. The father and mother were killed but the baby was in a cot in the middle bedroom with a cord from a picture frame round her neck. We heard her cry about 2 o'clock and she was rescued from the back of the house. The father was George Charman and the mother was Rhoda Charman. Also in the house was the grandmother but Mr Charman senior was working on the railway as a driver and didn't know about it until he was told at the top of the road!"

Mr Garner was quite right, the grandmother was in the house at the time; she had been in the back sitting room and had been blown through the french windows onto the garden, suffering severe injuries which kept her in hospital for some time.

The story of the "Baby" was quite true. She was found some time later and rescued, so I'm told by Sergeant Peters of the Horsham Police and was cared for by Dr. Williams and his wife until her grandmother was well enough to take over. The baby? Alive and well, still living in Horsham, happily married with her own family and now able to talk about the events of that night. Quite naturally, being only two years old she can recall little of the bomb, but remembers going to play with the family of Dr. Williams until returning to her grandparents.

In Mr Frank Holmes' book, The History of Horsham St Johns', he interviewed Sgt. Law who talked about Orchard Road, "We had with us the late Dr. Williams, and he was marvellous, he seemed to be everywhere, helping and encouraging. It was a shambles when we arrived; it was difficult to know where to start. There were a number of dead and injured; everyone had to work quickly but carefully, because of the extent of the damage and possible collapse. Several were of course trapped in the rubble, but eventually everyone was accounted for, except for the baby of a young couple who had been killed. A further search was made with Dr. Williams every few minutes calling for silence, so that we could listen for a movement or cry. I'm thankful to say that it was heard, and one of the rescue squads found the baby under a table that had protected it from the rubble. The parents must have placed her there a few seconds before they were bombed."

Sgt. Law went on "One incident that night that did affect me very much was when a man came up to me and said 'I can't do any more for my own boy, could I help you with the others?' With his own son killed a few minutes before, and his own home destroyed, I could hardly answer him. It was the sort of person that made our job seem worthwhile."

The following week the County Times told the story as best they could; remember The Censor vetted everything they wrote.

Of the Baby :- "She was in her cot, cold with bricks around the bedclothes and the string from a picture frame hanging round her neck. She was quickly taken to a place of safety and was cared for by a local doctor, with whose children she was seen playing the day afterwards."

"All the neighbours did what they could for the unfortunate ones and the Salvation Army quickly arrived on the scene, dispensing tea and refreshments. The bursting of the water main hindered the Fire Brigade who were obliged to fill buckets from a crater in the road made by one of the bombs, but in a very short space of time all the services were working efficiently. Fifteen people were treated for injuries, including the driver of a bus whose vehicle was damaged by the explosion".

The bus driver was extremely unlucky. The story is that he and the conductor had got to the end of their run, turned round and were at the top of Depot Road and Orchard Road and had got out to have a cigarette when the bomb dropped, the driver being injured.

Horsham was not a specific target that night; there were raids on Portsmouth and Southampton. This was after The Battle of Britain period, but the Blitz was in full swing and the Luftwaffe had turned its attention on the cities as well as London.

Having heard and read the personal accounts of that evening, here is how was it reported officially!

In The Action Officers Minute Book held at The Records Office at Chichester it is recorded thus:-

Nov. 29. 1940.

22.10. Horsham, Orchard Road. 2 H.E at 21.45.

Houses demolished. Gas escaping, casualties not yet known.

Nov. 30. 01.21.

Casualties 2 men and 2 children killed. 2 men and 6 women seriously wounded; 3 men and women and 1 child slightly wounded. Total 20.

Nov. 30. 16.30. Horsham. Amended Casualty Returns.

	Dead.	Ser. Wd.	Slt. wd.
Men.	3	4	1
Women.	0	7	3
Children.	3	1	1

Total Casualties in the incident:-

> 6 Dead.

> 12 Seriously Injured.

> 5 Slightly Wounded.

> Total. 23 Casualties.

Finally on December 2nd the last report:-

> 16.40. Horsham.

> Gas, electric and Water Services now restored.

> 1 Woman, seriously injured has since died.

The houses were made safe or demolished and weren't rebuilt until after the war. I asked a number of people what it looked like just after the raid and Mrs Jean Baxter recalled that there seemed to be paper and what looked like school material strewn everywhere. Today a definite line can be seen between the prewar houses and those that were built after the war. The road itself on which the bomb fell bears no tell tale signs. When Mrs Laura Snaddon saw the picture which did eventually appear in the County Times she was quite surprised to see the amount of devastation that was caused to the road and housing.

Some idea of the devastation caused by the bomb in Orchard Road.

From a West Sussex Times Photograph.

34   ADVERTISEMENT

SPECIAL INFORMATION

ELECTRICITY
will save you
Money,
   Work,
      Anxiety
It is Cheap
   It is Clean
      It is Safe

'PHONE - - HORSHAM 86
or Call at
HORSHAM U.D. COUNCIL
SHOWROOM . CARFAX

THE ORCHARD ROAD INCIDENT

*Mr and Mrs Charman
sitting in the rear
garden outside the
French Windows.*

THE BABY

*Little Betty Charman,
the baby found in her
cot with a picture frame
round her neck.*

The local fire brigade lost two brigade Chiefs during the war years. The first was Mr. J.G. Gadd, who had served for 35 years; the second in July 1944 was Mr. Ernest Denny. The photograph shows the latter. The flower bedecked fire engine approaching Horsham Parish Church with Mr. Ron Lampard at the wheel.

THE ORCHARD ROAD BUS.

Whenever I spoke to anyone concerning the Orchard Road bombing incident the story of the bus and the crew came up in our conversations; even the West Sussex County Times mentions it in its coverage of the events.

I had been told a number of conflicting versions, the first by the late Harold Champion who himself had been walking home down Depot Road that evening and he suggested that the crew of driver and conductor were having a smoke and it was the light from the cigarette that had attracted the aircraft!

To obtain the true facts I contacted The Southdown Bus Co. and they were very helpful, but unable to shed much light on the events, although they were kind enough to send me copies of the Timetable in use at the time. Apparently they had given away much of their archival material when they had moved from Brighton to Lewes. This left me with the task of tracing the people involved, if at all possible? In the event it turned out a little easier than I imagined, and as is often the case the solution was close at hand! One of the secretarial staff at Forest Community School, Mrs Jean Baxter, informed me that she knew the daughter of the driver, and that she lived near the School! Not only that but the widow of the driver lived with the daughter! Eventually, after making a number of enquiries I was invited round to meet Mrs Rose and the daughter Mrs Reynolds and the whole story unfolded.

The story was at variance with those that I had hear. The bus was standing in Orchard Road, not Depot Road as I had been led to believe! The bus was on the Horsham (Carfax) to the Highlands Estate Service, (72,72B,73) and Mr Harold Rose was the Driver/Conductor – not a Driver and Conductor service as I thought! How unlucky they were can be judged from the point that they arrived in Orchard Road at 9.33pm and were due to depart at 9.43 and the bomb fell at 9.40pm!

According to Mrs Rose, her husband had stopped in Orchard Road and alighted from the bus and was talking to his friend Mr Ron Weedon when they heard the whistle of the bomb coming down. Mr Rose ran to the front of the bus and Mr Weedon ran to the rear. This meant that

Mr Rose was in fact running towards the bomb and his friend away from it! Mr Rose's memory of the next few seconds were of being swept up into the air and seeing the roofs of the houses being lifted off by the force of the explosion. Mr Weedon was sheltered from the full impact of the explosion and was relatively uninjured, but Mr Rose was very seriously injured and spent some considerable time in the hospital. The injuries that he sustained to his arm and hand meant that to all intents and purposes he never regained the full use of them again, although he continued to work in the Southdown office in Horsham.

Mrs Rose not only related the facts of the story but was able to produce the National Registration Card that her husband was carrying that night, issued, so I noticed only two weeks before the incident.

Mrs Rose had herself worked during the wartime period, in one of the local cinemas, The Odeon. Like most of the girls of that generation she remembers the town with affection, safe to walk around at night, one where it was safe for a woman to walk home at night, even though the streets were blacked out and that people seemed to help one another, more than it appears today.

Margaret Harmsworth behind the wheel of a Horsham Ambulance.

THE ORCHARD ROAD BUS

A copy of the National Registration Card that Harold Rose was carrying on that night in November 1940.
Below, looking down Orchard Road in 1992 towards where the bus would be waiting. It was due out at 9.43; the bomb fell at 9.40!

SMOKE HOUSE FARM, BROOMERS CORNER.

Heinkel IIIH-5 crashed durinbg a raid on Southampton. The three holes in the roof show where the propeller came to rest!

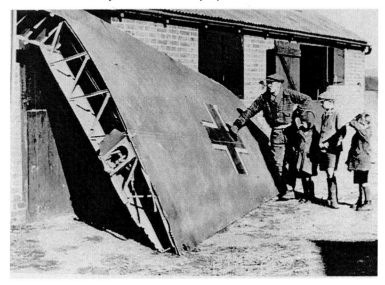

This large section of wing fell onto a nearby poultry farm.

COLGATE: THE AFTERMATH

*The District Nurse's House: a poignant picture; just the front gate left.
Below a picture looking towards the junction with the remains
of the Village Hall showing.*

COLGATE REMEMBERED.

On a dull overcast night in September 1940, the little village of Colgate was at the centre of a tragic air raid and the peace of this Sussex village was shattered. It was on the receiving end of a 'stick' of bombs and five people lost their lives.

Gerry and the late Edith Menezes had moved into The Post Office and General Stores around 1938/39, and Gerry still recalls that the salary in those days, as Postmaster was £52 a year! He also delivered the papers, collecting them from Faygate Station in the morning.

Gerry and Edith recalled the events of that September evening for me; "It was an evening in September 1940 when the calm was shattered. The first bomb was dropped on The District Nurse's House. The local Policeman from Roffey called and asked for help and I went down with him and another man and we managed to find the Nurse and we took her to The Village Hall which doubled as a First Aid Post. Unfortunately, a further two bombs dropped, one on the back of The Post Office and the other on The Village Hall, killing Nurse Hocken, and fatally wounding one of the first aid workers, Heather Barnes. A further bomb had been deposited close to the Church wall, this one killing three Auxiliary Firemen, including a young sixteen year old boy."

"The Assistant Postmaster and The Head Postmaster came out the next day and they were only concerned because the Date Stamp was missing! So we had to search in the rubble until we found it!"

Mrs Rose Stace recalled how, on that evening, her brother was out in the forest fighting some incendiary fires and it was only later that they learned that he had been killed. She recalled for me how Mr Barnes, The Chief Warden, had called round to tell them and also saying that his own daughter had 'caught a packet' when the Hall was bombed. It had been a terrible night for the villagers. The first bomb had demolished the Nurse's house and as PC Baird and Gerry had been rescuing the Nurse it returned and dropped a further three bombs onto the village. The first of these must have landed on the churchyard gate killing Ian Campbell, Jack Constable and young William Doick. The second landed on the Hall killing the already injured Nurse Hocken and tragically fatally injuring Heather Barnes. The third hit the Post Office at the rear. By this time Edith and Gerry had taken refuge in the forest. Not to be outdone the aircraft then returned and dropped two more bombs which did not detonate; one went off the next morning and, strangely one according to the account in the County Records Office exploded a long while after.

For her work on that night 'Nanny' White received The George Medal and Heather Barnes received posthumously the Guides V.C.

Gerry told me that as well as 'Nanny' White he felt that the Roffey Policeman deserved to have been decorated after that evening. I discovered, thanks to Edith and Gerry, some of the rubble from the old Post Office. It is in the garden of The Dragon, the village pub! You will find in the garden of the pub a small brick air raid shelter built from the rubble of The Post Office and it was built to provide some shelter for the villagers. Edith was quite incensed when after collecting the bricks free of charge the builder then charged £25 for their contribution to its construction! A seat was presented to the Church and this was consecrated by the Bishop of Lewes.

THE AIR WAR
Hit and Run Raiders.

Although the most serious raids had been Headline news there were, never the less, a number of minor incidents, some of which resulted in the loss of life.

Two nasty incidents involving railwaymen made headline news, when attacks on trains, one at Bramley and one at West Grinstead resulted in the death of 7 people.

"Cannon fire and machine gun fire was rained down on a train and station, and one eye witness said the sound of empty cases showering down was like a hail of broken glass. People on the bridge near the station took cover and men working in the Goods Yard nearby sheltered under the trucks", so reported The County Times.

"The planes, upon which the black crosses could be clearly seen, approached from the south west and on their way to the village fired several bursts at a school, only damaging the branches of the trees about 50 yards away."

In Aug. '92, Mr Chris Lawrence of Partridge Green recounted how, as a member of staff at the school, which was St. Thomas Mores Approved School, he had been conducting a woodwork lesson in his workshop when he heard the sound of gun fire. He heard the planes approaching and shouted for the lads to "Get down". The planes passed low overhead, and when he went outside to look for damage, all along the wall there was a thick carpet of pine needles and spent cartridge cases!".

At the station, Mr G. Court was in the signal box when the raiders came over and took shelter in the corner of the box - the door was open and several shots hit the box, one passing through the door, missing Mr Court, hitting one of the levers leaving a large dent.

Mr Court told one of the County Times reporters that the train had been going to Brighton and had stopped about 100 yds. from his box. The driver Mr George Ansbridge of Horsham, had been dismounting from the engine to take shelter when he was hit, but the fireman was uninjured. Later it was found that a platelayers hut was also riddled with holes.

On the safety of Signalmen, I asked Frank Holmes, who had worked throughout the war in Boxes all over the south, if they were given any special protection? "No" said Frank in his own laconic manner, "Just a tin hat and a gas mask!".

I also asked if there were any boxes which were more dangerous than others? Frank thought maybe Arundel Junction was the worst. "A bloody nuisance that place" was Frank's comment. "They bombed that every day, every day they came over, a little old box, right out in the "sticks" - no protection."

"If we thought we were going to be in the way, we'd go down and crouch beside the wall, the thickest bit of the wall!"

"No protection, a tin hat and a gas mask, no shelters, a bit pointless really", said Frank with a smile.

"Everything was covered, catered for – sabotage, bombing, in case of invasion – it was all planned. At Arundel it was easy for them to come in and out again, over the coast, before even the Radar could catch 'em. In fact they could have dropped their bombs on the coast and land them on Arundel Junction if they'd been better shots, without coming inland at all. They stopped Arundel once. They blew a hole in the banking, they never did score a direct hit on the place. At Pulborough we had a bit of a rough afternoon once - they were Stukas, I think, machine gunning and bombing, but the Bofors Gun, which the Canadians were looking after stayed silent all the time; they were in my mates house, under a table."

Another serious attack on a train resulted in the death of 5 people. These included, Mr George Budd, the driver and Mr G. Jeal, the guard and on this occasion 5 passengers, including a young scholar from Christ's Hospital School. This incident occurred at Bramley, on the Horsham to Guildford line. The same aircraft may well have been among those which "shot up" Horsham on the same day.

Tony Jupp was a pupil at Chesworth School and remembers clearly all diving under desks. Mr New, The Headmaster was sitting at an old fashioned chair, he moved fast, shouting "Duck" and hit the floor". Tony remembers that a shell went through the roof and ceiling and some wooden partitioning. At the same time the junior children at The High School were having their Christmas Party and the VIth Form were preparing to put on "Babes in The Wood". By one of those strokes of good fortune, no one was injured, they could have been, one bullet passing through an unoccupied classroom, though a blackboard and wall. I have been told by a number of former girls, that the hole was visible for quite some time, even after the war.

The County Times reported the following week, "Those at work in the School saw only one plane which was so low that the flashes of the machine guns in the rear cockpit could clearly be seen", and went on "Several of the children said they considered the party "the most exciting they had ever had!".

Among the "casualties" that day were the Mineral Bottling Plant of King and Barnes and the Gasworks, but again without sustaining injuries.

Gradually, bit by bit, the Air War was slowly coming to an end; German aircraft were to be seen less and less in the skies of Southern England and the people of Horsham were just beginning to relax when a new and far more sinister sound sent a shiver through the townspeople: the "doodle bug" had arrived!

Not really within the area that I am covering, but readers might not be aware that one of the worst and most tragic raids in West Sussex occurred at Petworth. In one very sad incident the Boys School was bombed. 26 children and adults were killed and 33 were injured. In Petworth a total of 15 incidents were reported.

The last major bombing incident of the war happened on the afternoon of 10th of February, 1943 when at about 4 o'clock a single aircraft swept low over the town and deposited 2 bombs on the north of the town. One demolished one house in Wimblehurst Road and one in Richmond Road. Fortunately no one was killed although a number of ladies at a Bridge Party had a lucky escape! The aircraft came in very low and was seen by many people, Una Penny as she sat on her balcony and Syd Weller from The Post Office. Looking at an aerial photograph of Horsham it does seem as though C.I.B.A. could have been the intended target.

Damage at Colgate

THE AIR RAIDS 1940

339

1940

use of the Hall after 'Break' each morning and afternoon — and for assemblies on Tues., Thurs. and Fri. A.M., and Friday P.M.

26. Sept.   Air Raid Warning 4·01 p.m – 4·45 p.m. Boys retained in shelters. S.A.O. called

27. Sept.   Air Raid Warning 9·14 A.M. – 10·04 A.M. Play was therefore curtailed. Warning 3·20–3·50 p.m. Mr. Honeybun, practising teacher, concluded his period of three weeks today.
Attendance
Roll 163   Av. 147·5   91·05%.

30. Sept.   Air Raid Warnings 9·15 A.M. – 10·13 A.M. and 10·18 – 11·06 A.M. also 1·23 p.m. – 2·08 p.m.

6 et-1 st   E. f West. visited p.m. Air Raid. Air Raid Warnings 1·3 – 1·56 p.m. 2·10 – 3·25 p.m.

2. Oct.   Warnings 9·7 – 9·37 : 10·01 – 10·53 : 2·07 – 2·21 : 3·03 : 3·30.

4. Oct.   Attendance
Roll 165   Av. 147·4   89·6%.
Air Raid Warning 1·58 p.m. – 5·35 p.m. After 4·45 p.m. boys who wished to go were sent home a few at a time. Mr. Hebden received calling up notice.

7. Oct.   Air Raid Warnings. 10·20 A.M. – 11·15 A.M. 1·28 p.m. – 2·25 p.m.

To give some idea of the disruption to normal schooling, I have selected a page out of the Oxford Road Log Book, as written up by Mr. Hawkins.

THE AIR WAR – THE SAD SIDE.

In my efforts to seek out the truth behind many of the stories a number of rather sad events were related to me, both concerning the British and the German side. How many of them are entirely accurate I will leave the reader to judge.

I was told early in my research about the aircraft that came down at Slaughter Bridge – an inappropriate name to start with! The story teller was a lady from Warnham and she remembered the local school children being taken down to help clear up the debris for a farmer; at that point it was assumed that the crew had baled out safely, but this was not the case. The crew were discovered impaled in the trees. On checking the story with a local aviation group they thought that as the aircraft crashed through a copse and that in this type of aircraft the crew were sitting in a glazed nose section with very little protection, the story was quite plausible. Nasty!

Another tale this time from Partridge Green was related by Mrs Illingworth, now a resident in Worthing, but in those days a youngster at Jolesfield School. She remembered very clearly the Junkers 88 which crashed one morning near the Station. She was on her way to school and they went to have a look at the wreck. It had crashed into one the small cottages and the pilot was found dead in one of the upstairs bedrooms. She remembers getting into terrible trouble with her father because they had been warned to stay away, and Mrs Illingworth recalls seeing flesh and bits of skin lying around.

Peter Baxter recalled going to see the site of the Hurricane which had crashed at Holbrook and seeing the indentation in the ground where the poor unfortunate pilot had died.

The thoughts of John Christian who saw the young pilot from an Me109, which crashed at Plummers Plain; it was the first time that John had ever seen a fatally wounded man. John remembers that he was in a terrible state.

Today, well over forty years after the event, Don Bateman can remember seeing the two Halifax crew members lying with their parachute canopies draped over them on the Golf Course, having tried and failed to escape from their doomed aircraft.

Who could fail to be moved by the story of Colgate, and of Gerry Menezes and Sgt. Baird from Crawley after going to the rescue of the Village Nurse and taking her to the Village Hall to be treated and leaving her in the care of Heather Barnes to watch and see the destruction of that same Hall fifteen minutes later, and then be touched by the story told to me by Mrs Rose Stace that it was Mr Barnes, the village Warden who had to go and break the news to her that her brother had also been killed, and knowing that his daughter was also dead. Terrible times.

Also from Partridge Green came a story of German Spies and the strange unexplained death of a young German airman at the hands of the Canadians. Strange!

On a happier note, the story of the Me109 which crashed at Romans Gate and the engine which demolished the privy!!

The lucky escape of the young baby in a pram at Amies Mill Farm. Normally she was put to bed upstairs but on that evening in 1944 she was fast asleep in a pram downstairs when one of the engines from one of the two Mitchells crashed through the roof!

Finally, the escape of Ken Parfitt, a Fireman, looking into a bomb crater at Nuthurst when the bomb exploded!

Are the stories true? Who can tell, certainly not me, but they may stir a few memories.

WIMBLEHURST ROAD INCIDENT

It was on this corner on the right that the first of two bombs was deposited on the afternoon of 10th February 1943. The second fell in Richmond Road, in a straight line with CIBA!

THE GUILDFORD ROAD INCIDENT

It was on the left behind the trees that a lone FW190 either dropped its bomb or engine before crashing in Broadbridge Heath.
Two people were slightly injured but 200 houses were damaged; the pilot was captured at Billingshurst.

THE WORTHING ROAD INCIDENT.

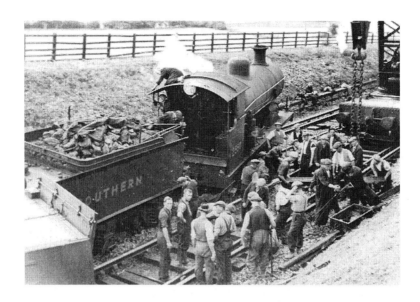

Amies Farm today.

Part of the engine of one of the Mitchell bombers tore through the end the house. Just a few different coloured tiles give any clue to the damage.

WAR IN THE AIR.

The town and the villages had a grandstand view as the war in the air unfolded, as I began the research I quickly discovered that a large number of aircraft had crashed in the area. The details of each crash are to be found in various books and booklets, so I have set below just the bare essentials. It all began in 1939 when a Lysander force landed at Broadbridge Heath.

27.10.39   Lysander.L6862 at Broadbridge Heath.

21.04.40   Hurricane N2500 at Cowfold.

27.06.40   Gladiator at Lower Beeding.

09.09.40   Junkers JU88 at Newells Farm, Nuthurst,

09.09.40   Messerschmitt l09E at Romans Gate.

09.09.40   Messerschmitt 109E at Cootham.

30.08.40   Heinkel III at Mannings Heath.

30.08.40   Heinkel 111 at Swires Farm, Capel.

29.10.40   Messerschmitt l09E at Plummers Plain.

27.08.40   Hurricane at Holbrook.

17.04.41   Junkers JU88 at Slaughter Bridge.

13.03.41   Heinkel III at Smoke House Farm, Shipley.

10.04.41   Heinkel III at Alfold Crossroads.

28.08.41   Junkers JU88 at Partridge Green.

13.02.41   Beaufighter lF at Partridge Green.

13.08.43   Lancasteer ED361 at Plaistow.

19.11 43   Lancaster JB605, at Oakwood Hill.

06.12.43   Spitfire XII at Roffey Corner (Forest Road)

06.12.43   Spitfire XII collided with above, at Colgate.

20.11.43   Focke Wulf 190 at Broadbridge Heath.

07.01.44 Mitchell in the grounds of Rikkyo School.

07.01.44 Mitchell collided with above, same place.

19.04.44 Messerschmitt 410 at Cooks Farm, Nuthurst.

08.06.44 Mitchell II at Worthing Road, Horsham.

08.06.44 Mitchell II collided with above, at Kerves Lane.

17.02.45 Halifax III at Golf Course, Mannings Heath.

Others that have come to light since include:-

17.04.41 Defiant I at Slaugham.

19.04.44 Mustang at Honeywood House, Rowhook.

24.12.43 Spitfire Vb at Munthorne Farm, Horsham.

13.02.41 Beaufighter IF at Partridge Green.

13.08.40 Whitley bomber at Ifield.

03.08.08 Spitfire at Billingshurst.

24.05.44 Spitfire at Maplehurst.

09.09.40 Spitfire at Loxwood.

01.10.40 Spitfire at Henfield.

There was another Spitfire which landed at Billingshurst and a number of aircraft crashed onto the newly opened airfield at Coolham, the largest being a four engined USAF Liberator! This in fact made an emergency landing and some days later managed to take off! This is the list at the moment of writing, and does not include an Italian aircraft that is purported to have crashed at Hills Farm.

MADE IN GERMANY, SCRAPPED IN ENGLAND!

Scrap from the Mannings Heath Heinkel III.
This aircraft broke up in the air and scattered the debris over the village.

The remains of the Junkers 88 at Partridge Green.
A number of badly damaged houses can be seen in the background.

Photographs courtesy of Andy Saunders.

HILL'S CEMETERY AND THE GERMAN GRAVES.

Many of the older residents know of the German War Graves in Hill's Cemetery but are often surprised and quite often disappointed to learn that they are no longer there.

There were at one time 19 graves in the cemetery, all German aircrew and in the 1950's they were reburied in the German War Cemetery at Cannock Chase. I have yet to discover if they were given a Military Funeral; perhaps someone can remember?

The following is the list of those who were buried in the cemetry and whose names appear in The Register, still held today by The Superintendent, who kindly allowed me to copy the names. I have been able to add the location and aircraft to each name.

No.1. 30.08.40.   Oblt. Paul Waechter.

No.2. 30.08.40.   Gefr. G. Maehlbeck.

                    He 111, crashed at Mannings Heath.

No.3. 09.09.40.   Uffz. Karl Born.

                    Me 109, crashed at Romans Gate.

No.4. 29.10.40.   Uffz. Alfred Lenz.

                    Me 109, crashed in flames at Plummers Plain.

No.5. 12.03.41.   Fw. Alexander Dussel. He.111, Ockley, parachute failed to open and landed in Lintotts Field, Fivens Green, Holbrook.

No.6. 13.03.41.   Uffz. Eric Hermann.

No.7. " "   Uffz. Graf Callice.

No.8. " "   Gefr. Leopold Schmid.

No.9. " "   Obergefr. W. Hallert.

                    All from He.111 which crashed at Broomers Corner.

No.10. 19.04.41.   Fw. Heinz Bukart.

No.ll. 19.04.41.   Obertw. Wolfgang Haselsteiner.

No.12. " "   Ober. Walter Rudi Scheitauer.

No.13. " "   Obergefr. Bruno Kalmus.

All from Ju.88 which crashed at Slaughter Bridge, Slinfold.

No.14. 28.07.41.   Oberfw. Eitel Fredrich Mielke.

No.15. " "   Uffz. Josez Stepniewicz.

No.16. " "   Uffz. Walter Dankenbrink.

No.17. " "   Uffz. O.Haefker.

All from Ju.88 which crashed at Partridge Green.

No.18. 19.04.44.   Uffz. Ernest Tesch.

No.l9. " "   Lt. Reinhold Witt.

Both from Me.410 which crashed at Nuthurst.

THREE ENEMY PLANES DOWN

Three German planes were shot down during dog fights and raids that took place over a south east town and nearby villages on the evening of September 9 and into the early hours of the morning, and there were several casualties. Three German prisoners were taken to a local police station one to a hospital and another was killed.

(Extract taken from The West Sussex County Times;
it was usual to refer to the town as "a south east town").

KARL BRUNING.

St.Fw. Karl Bruning was the pilot of the Heinkel III which was shot down by F/O F.D. Hughes and Sgt. F. Gash in a Defiant during a raid on Liverpool on March 12th 1941. The aircraft crashed at Ockley. Karl was wounded and was taken to a nearby Home Guard Post where he was treated kindly. He was then transferred to Horsham Police Station under guard by the Canadians. He was subsequently transferred to Horsham Hospital where he was operated on immediately and a friendly nursing sister brought him a glass of milk and some cigarettes.

A former nurse, Mrs Marjorie Bowyer recalled that although she hated the Germans they seemed so young and so frightened when they came in. One even refused to have an injection, he thought that it was lethal!

(Photo and details from Andy Saunders)

RESCUED GERMAN PILOT FROM BLAZING PLANE.
THREE SUSSEX MEN AWARDED COMMENDATIONS.
CARRIED ON DESPITE HAIL OF BULLETS.

Three Sussex men who rescued the pilot of a crashed Me109 have been awarded commendations. The announcement is made in a supplement to The London Gazette.

The three men are:-

> Frank Burgess, Cowman of Plummers Plain.
>
> Thomas Gilbert Childs, Labourer, a member of the Home Guard, of South Street, Partridge Green,
>
> Charles Gardener, Labourer, a member of the Home Guard of Littleworth, Partridge Green.

The rescue took place on October 29th, 1940, when the Me109 crashed at Plummers Plain and caught fire. The Pilot could not free himself and must have burned to death if there had not been close at hand men ready to face danger to save him. Mr Childs and Mr Gardener were doing building work on the Plain, Mr Burgess, the cowman was in a neighbouring field. All three at once went up to the aircraft, which was burning with increasing fierceness and endeavoured to release the pilot.

In the crash one of the wings of the aircraft had been wrenched off with the result that the cockpit was tilted at an angle making it difficult to remove the pilot. Two of the men held up the wing while the other pulled the pilot from the burning aircraft. By this time all the pilot's outer clothing was on fire.

Before the rescuers had carried the pilot more than a few yards from the aircraft a shower of machine gun bullets compelled them to leave him for a few seconds, but they went back despite the danger of further bullets exploding or of an explosion and dragged the pilot to a safer distance. They then stripped off his burning clothing. Had the men been one minute later in attempting the rescue of this enemy pilot their effort must have failed on account of the increasing fire. Mr Gardener was burned on the wrist.

This report appeared in the West Sussex County Times. The aircraft in question had been shot down by P/O Guy Marsland of 253 Squadron. The German Pilot, Uffz. Alfred Lenz was taken to Horsham Hospital but was so badly burned that he died of his wounds the next day. He was buried, so I am informed, with Full Military Honours in Hill's cemetery.

Mr. Thomas Gilbert Child

One of the three men awarded Commendations for their rescue of Alfred Lenz, the young German pilot, from his burning Me109 at Plummers Plain.

THE FLYING BOMB SAGA

Shortly after the start of the "D Day" landings, Hitler launched his revenge weapon, the flying bomb on the country. Because of it's strategic position Horsham and the district found themselves once again in the firing line.

Many are vividly remembered by the locals and most remember how vulnerable they felt. The Observer Corps in Denne Road had been warned to be on their guard and the code word "Diver" had been pre-arranged to signal the start of the offensive.

Mrs Nellie Gill, then Nellie Jackson, remembered the night when the word came through from the outlying posts that the first bomb had been sighted and the tension in the Centre as she plotted it up from the coast. Tommy Hol was also on duty that night and he can still recall and feel the tension as the bomb was plotted slowly up the board, steadily on, step by step onwards towards Horsham. Tom recalled how the Centre became suddenly quiet as Nellie plotted its cours. The "doodle bug" passing overhead on its way to London.

Nellie still maintains to this day, that it was the Centre at Horsham not Maidstone that plotted the first of these weapons, although Maidstone claimed the honour!

A number fell in and around the town. One came to earth in Chesworth Farm, exploding with its engine still running, demolishing some farm buildings.

The village of Barns Green was also a target, a number of cottages being demolished. One of the first to figure in the A.R.P. Logs came down at Marlands at Itchingfield.

The last one in the area is recorded at Rudgwick on the 13th August 1944, doing considerable damage to houses, shops and the church.

One story that was told to me by Mr Arthur Leighton-Porter, at that time flying Typhoon fighter bombers, based at Redhill, puts a slightly different complexion on the picture, which somewhat amused me! Arthur's squadron had been trying to intercept these bombs, with some success.

Unfortunately, the residents of Redhill viewed their efforts rather differently! As far as they were concerned, the bombs were targeted on London and the Royal Air Force should leave well alone!

As far as I can ascertain, none of the more lethal follow-up weapons, the awesome V2's, fell in the district, but if they did, perhaps someone will tell me!

CHESWORTH FARM, 1992.

In the early hours of 21st of July 1944, this peaceful edge of town scene was shattered by one of Hitler's dreaded V1's.

Little remains today of the incident. At the time it was recorded that "Considerable damage to field of wheat at Chesworth Farm. 05.56.". Half a mile further and Gorings Mead would have been on the receiving end!

THE FLYING BOMBS.

The West Sussex County Times carried an article in late 1945 and I thought that it was well worth including. The war was at an end so censorship was less strict, I quote:-

HORSHAM DISTRICT HAD 23 FLY-BOMBS.
Seven Women Die at Crawley.
Children among the injured.

Twenty three flying bombs fell in Horsham and the rural district during the three months that the attack by the Germans' much vaunted "terror weapon" was at its height. They caused seven fatal casualties - all of them women, who died as a result of one incident at Crawley - twenty five people were seriously injured and thirty four, including three children were slightly injured.

Only one flying bomb came down in Horsham itself. That was in the middle of July when one crashed at Chesworth Farm and caused damage to a field of wheat. There were no casualties.

The rural population bore the brunt of the attack for although nearly every flying bomb landed on open ground, nearby farms, farm buildings and cottages were damaged and sometimes wrecked by blast.

The seven fatal casualties occurred at Crawley when a bomb which had been shot down by a fighter fell at the junction of Oak Road and West Street. Twelve houses were totally demolished together with a small workshop. Forty five people were injured, 15 women and eight men seriously.

The way in which the Civil Defence services and the W.V.S. rose to the occasion and the calm manner in which residents behaved has been the subject of considerable praise.

The first of the robots to land in the district came down at Marlands, Itchingfield on June 6th causing damage to the stables and houses on the estate and killing about fifty chicken. This was before the official news that flying bombs were being used had been released and when it flew over many people hearing the peculiar noise of its engine thought it was a plane in trouble.

Christ's Hospital was damaged and a woman was slightly hurt on June 20th when a flying bomb exploded in midair after being shot up by a fighter and at the end of August houses on the Holmbush estate including that of the owner Brig. General H. Clifton Brown, M.P. were slightly damaged when a bomb exploded in a wood.

Villages that have also suffered include Itchingfield, Ifield, Billingshurst, Cowfold, Barns Green, Partridge Green, where Jolesfield House was badly damaged, Colgate, Warnham, Shipley, Mannings Heath, Slinfold, Rusper and Rudgwick.

News was also released this week that Horsham has had 700 air raid warnings since September 3rd 1939.

Bits and Pieces!

In my travels I collected so much material that it was very difficult to select the most appropriate or the funniest. I had in the end enough material for two books, but there were a number of quotes which I thought I would pop into the book somewhere. My apologies to those that I may have missed, but I have tried to select something from all my interviews.

~Always Monday, one shirt during the week and a clean one for Sunday." *Shirley Glaysher on Wash Days.*

"She was always giving something away, she was too generous" *Alf Murrell on Nellie Laughton.*

"It started life as The Air Defence Cadet Corps, then became 87 Squadron A.T.C."
George Coomber on Collyers A.T.C.

"It was called "The Yellow Peril" a converted fever ambulance, it was so comfortable that people slept in it!".
Margaret Buchanan on the Ambulance.

"Coupons were a problem, we spent hours counting them, and when we had "blackout" material we had long queues outside. Girls made frocks out of it!"
Mrs Laker on the problems of Shopkeeping.

"German P.O.Ws built part of Bennetts Road, at the top end, Nice bunch of lads.
Tony Jupp on the German P.O.W's.

"The doodle bug at Barns Green damaged 2 farm cottages. We rescued a young mother and baby; the one at New Town flattened all the allotments".
Ken Parfitt on the "Doodle Bugs".

"I remember dancing round the bandstand. It was a great night, events in the Park, there were flags and bunting everywhere".
Sheil Elphick on V.E.Day.

"If you didn't go to the High School, you took The Civil Service Exam."
June Evans on leaving school.

"What a delicious smell, a cross between sump oil and leather seats!"
Margaret Woolven on "Comfy Coaches".

"Horsham, Australia sent food parcels to Horsham W.I. during the war, mainly dried fruit."
Mrs Percy Spriggs on Horsham W.I.

"Search light camp at B.B.H, "Searchlight Dances" were held, Bomb Disposal came after the war."
Trish Chanter on B.B.H Army Camp.

"Registers in Schools had to be taken to the shelters, in case of air raid."
John Elphick on Oxford Road School.

A TALE OF A TAIL GUNNER

Very early in my research I had occasion to interview Mr Ken Lane. It was in connection with his early years as a schoolboy at Collyer's Grammar School in Horsham and in particular about a School Journey to Germany, which had to dash home in August 1939. It was while we were discussing the trip that Ken produced a little blue paper back from a book case. The book was entitled "Tail Gunner" by Flt. Lt. R.C. Rivaz D.F.C., priced 1/6d! It appeared that the author had been a Master at Collyer's before the war and had been one of the Masters on the trip to Germany.

I borrowed the book and promised Ken that I would find out a little more about the author and his activities during the war. Ken seemed to think that he had survived the war and had been killed sometime after the end of hostilities.

I read the book with interest, but it gave few clues. It had been written during the war, the censor had deleted all that would have been of any use to the enemy, names, places, aircraft and squadrons. The author had served in Bomber Command and his story started shortly after being posted to his first squadron. He goes on to recall his first skipper, "Whom I was later to know as Leonard" and somewhat later "noticed that he seemed to know everyone and that most people called him simply "Cheese"! I read on and became more and more convinced that I might have come across his name before. It took almost a year and after a number of attempts I managed to make contact with one of his former colleagues, now retired and living in The West Country, Mr A.N. Willson.

Mr Willson very kindly wrote a long letter, about life in Horsham during the war and the young Art and P.E. Teacher, "He left us to join the R.A.F. in 1940, but visited us during his service years and intended to come back to Collyer's when the war was over, but in 1945 he took a job editing an R.A.F. magazine and would pick up lifts in Service Aircraft to visit R.A.F. Stations. It was sadly, during one of these flights in a Liberator that he lost his life".

The letter went on to say "He did indeed fly with Leonard Cheshire V.C., at the time Bomber Command was changing over from Whitley's to Halifaxes and I had the experience of flying with them on a training flight or two at Linton on Ouse near York. I was at the time C.O. of the School A.T.C. and Ronnie Rivaz specially got me invited to stay there as I was very inexperienced in the ways of the R.A.F., a typical friendly act!"

So my suspicions were confirmed and thanks to a good friend in the R.A.F.A. I was able to write to Group Captain Cheshire, V.C. and ask if he could tell me a little more about Ronnie Rivaz and I am delighted to say that he took the time and trouble to reply.

The trip to Germany!!! Let Austin Willson tell the tale, "The Collyer's School Journey on the Continent led by my late dear friend Andrew Henderson which hurried home in 1939 was certainly not from Germany, but was from Switzerland. "Hendy" as he was called, would not have ventured into Germany as he was in bad odour with the German Authorities. He had some problems with a certain "youth movement", he felt he was high on their "wanted list!"

TAIL GUNNER.

Standing proudly beneath their Whitley bomber, flight and ground crew of Leonard Cheshire in the centre and on the right R.C. Rivaz. (Imperial War Museum Photograph)

TAIL GUNNER TAKES OVER.

That was the title of Flt. Lt. R.J. Rivaz's second book and dealt with his time whilst training as a pilot. The book closes with him waiting to join an operational squadron.

I made strenuous efforts in the press and sent a number of letters to various quarters but in the end I had to rely on The Librarian at the R.A.F. Museum at Hendon to furnish some details of his career. There had been some correspondence between his publisher and the R.A.F. in 1955 and through this I was able to trace part of his career.

He joined No.9 Bombing and Gunnery School in Wales, Penrhos in May 1940 and went to No.10 OTU Abingdon in June 1940.

He joined No.102 Squadron at Topcliffe in August 1940. It was from the airfield at Stanton Harcourt that the daylight raid was made on the Scharnhorst, in which he won the D.F.C.

His final rank was Acting Squadron Leader, Decorations M.I.D. 24.9.41. D.F.C. 24.10.41.

He was tragically killed in a flying accident on October 13th, 1945 in a Liberator at Brussels.

"ENGINEER FLIES BOMBER HOME."

The story of Flight Engineer Gilbert Steere from Rusper is told in "To Shatter The Sky" by Bruce Barrymore Halpenny, a book that chronicles the experiences of aircrew during the war.

One of the contributors to the book is a Canadian, Pilot Officer Gordon J. Ritchie, who was the rear gunner on the same aircraft. According to his account they were serving on 429 (Bison) Squadron, Royal Canadian Air Force, stationed at R.A.F. Leeming in Yorkshire, flying Halifax bombers.

On the night in question they were detailed to Acheres, a marshalling yard behind the German lines in France, shortly after 'D' Day. (June 8/ 9th)

The pilot Sq. Ldr. W.B. Anderson had been appointed flight commander and had taken the crew through some 'dicey' do's to targets such as Berlin, Leipzig and The Ruhr and had been awarded the D.F.C, of which he learnt shortly before take off.

As they crossed the French coast at Dieppe they were hit by flak and the pilot was caught by a large fragment in his side and gave the order to bale out. The aircraft went into a vertical dive and it became difficult for the crew to get out of the aircraft and it was at this point that Gilbert Steere took over. He pulled the pilot out of his seat and levelled out the aircraft, but by this time the navigator, bomb aimer and wireless operator had managed to get out over France. The mid-upper gunner Flt. Sgt Mangione from Ottawa and Gordon Ritchie went forward to render first aid. They then jettisoned the bomb load near Dieppe and headed for England.

Gilbert Steere was flying the aircraft sitting in a bucket seat wearing a chest-pack parachute and was unable to see out of the aircraft, flying solely by the artificial horizon.

They managed to drag the skipper back down the aircraft and attach him to a static line although by this time he was in a bad state. They made a Mayday call to several airfields before they eased the stricken pilot out of the aircraft. By this time Gilbert Steere was getting concerned about the amount of fuel left on board.

It was then time for them to leave and after trying the various emergency exits left by the rear hatch. The last to leave was Flight Sergeant Steere.

The aircraft, Halifax, LW128 AL-V, 'Impatient Virgin' crashed near Wallingford in Oxfordshire. The three remaining members were reunited at R.A.F. Benson. The bomb aimer and wireless operator after a few days freedom were taken prisoner, but the navigator with the help of the French Resistance was back in England within six weeks.

The pilot, Squadron Leader W.B. Anderson, DFC is buried in Brookwood Cemetery in Woking, Surrey. Within a week Gilbert Steere was awarded the Conspicous Gallantry Medal and John Mangione and Gordon Ritchie the Distinguished Flying Medal.

In 1993 I had the pleasure of visiting the village School at Rusper and was shown by the Headmistress a Cup which had been presented by Lady Hurst to commemorate Gilbert Steere and that it was still being presented on Sports Day to the winning House.

PICTURED below, the County Times of January 9, 1942 carried this picture and caption, issued by the Ministry of Aircraft Production, showing Horsham's Spitfire. "Now on service" proclaimed the headline. The plane had, however, been shot down off the coast of France over two months earlier.

HORSHAM'S SPITFIRE—NOW ON SERVICE

Horsham's Spitfire is now on active service. Mr. S. Parsons (secretary of Horsham and District Spitfire Fund), recently received an engraved tablet, seven inches by five-and-a-half inches, mounted on light oak, in recognition of Horsham's effort in raising more than £5,000. The tablet bears the following inscription: "In the hour of peril the people of Horsham and District earned the gratitude of the British Nations sustaining the valour of the Royal Air Force, and for fortifying the cause of freedom by the gift of a Spitfire aircraft. 'They shall mount with wings as eagles'. Issued by the Ministry of Aircraft Production."

SPITFIRE W3327: "HORSHAM AND DISTRICT."

Like many other towns, cities, organisations and even some private individuals, Horsham presented the Royal Air Force with a Spitfire in the early years of the war. A campaign was launched to persuade people to invest in a variety of ways towards the war effort; "buying" a Spitfire was one.

Under the guiding hand of Mr W.S. Parsons the town raised the grand total of over £5.000.

The Spitfire that was allocated was a Mk. Vb. It joined No. 611 Squadron at Hornchurch on June 25th 1941, too late to take part in The Battle of Britain. No. 611 Squadron were formed at Hendon as an Auxiliary Air Force Squadron and were the West Lancashire Squadron.

By contemporary standards, it lasted remarkably well. It flew almost continuously from 2nd July until it was shot down late in October 1941. During its operational life it was flown mainly by P/O John Frederick Reeves. W3327, the serial number of Horsham and District, flew on a total of 61 operational sorties during its career.

The last operational flight is recorded thus in The Squadron Operational Book, held at The Public Records Office at Kew: "12 Spitfires took off at about 16.00hrs to form a Channel Air Sea Rescue Escort. P/O Reeves and P/O Smith are listed as missing. All other aircraft returned to base at about 18.10hrs."

I have made strenuous efforts to trace the family of John Reeves both in the press and radio, but so far without any success. I do know that sometime in 1950 his parents were living in Bexhill, perhaps having retired to Sussex after the war.

The Air Historical Branch of The Ministry of Defence kindly supplied the following information :- "Our records show that at 17.00hrs on 21st October 1941, Spitfire W3327 was being piloted by 86670 P/O J.F. Reeves No. 611 Squadron when the aircraft was seen to crash into the channel, 4 miles off Boulogne, France. P/O Reeves is still reported as lost at sea and is commemorated on Panel 30 of the war memorial at Runnymede".

I have recently come across another report of the last flight of W3327 and read thus," At 16.10hrs the squadron again took off to escort two Air Sea Rescue boats in the Channel.

They escorted them for 55 minutes within four miles of the French coast. They were jumped by six Me 109's who dived on them out of the sun and then shot away into France. Red and Blue Sections were at 2000 feet. P/O Reeves and P/O Smith failed to return".

The operational history has been researched, every flight logged and the pilots who flew it can be read in a small booklet which can be obtained in the Library or in Horsham Museum.

The total amount collected was £5,075 8s 5d, of which the sum of £4,417 15s 4d was received from donations. Horsham contributed £2,319 2s 8d, the remainder came from the villages, Itchingfield, Barns Green, Christ's Hospital leading the way with £516 1s 7d.

One of the fitters at Hornchurch in 1941 with 611 Squadron was Max Bygraves. Max very kindly wrote to say that at the time there were so many young pilots going through the station that it was difficult to keep track of individuals.

THE HORSHAM SPITFIRE PILOTS

*Sergeant Pilot Joe Leigh in the cockpit taken at Hornchurch
(Photo courtesy of Joe Leigh).*

Pilots pictured with the 611 Squadron 'score board' outside 'A' flight Dispersal at Hornchurch. Seated far right, front row is Sq. Ldr. Thomas, DFC, another of the "Horsham" pilots.

Plaque presented to Stan Parsons.
Horsham and District Spitfire Fund.

RAISING THE MONEY.

Once the town had decided to 'buy' a Spitfire a small committee was set up with Stan Parsons at the helm. Five thousand pounds was no easy sum to raise, especially if it meant pennies rather than pounds!

But the town set to with a will, the villages played their part, whist drives, raffles, dances, you name it, they did it! Individuals gave, clubs gave, schools gave and if it would raise money they did it. One of the funniest stories told to me by Stan was when he asked the Air Force to lend him a German aircraft to put on display. He was in his shop when in came an airman to announce that he had an aircraft for Stan. Stan duly explained where the aircraft would be displayed and off they went, an hour or so later another airman turns up at the shop to announce that he too had a German aircraft for Stan!!!! Two for the price of one! The town displayed a Heinkel III and also a Messerschmitt 109. This one was used in a number of towns in the south. Each week the County Times reported on the progress, and I have included a few of the more interesting items from the paper.

From the WSCT dated October 11th, 1940.

HEINKEL COLLECTS MORE THAT £80 FOR SPITFIRE FUND.
GRAND TOTAL NOW STANDS AT £3,338.
MESSERSCHMITT ON VIEW NEXT WEEK.

"Horsham's Spitfire is well on the way to the aerodrome. The fund, up till yesterday amounted to £3,338 18s 2d. Contributions have been received from many sources this week. The Odeon Theatre's box amounted to £7 11s 11½d. One lady brought in her gold trinkets to be sold in aid of the fund. Children at Rudgwick School organised a jumble sale of their personal belongings in order to raise their collection for the Horsham and District Spitfire Fund, and the proceeds amounted to £1. In this and many other interesting ways they collected altogether £3 16s. One scheme was of making a cake and guessing the number of currants in it, another involved guessing the number of sweets in a jar. A concert was staged with the entrance fee of one penny, the entertainment being provided by the scholars themselves.

The Heinkel III, which was displayed at Springfield Road, Horsham in aid of the Fund did remarkably well. Within a few days it realised over £80. Many people were disappointed when it was taken away on Monday morning, but are now looking forward to the Messerschmitt 109 which is intended to be displayed in the Kings Head car park as from the beginning of next week."

And so it went on until Stan had collected £5,075 8s 5d and the first of the town's efforts came to an end, but there would be more as the years progressed.

COME AND SEE THE

HEINKEL 111

(The Giant German Bomber)

SPRINGFIELD ROAD

Near Catholic Church

MINIMUM ADMISSION 6d.   **CHILDREN 3d.**

(PLEASE GIVE MORE IF YOU ARE ABLE)

(All Proceeds to Horsham & District Spitfire Fund)

West Sussex County Times and Standard, Friday, October 4, 1940

This remarkable photograph was taken by Ron Lampard from his workshop in Springfield Road.

From the WSCT dated April 11,1941

£5,000 CHEQUE SENT TO LORD BEAVERBROOK

7,000 Spitfire Subscribers Average 12s 6d a Head

VILLAGE CONTRIBUTIONS

A cheque for £5,000 was sent to the Minister for Aircraft Production on Friday, Horsham's goal in the Spitfire Fund having been reached.

A letter was received on Wednesday from the Ministry of Aircraft production. The Spitfire will be called "Horsham and District".

The total amount collected was £5,075 8s 5d, of which £4,417 15s 4d was received from donations. Horsham contributed £2,319 2s 8d and the adjoining villages contributed the following sums:-

Billingshurst	76	2	11
Broadbridge Heath	74	4	0
Colgate and Faygate	117	0	10
Cowfold	81	12	6
Itchingfield, Barns Green, Christ's Hospital	516	1	7
Lower Beeding and Nuthurst	178	5	7
Partridge Green and West Grinstead	248	8	6
Rudgwick	371	7	4
Rusper	62	17	0
Slinfold	15	13	2
Southwater	64	12	1
Warnham	130	15	1
Coolham and Shipley	161	12	1

Other receipts, from the Odeon matinee, dances, competitions, etc., were £657 13s 1d.

The expenses were only £47 9s and the balance of £27 19s 5d together with any other outstanding amounts will be sent to the Minister of Aircraft Production shortly.

There was a greater proportion of voluntary subscribers to the fund than in many towns, where a large proportion of the money was obtained by sideshows, competitions and entertainments. Approximately 7,000 people in Horsham and District have subscribed, which worked out at 12s 6d per head.

No report of the Spitfire Fund would be complete without mentioning Mr S. Parsons, whose work as secretary of the Spitfire Committee is greatly appreciated in Horsham.

WHAT THE PAPER SAID: 1942.

Jan. 2nd.

"Do A.R.P. Wardens really want Uniforms?"

2 out of 6 declined Official Forms.

Jan. 9th.

Horsham spent a Happy and Hospitable Christmas.

Jan. 2.

HENRY HALL and his Broadcasting Orchestra at Odeon. Photo. HORSHAM SPITFIRE - NOW ON SERVICE. Horsham forms Unit of Women's Junior Air Corps Girls 14 to 17½ years.

Jan. 16th.

Horsham Warship Week — Target £345,000.

Jan. 23rd.

Warship Week Details Announced. Henry Hall's Guest Night "On the Air" Live broadcast. Broadcast live from the Odeon Theatre. Horsham and Crawley Cinemas may close on Sundays. Magistrates say they must pay £1,150 to charities if they keep open. Firemen give New Year Party. Gift of toy for every youngster.

Feb. 13th.

Submarine Week Programme will be a big Social success. Horsham's SOBER War Time record. Cinemas to remain closed on Sundays.

Feb. 20th.

Parade of 1,400 to inaugurate Warship Week tomorrow. Modern youth is weak in Mathematics. "Want" revealed in present educational system.

Feb. 27th.

"Una" is almost ours! Warship Week total passes the £300,000 mark. Thousands line the streets to watch parade.

March 13th.

WEST SUSSEX COUNTY TIMES FORCED TO MAKE 10% CUT IN NEWSPRINT. FROM THE 20th THE PAPER WILL BE REDUCED IN SIZE. NEWS TO BE ON THE FRONT PAGE. ONLY ONE ADVERT ON FRONT PAGE.

April 3rd.

Stocks and Bullring removed from the Carfax. Important reminder to motorists, Cars must be immobilised.

April 10th.

Horsham Bakers state their case for 4½d, 2lb loaf. More weddings than usual this Easter. Comforts for H.M.S. Una's crew - to be provided with unclaimed prize money.

April 17th.

Town pay respects to memory of Station Master. Mr H.J. Layton who died last week, gave 14 years Public Service. Notice. "Are you a Patriot Engineer?" Volunteers are needed to drill munition parts.

April 28th.

Letter to the Editor, Canadian soldier speaks his mind. Corporal Forward puts a Soldier's Point of View. "We'd like to play Golf and visit your Clubs."

May 1st.

"Council run by selected few", Chairman accused of wanting to "Rule the Roost". Emergency Committee criticised.

May 8th.

"Blitz" on Horsham! Realistic display by A.R.P. Mobile Reserve. "Casualties rescued from debris, Victory Road School site used for display. CRIME reported this week included the following:- Cafe proprietor sent for trial. Assault on woman alleged. Soldiers gaoled for cycle stealing. Heavy fines for having Army goods. Boy exchanged rabbit for watches.

May 15th.

"Any complaints Horsham?" asks Lord Woolton on a short visit to the town. Police accused of Gestapo methods. Sergeant Major killed by anti-tank grenade, when attempting to blow up stopped sump pit. Canadian dispatch rider killed - speeding. Canadian trooper shot himself by accident - whilst out shooting rabbits.

May 22nd.

Horsham W.E.A. carries on despite difficulties. Hunting continues despite the war.

May 29th.

Horsham Officer awarded the D.F.C. Member of the well known brewery firm Flt Lt. J.G.B. King for his "Gallantry and Devotion". Bombed the Renault works and raided Vaagsa.

June 5th.
Cinemas to open again on Sunday.

June 12th.

Factory without wages or profit. Horsham Patriot Engineers begin production.

June 19th.

Raising of school leaving age urged, Miss E.M. Marchant BA. tells Townswomens' Guild. Miss Marchant was Headmistress at Horsham High School for Girls.

June 26th.

British Restaurant to be opened in Horsham. Water shortage affects allotments.

July 3rd.

Butchers fined for selling above fixed prices. Warnham School win Health and Happiness Trophy.

July 17th.

Conscientious Objector gets prison sentence for refusing Fire Guard Duty. Canadians advertise Baseball, two teams to play a game on the Horsham F.C. Ground.

Aug. 14th

Horsham man dies following triple collision. Army motor cyclist (Canadian) hits cyclist, pedestrian and then collides with stationary car.

Aug. 21.

"Great hearted public" turn out their pockets to help raise £1,500 at the Horsham Hospital Jubilee-Fete.

Aug. 28th.

"Tanks For Attack" Appeal verging on failure! Super effort needed to raise £40,000 in the next four weeks. Film. Advert announcing the forthcoming attraction at The Ritz.... "Gone With The Wind".

Sept. 4th.

First Southwater Flax crop for 50 years.

Sept. 11th.

3.000 Horsham women to Fire Watch. Compulsory Registration for women, dates announced for signing on.

Sept. 18th.

Horsham no longer music starved. Large audience at Music Circle Concerts.

Sept. 18th.

Films this week. Odeon show "First of the Few" and at The Ritz, "Gone with the wind".

Oct. 2nd.

Better building wanted for Victory Road Schools.

Oct. 9th.

Kiddies are happy in new War Time Nursery School.

Oct. 16th.

"Public School has produced sterility in Middle Classes" Education Reforms outlined by Mr P.A. Tharp at Collyers Founders' Day.

Oct. 30th.

Rural Chief Warden to be relieved of Post. Too many functions for one man to perform. Capt. J.E. Pugh to be appointed. Lady Baden Powell, Chief Guide visits Horsham.

Nov. 6th.

Threepenny Baths for the public! Voluntary helpers to man Cleansing Centre.

Nov. 13th.

"Victory Bells" to be rung on Sunday between 10 & 11 am. at Horsham Parish Church. Remembrance Day Service, Canadian Padre gives Sermon at Horsham.

Nov.20th.

Horsham British Legion, largest branch in Sussex. Record membership since last war.

Nov.27th.

First "Panto" of the season - "Dick Whittington", Ashley Juveniles at Roffey Institute.

Dec. 4th.

Horsham Engine Driver killed by German raider. Train machine gunned in S.E. Station. Mr G Ansbridge of Curzon Avenue. As with all these reports The County Times was still subject to strict censorship. It was still referred to as a South East Town, but in fact this was the event at West Grinstead Station. Canadians guests at Rotarian Luncheon.

Dec. 11th.

Man fined £200 for breaches of petrol rationing regulations. Canadians now have their own Y.M.C.A. Hall, the Horsham Winter Gardens in Battle Dress.

Dec. 18th.

Low level attack on school and train. Horsham man's fatal injuries from machine gun bullets. Girl Scholars quell roof fire. Horsham High School. Horsham Urban District Council concludes business in eighteen minutes! The shortest meeting on record! Horsham to have Citizens Advice Bureau.

Dec. 25th.

A Christmas Day Edition. Train attack victims buried. Horsham High School present "Babes in the Wood". The paper finally ended with a request for toys. "Christmas Toy Shortage". A number of local organisations were "doing their bit" such as the Firemen and the Canadians, but toys such as Dinky and train sets had by this time become a thing of the past.

BITS AND PIECES.

"One day Walter Jarrett came into the shop and said there's a Messerschmitt down at Plummers Plain. So we got in the car and went and cut a lump off the wing, quite illegal! Anyway we were driving back down East Street to my shop when we saw this copper coming down the street; we had this wing still on the back seat, and he sees it! He gets to the car and sees what we had in the back, "Where you going with that?" "To my shop" I told him. "Well you leave it there until I come round" he says. "Anyway Walt and me we get the wing out of the back and into the yard and we still had the metal cutters with us so we cut it up into little strips and sold it at sixpence a time for my Spitfire Fund, including the bits with the crosses on! When the copper gets back he wants to know where his aircraft bits are? When he saw what was left he threatened to report us. I said "You do that and I'll make you the most unpopular 'copper' in the County". He said "What did you say?" I said "You heard" and he shot off down the yards!

Stan Parsons on collecting for The Spitfire Fund.

HMS UNA

The Horsham Warship Week's contribution to the war effort, H.M.S. Una sails home to Rosyth, after a successful foray in the Mediterranean. Note it is proudly flying the 'skull and crossbones' indicating that it had sunk enemy ships. It was returning home for a refit, after which it became a training submarine, operating from home waters. (Imperial War Museum photo)

THE SUBMARINE AND 'WARSHIP WEEK'.

It came as quite a surprise to me after researching the Spitfire story when one evening Terry Hardy from Roffey mentioned the 'Horsham Submarine'. Not being a local lad I knew nothing about a submarine. So off I went on yet another search. Aeroplanes I understood, submarines?

I made enquiries and it transpired that the submarine in question was HMS Una.

The Submarine Museum at Gosport were extremely helpful and provided me with a photo copy of Una's Working Up Log and a few items from various newspapers of the time. It appeared that Una served in the Middle East Theatre and had sunk a number of axis shipping, mainly Italian.

She then came home to serve as a training ship, this time operating out of Scottoish ports. Her role was to act as a target ship, being hunted by surface ships and aircraft. She trained her personnel before they moved on to more modern craft. She did survive the war, unlike Stan's Spitfire and was eventually being broken up for scrap. She had her moments of glory and she featured in one of the war's better known films, 'Western Approaches', playing the part of a German "U Boat".

Thanks to the help that I received from the Submarines Old Comrades Association I was able to trace some of the former crew of H.M.S.Una, some now living abroad, who very kindly told the story.

It says a great deal for the good people of Horsham and Crawley that a sum in excess of £300,000 was raised in this venture. The Horshan Sea Cadets were originaly named after H.M.S.Una and for many years a plaque which was presented during the war hung in The Town Hall. It now resides in the museum at Gosport.

For those who have an interest in these things and boats in particular I can furnish some details of 'our' submarine.

She was built at Chatham Dockyard and launched on the 10th of June 1940. She was a small boat by the standards of the day, being 196 feet 9 inches in length and had a crew of 31. She had two diesel and two electric engines driving twin screws. She was capable of almost twelve knots surfaced and nine knots submerged.

She was credited with a number of sinkings and these included on 12th of February 1942 the tanker 'Lucania' in the Gulf of Taranto, the 'Ninetto' off Calabria in April and the motor vessel 'Cosala' east of Calabria in February 1943.

She was commanded during this period by Lieutenent G.D. Marin who on his return to home waters was awarded the DSC.

At an informal reception held at The Black Horse Lieut. Martin thanked the people of Horsham and related some of the stories and adventures the 'Una' had encountered during her 18 months in the Mediterranean. He said the whole of the work had been interrupting enemy supplies to Tunisia. 'Una' then became a training ship, operating out of Scottish waters and was finally sold for scrap on 11th April, 1949.

Why a submarine?

There had been a number of very successful Horsham campaigns to raise money, The Spitfire Fund, War Weapons Week and so they began to make plans for Warship Week,to be held in Feb.1942. The object was to raise through War Savings a sum which it was hoped would represent the cost of a battleship.

The Admiralty had undertaken to allow the area to adopt a battleship. The district would be the same as for War Weapons Week, Horham Urban & Rural, including Crawley and the week chosen was Feb.21 to 28th, 1942.

The amount they had set themselves was £345,000, which would "buy" the hull and machinery of a submarine, but if an extra £8,000 could be raised, they could buy a complete submarine.

The Council decided that they wanted a complete battleship and so did the Navy.

A committee was formed and a large number of events both big and small was organised. The local cinema managers cooperated and all the villages took part.

The question of when and who decided upon H.M.S.Una had bothered me for some time, but it would appear that little or no discussion took place. The Admiralty allocated the boat, and that was it!

At the inaurgural meeting held at the Odeon, Mr E.T. Nethercoat. C.BE. J.P. the Chairman of the Committee announced that the Admiralty had already allocated a submarine called "Una".

On the Sunday there was a large parade, and it will give you some idea of the numbers that could be called upon on these occasions. In the parade were, The Navy, Sea Cadets, WRNS, Royal Winnipeg Rifles, Home Guard, Canadian Scottish Regiment, R.A.F., R.O.C., A.T.C., Red Cross, St John's A.B., Civil Defence, led by Capt Pugh, Motor Transport Corps,W.V.S., Womens Land Army, British Legion, Scouts, Guides and NFS with two engines and The Police.

The saluting base was opposite the Post Office and the Guard of Honour was inspected by Admiral Hornell.

Events were held all over the town and ended with a Dance at The Drill Hall on the Saturday, with a band from The Royal Air Force.

The money was found, Una was at sea with the 10th Flotila sailing out of Malta and came home 16 months later, when her Commander and some of her crew were guests of the town. A crest was exchanged, HMS Una's hung in the Town Hall for many years, but after languishing in a cupboard for some time, found a permanent home at The Submarine Museum at Gosport, coming back to the town, for possibly the last time in Feb. 1992, to celebrate the fiftieth anninversary of Submarine Week at Forest Community School.

What of Una's part in the war? I wrote to a number of her former crew and I will allow their letters to tell some of the story.

This is part of a letter that I received from Mr Jack Reeves, one of the few survivors from the period when Una served in the Mediteranean and took part in some of the actions.

"I was returned to Base in Malta after being sunk in the "Pandora". (31st March, 1942, sunk by air attack in Lazaretto Creek.) and after 2 days was put into another operational submarine, P34 a U class boat, much to my displeasure. I mention this, because once again my life was saved. Some of the ex- Pandora crew were put on the sub "Olympus" and I would have probably been amongst them. She hit a mine 9 miles outside Malta and only 7 survived, they actually swam back to Malta. (8th May, 1942.) It was after the patrol in P34 that I joined "Una" as second coxswain. It is recorded that Una sank 13,000 tons of shipping and did the most patrols from Malta in 1942. The tonnage doesn't seem a lot compared to other Subs in The Flotilla, but it was mostly small ships that were running supplies to North Africa and Crete in the Aegean."

"We took part in several commando operations, landing them from 2 man canvas canoes. Their object was to blow up the aircraft on Catania Air Strip in Sicily. Each plane was heavily guarded. Having got to about ½ mile from the beach or thereabouts, so long as we had enough water to dive, all at night of course, we would put the Commandos in their boats, load them up with home made bombs, not forgetting the local currency, rolled up and put in "condoms" to keep them dry, keep the notes dry. Then we would withdraw out to sea, having arranged a pick up point further down the coast. They would flash a light out to sea giving a coded message or signal after the job was done.

I always thought these guys were mad, proper "Death or Glory" boys, all volunteers and at that time no extra money. Nevertheless they were very brave, unfortuneately we didn't very often pick them up. We knew they had done their job because we watched all the explosions and we could only stay for a couple of days in the area, as the enemy knew that the lads had been landed by submarine and were soon sending out Naval Craft to look for us. On one trip we took an officer(Heir to a whisky company) and his men plus his lucky mascot, a litle dog! One rating was detailed to lay newspaper in the wireless office as a dog toilet (we were short of grass!). The poor little hound pined a lot for her master who didn't return from the mission.

Instructions had been left for the dog to be sent to Egypt, and I believe that it eventually turned up in Alexandria."

"The early boats, "U Class Subs" had no Radar installed and relied on alert "Look Outs" for enemy aircraft, but after two weeks at sea these Look Outs weren't at their best, but we did have a big advantage over larger boats, we could dive very quickly and be under the waves in seconds. The faster we were travelling on the surface the quicker we went down, sometimes only just getting the conning tower hatch shut as the sea came over. You'd be surprised just how fast ratings used to slide down the ladders from the bridge. Things were getting very bad in Malta in 1942, and the boats were in need of repair and engine overhaul. This had to be done by the crew diving the boat to the bottom of the creek off Manod Island, to avoid air attacks during daylight hours and we surfaced at dusk, having been given the "All Clear" by a small charge dropped in the creek, a very sweet sound after the bombs that were being dropped during the day."

"However things got so bad for the "U"s of the 10th Flotilla, it was decided we should leave Malta and go to Alexandria to the Depot Ship,"Medway'. 4 subs went but only 3 arrived safe, the "Urge" was lost en-route. We were all carrying spare crews so it was a double loss when the "Urge" went down. (Urge was sunk by the Italian torpedo boat Pegaso on 28th April, 1942.)

There was an amazing gesture on our Captain's part when we approaching Alexandria Harbour. We had draped sea weed around the Periscope Standards, usually the boats have a good clean up inside before entering harbour, and on arrival at the Depot Ship, Medway the Flotilla Commander welcomed us on board and asked our Skipper "What the hell's that seaweed about?" Our Skipper's reply was "Sorry, Sir but we have just done 75 days at sea", meaning that we were diving even in harbour! Our stay in Alexandria was short lived. The Germans were pushing on towards the port, so we once again had to evacuate to Port Said in Egypt. Medway, our Depot Ship was sunk 2 miles outside the harbour, a big loss to the Submarine Service, with all our spare parts and torpedoes on board. H.M.S.Medway was sunk on 30th June 1942 on its way to Haifa by U 372.

We were back to square one again: no spares; it was just make do and mend. I actually rewired our forward periscope. This is normally a dockyard job, it's amazing what you have to do under pressure; I often think "How the hell did I do it?"

"Anyway a nice rest at Haifa and it was back to business in Malta. When we returned the bombing was very scarce and opposite our old

Fifty Years On. Shipmates meet.

Fifty years on from Warship Week 1942, two Submarine Old Comrades meet up at Horsham. Jack Reeves, who served in "Una" in the Mediterranean Theatre of operations and Jim Rourke met at Forest School for a reunion organised by the Gatwick Branch of the Association.

Base the Maltese had actually started digging Submarine Pens under the cliffs,(about 2 years too late!) We were soon into our old routines of Patrolling from Malta, but as the invasion of Sicily was getting underway and 10th Flotilla being very involved our attention was being drawn to the Aegean where we had to stop supplies getting to Crete from Greece.

Basically, the Aegean was sealed off by mine fields at the west of Crete and east of Rhodes. To enter the Aegean we had to dive under the minefield net at Andikithra Channel. We could hear the mine wires scraping down our sides as we wormed our way out and clear, thanks and blessings to our Asdic Operator. We had to take up our billet at the eastern end of Crete. 4 submarines were always in position to cover the north of Crete, hence we stopped the flow of supplies to the Germans in the island. The routine was boats coming from Malta would take up position at the eastern end of Crete and the other three would all move up a billet and the one at the end would move back to Malta. This seemed to work O.K., but perhaps you would move into a billet where they had sunk something, then when you moved into the area and receive all the depth charges! (Oh Happy Days!)"

"We were lucky on one patrol. Shipping was getting scarce and big ships were hard to find. It was our luck to lie in the billet by Suda Bay when a 4,000 ton tanker came out the Bay with a destroyer escort. We started the attack and managed to get 2 torpedoes off, one hit the tanker midships. Immediately we took evasive action, diving deep and closing all water tight doors for depth charges and kept "Silent Routine". After a while no charges were dropped so we crept up to Periscope Depth, the Captain couldn't believe our luck, no charges and no destroyer. We assumed she had fled back to Suda Bay."

"There were just short patrols after this, North Africa, the invasion of Sicily and the boat still in a bad way. We had the good news that we were being sent back to England, arriving back, I think in February, 1943. After some pleasant leave we were repaired and then sent back up to the Sub. Training Base in Scotland, training new submarines and surface ships."

Jack returned to the main base at Gosport later in 1943 to join a new submarine and spent the rest of the war in the Service.

WHAT THE PAPER SAID: 1943.

Jan. 1st.

Masked gunmen hold up Cinema Staff in 8 hour Raid. Night watchman and woman cleaner bound in chairs. Horsham Hunt Meet on Boxing Day. Horsham Home Guard Company to be renamed "A" Headquarters Company.

Jan. 8th.

N.F.S. Tribute to former Brigade Chief. Mr J.G. Gadd's 35 years service. Coffin borne on Fire Engine. New Police Chief for Horsham, Supt. W.H. Wright to take over from Supt. Heritage. Army Cadet Corps to be formed in Horsham.

Jan. 15th.

"Nothing finer in Royal Naval Annals." Captain Sherbrooke's Gallant Action Wins V.C. Capt. Sherbrooke was married to a Broadbridge Heath girl. Reason for story. He won the honour in the North Atlantic battle.

Jan. 22nd.

Sergeant Major killed by own revolver! Sequel to "Fooling About" with Canadian comrade.

Jan. 29th.

Ruthless removal of railings in Urban area. H.U.D.C. bombarded with complaints. "Bench" renews cinema licences. £460 allocated to local charities. Hospital gets £49. British Restaurant to be open soon. Rural Council pays £11 for rats tails!.

Feb. 12th.

A.T.C. Breaking all records! Squadron's second birthday. N.F.S. fight blaze for five hours. Clock House at Cowfold damaged by fire.

Feb 12th.

TWO KILLED, 18 INJURED IN RAID ON TWO SUSSEX TOWNS. Post Office, School and houses demolished. (Crawley). Bridge Party bombed out - but no casualties. In garden when house received direct hit. Remarkable Escape in Wednesday raid. (Wimblehurst Road.)

Feb 19th.

Earl Winterton, P.C,. M.P. Inspects Home Guard. "Be prepared message to Holbrook Platoon".

Feb. 26th.

"Patriots" in full swing. After a lull of twelve months, production is now in full swing.

Mar. 12th.

British Restaurant opens to Public today. Meals will be full of vitamins. Bowling Club has record year.

Mar. 19th.

Horsham Aims to Fly High! £350,000 "Wings For Victory" Target. Flt Lt. R.C. Rivaz DFC. Story of a Tail Gunner" goes on sale in Horsham.

April 2nd.

Horsham Rates unchanged at lOs.5d in the £1. Canadian children's gift to Home Guard. Mobile kitchen handed over at Horsham to Sussex Home Guard.

April 9th.

Princess Royal at Colgate School. "The Toppers" are a fighting family!" Seven sons serving with the Army.

April 16th.

Baby found abandoned at Horsham Station. In the care of the nurses at hospital.

April 23rd.

The Bells to Ring On Sunday!!!!! Bell Ringers volunteer after Government lift restriction.

April 30th.

Boxing Champion Tommy Farr referees boxing at Billingshurst Fete and Sports.

May 7th.

H.M.S. Una comes home after 16 months at sea. Wooden houses suggested for civilian population.

May 14th.

Horsham's only Maternity Hospital closing.

May 21st.

Horsham greets H.M.S. Una. Commander Lieut. G.D. Martin wins D.S.C.

May 28th.

"The Target is in Sight!" Latest Wings Week total £271,000.

June 25th.

Autograph hunters pursue Una's crew. Flying start to Wings For Victory Week.

July 2nd.

Plaque H.M.S. Una presented to the town.

July 9th.

Public Meeting calls for Maternity Hospital.

July 23rd.

Childrens' Day in the Park. 1,000 take part in Displays and Parades.

July 30th.

£12,800 expenditure on Maternity Hospital.

Aug. 13th.

Housewives complain of milk supplies! "Dirty bottles are NOT used."

Aug.20th.

Model cottages for Farm Workers!

Aug. 27th.

More sour milk complaints..

Sept. 3rd.

No indication where Maternity Hospital will be built.

Sept. 10th.

Earl Winterton to head Farmers Cause.

Sept. 17th.

Low water pressure hampers Fire Fighters. Big blaze in centre of Horsham. Vulcanising Shop Gutted. Sussex Tyre Co. Linden Rd.

Sept. 24th.
R.D.C. wants improved bus service.

Oct. lst. "Farcial conditions at Crown Garage Fire". Councillors criticise water supply. Battle of Britain commemorated. Open Air Service.

Oct. 8th.

Police drive to hunt down cycle thieves.

Nov. 5th.

British Legion turn down Sunday opening.

Nov. 12th.

Ten wins, twice beaten. Cricket Club's successful season.

Nov. 19th.
"A shilling an hour for Home Helps" "Ridiculously low" say Horsham women!

Nov. 26th.
Crowds cheer as raider crashes in flames. Bomb damages houses and shops. No serious injuries!

Dec. 10th.

Midnight struggle on staircase. Capt. C.E. Lucas attempts to capture intruder. Police hunt for soldier. An intruder had entered the house in Broadbridge Heath and entered his 17 year old daughter's bedroom. Horsham protest against Mosley's release.

Dec. 17th.

Austerity cooking this Christmas - Tasty dishes from simple recipes.

Dec. 24th.

Expectant mother dumped in a Hostel. Anxiety over Maternity Home delay.

Dec. 31st.

The Army join in the fun - Canadians' party for 350 children.

And so 1943 drew to a close. The town had survived, the bells had rung, invasion had receded and thoughts of Victory and the aftermath were being discussed.

BITS AND PIECES.

"I used to take the School Registers to an Air Raid Shelter in Clarence Road, a surface shelter. This was in case the School was bombed, they would then know who was in the building."

Peter Wilkins on school days at Oxford Road.

"I used to go all over playing for the Troops. If it was in school time I had been given special permission by County to have time off school. I was only twelve. We had a van which used to pick us up. We also played at the cinemas in the evenings. I enjoyed that because we used to get a fish and chip supper!"

Alan Woolven on playing accordion with
Mrs Layton's Accordion Band and for ENSA.

Village life.

It was perhaps only coincidence, but the little village of Mannings Heath seems to recur quite often in my meanderings. Perhaps it was typical of life in the country at the time, although as far as my story goes, far from typical.

In those days it had its own School, now only the School House remains, opposite the cricket pitch. The village had its own Police House and Constable, P/C Joe Lemm. Joe recalled that the first problem that arose was the black out and he had to ensure that all lights were concealed. Most cooperated but he had some difficulty with the vicar. Having made a number of requests to improve the blackout at the vicarage Joe had to eventually threaten prosecution! A number of residents drove cars and were only entitled to a petrol allowance for business purposes. It annoyed Joe to find them driving around and propping up the bar in The Dun Horse!

For Joe life became hectic with the arrival of the men of the Canadian Army. Large camps were erected all around the area, Monks Gate and on the common at Plummers Plain. He told the school children of Nuthurst School when he visited them in 1990 that he quite liked the soldiers, the only trouble he experienced was after they had been paid and tended to get a little drunk! He also said that of course his only mode of transport was his bike, and on one occasion when he needed to bring back some German prisoners he had to find a taxi!

The village had its own "Fire Brigade" and Home Guard Platoon. Gilbert Newberry was a member of the former, John Christian a member of the latter. Gilbert Newberry recalled "In the early days of the war, 10 of us formed the Mannings Heath section of the A.F.S. with our headquarters in a shed opposite the Dun Horse Public House. In those days we were not very well equipped, only having a manual pump. Later we were provided with a Coventry Climax trailer pump and were split up into three crews of three firemen and a messenger boy, all part time people. This meant all night duty every third night, 9pm to 9am, then we signed off to go to work."

"At this time we were incorporated into the N.F.S and came under The

Horsham Fire Station. One afternoon a German plane was shot down and crashed at Newells Farm, Plummers Plain. By the time we arrived the army had taken the airmen prisoner."

"Later on, during the night raids on London, another was brought down behind Cooks Farm, Nuthurst. Our crew was called out and as we approached three bombs exploded. Fortunately none of us was hurt, but the crew were blown to pieces. In one raid at night seven bombs were dropped across Home Farm and the golf course, luckily none exploded."

"I was on duty the night the first flying bomb landed near Cuckfield. We had an alert just after 9 o'clock at night and it lasted until 6 o'clock the next morning. No one, including the army or police, knew anything about what was happening."

"Three nights later when on duty again another passed over us and landed somewhere the other side of Horsham. By this time we had been warned what to expect. One afternoon while working at "Swallowfield" I watched a flying bomb come from the direction of Plummers Plain, tip over and land on the boundary of "Swallowfield" and Seamans Farm. This did considerable damage to properties in Mannings Heath."

The village had its Village Hall, which held dances. The Golf Club continued throughout the war, the Canadian Officers playing regularly, the young lads finding and selling lost golf balls!

The ponds were used on a number of occasions by the military to test various weapons, The river was widened and tank traps set up to deter any invader. A number of "pill boxes" were built round the village at strategic points and some have survived and can be seen today. Canadian soldiers dressed as Germans played "war games" in the fields off Goldings Lane attacking the pill boxes as a preliminary to the Dieppe Raid.

Large concrete blocks were also in position around the village as deterrents and oil drums filled with petrol were also positioned.

Later in the war, there were prisoner of war camps in the forest, "White Russians" at Sun Oak. It was from this camp that some very fine toys were produced and some of these are still to be found in Horsham today.

One young schoolboy in those days was Dennis Vallance. He had some memories of the village and writes," I was informed by a Canadian Army Sergeant that a German aircraft had crashed on Plummers Plain - like all 14 year old lads at that time I was a keen souvenir hunter."

"Cycling from Crawley to Plummers Plain I found the complete tail section of the Heinkel. Determined to secure a decent "lump" of the aircraft I returned to my home for a tool. Suitably armed once again rode back to the site and set about removing the "swastika" from the tail fin - alas my mother's one and only tin-opener was no match for the tough 16swg Aluminium - snapping in two on the first attempt!"

"Not to be outdone, however, I managed to procure two sizeable pieces of the tail plane, main ribs and triumphantly returned home with my prizes."

"I had the souvenirs up until 1973 - when my mother sold the family home, also disposing of my precious wartime treasures to the dust-man — sweet revenge I suppose for breaking her tin opener 33 years before!"

The local M.P, Earl Winterton recalled in his book "Orders Of The Day", of visiting the village. He attended a public meeting on May 27th, 1940.

"Went to a public meeting at Mannings Heath. The old ladies present were all genuinely ready to "do or die" for the country; in Sussex the ominous thunder of the guns in France and on the Channel come nearer every day; but the nightingales continue to pour out their hearts in the Weald on the lovely still Spring evenings of May 1940".

"The old ladies present, as well as the few men in attendance, were magnificent - an epitome of the spirit of England; none were under fifty, many were over seventy, because the younger men and women of the village were on war service somewhere."

"I told them that, if the Germans invaded us, Sussex would obviously be very much in the front line; that we must, in that event, obey the military authorities implicitly and not worry about our lives and properties; it ought not, I added, to be difficult for our generation, as we had been through all this in an earlier war. We had heard the Flanders guns in the Weald before, and some of our best friends' bones lay across the Channel. But England had survived then and would again. My speech was badly delivered and over-emotional owing to the tension we had all been going through, whilst Sussex audiences are not noticeable for their enthusiasm; but the fifty or sixty old people present cheered me to the echo, drowning the dull "thud-thudding" of the noise of the guns from across the Channel. This little incident and the ceremony of signifying the Royal Assent described below in my diary heartened me enormously in this period of grave anxiety."

June 30th 1940. "Went as a "front bencher" with others to hear the Royal Assent given to certain Acts; John Simon, very handsome and dignified and with admirable enunciation, performed his duties as Lord Chancellor. Memories of Gallipoli came flooding back to me. The ceremony was as usual simple, dignified and impressive. The pageantry and custom of hundreds of years was completely unaffected by the frightful proximity of the war to London."

On the bicycle provided!

Joe Lemm reminded me how large his patch was, "It was quite big, it covered Monksgate, Mannings Heath, Plummers Plain, Lower Beeding, Maplehurst, Copsale, Nuthurst, to the border of Southwater, to Colgate and part of Horsham rural, Kerves Lane and Denne Park, the biggest "beat" in The Division, all on a bicycle!"

"I was on a course and the Superintendent asked what would we do if a bomber or some such came down on our beat? What would you do Lemm? "Well sir" I said "I would go to the scene with all due speed, on the bicycle provided!". All the blokes laughed, including the 'Super'. Most of the petty crime was done by soldiers, chicken and rabbit stealing. 'Lor, the Canadians were always stealing 'em. I was quite fortunate, I had a 75% detection clear up rate, that was the highest in the Division as well."

"Besides The Vicar, I nicked quite a few for petrol offences. They kept coming up to the golf club for social evenings, not for golf, just for drinking, and a lot of villagers were upset so I thought I'd better do something about it. I kept watch, took their numbers and reported them. Of course they was a bit annoyed."

"They used to use paraffin as well in their cars, "Cor, you could smell it a mile off! The Canadians used to fight a bit but only when they were boozed up, but I had no real trouble with them."

"I did quite a lot of night duty at Horsham Station (Police) in charge. Not only that, we used to have to do the cleaning as well, "fatigues" they called it. We had no cleaners in them days – it was done by the bloke on night duty, floors, tables, clean the place up, it's different now of course."

Joe recalled for me the planes which had crashed, "We had four I think? We had a Junkers at Newells Farm almost intact, a Me109 at Plummers Plain, the guns were still firing, probably an electrical fault no doubt. I was riding down the village on my bike and this blasted thing was popping away, I thought he was shooting at me! It landed intact just below the Stud Farm at Plummers Plain. Of course I went down and took charge, but the pilot was badly burned, but it wasn't on fire. I was on duty when one crashed at Cook's Farm. I heard the machine gunning above and it crashed in a little field and made a deep crater. At the time we had the Canadians all around. It was swarming with blokes and I had a job to get rid of 'em. Whether it was a bomb or an explosion in the aircraft, but there was a great explosion and great lumps of clay went up in the air, 'Gor that soon dispersed them! We had a doodle bug at Swallowfields and another at Colgate in a field of wheat. The Swallowfields went low over the Police House when I was in the garden doing a bit of gardening. We had a few bombs at Prongers Corner, which injured or killed a few sheep and old Bertie Brown, the butcher, was one of my Specials and he was shooting the sheep that had been injured. Well old Sergeant Trott was close by, and you know how your nerves are on edge with all these bombs around, and old Bertie shot one right behind Sergeant Trott. Crikey, I thought he was going to have a heart attack, he almost jumped out of his skin!"

On the left: PC. Joe Lemm pictured in the garden of the Police House at Mannings Heath shortly after moving in with his family- Joe told me that it was a happy time in the village, some of the happiest days of his life. "I went there in February 1938 and stayed until October 1948. You know Mannings Heath was a pleasant place to be, they were all country people and once you get to know country people they put their trust in you. We loved it there, it was lovely! In those days it was a 24 hours a day job, but a lovely place to be in".

Another local man that I had the pleasure of meeting at his home at Brookfield Farm was John Christian. John and his family have been farming in the village for many years, so I asked about life on the land during the war?

"Farming was poor. The first money started to come into farming about 1938 when the war looked imminent and the Government decreed that to plough up land we would be given £2 an acre, which was a lot then. We were mowing for six shillings an acre (30p) and farm wages were 32s.6d per week.

We had Land Girls in about 1941. I think their role was to entertain the farmers' sons! In the main the girls did very well."

"I joined the Home Guard when I was 16, at Colgate. I loathed the Army, being told what to do or crawl about in the mud. I wasn't too keen on the uniform either! Anyway they asked for a volunteer dispatch rider and I got the job. They gave me a brand new civilian A.J.S. motor bike – all chrome. Do you know, I kept that bike so clean Hitler could have seen it from the other side of the Channel! The Horsham Home Guard marched out one day with a Smith's Gun. It had made up wheels, a barrel and when you met the enemy you turned it on its

side and fired. It fired a 7lb jam tin full of nails! That's how well prepared we were."

John also told me about some of the incidents. He remembered the
aircraft crashes, "The Heinkel was the first and that came down in the
Hammerpond woods. It came down intact and then blew up, the tail
flew off over my head – at that time it looked gigantic! The MelO9 was
shot up over here. I picked the cockpit up near our gate; it had come
off and he just skimmed across onto what was being prepared as an
emergency landing ground and he just 'bellied' into the ground, dug a
big furrow and went across two hayricks of corn and luckily swung
round. His ammunition went off and that was the first time I'd seen a
man critically injured. He was in a terrible state."

"The Canadians came in a big V8 car to give him his last ride, the local
policeman came and took him away from them; we nearly started another war!"

"We had Canadian Scottish Highlanders here for months, you could hear
their bagpipes from morning till night. I can remember so well a little old
lady in the village had about six hens and they went missing one morning. She went to the local policeman who took her up to the camp. The
Commanding Officer brings the whole lot out – next day she had 36!"

"We had Italian Prisoners of War in the village. They were very good
at weaving baskets, getting five shillings a basket, and they also tapped
all the birch trees for some kind of hooch. We employed one of them,
they were quite docile. They left and then we had the German prisoners. They had a tremendous following among the girls. Then we had
some Polish lads, they were very sad, they were going to be sent home,
many didn't want to go, "White Poles" I suppose. One man dressed
himself in his best uniform and carefully hung himself rather than be
sent back. We had a great village life; country boys had no money so
we didn't stand a chance with the Canadians around, but we had
dances, 'hops' and if you were well in you were invited to the camps
for ENSA parties. There was a tremendous bus service, three pence
into Horsham, six pence return. On the farm we kept pigs, cattle and
horses. There were restrictions on what you could keep and what you
could do with them, but being simple country folk who couldn't read
all these forms, what did we know?"

WHEN THE GERMANS ATTACKED MANNINGS HEATH.

Still in place today in the village are the remains of at least two of the defensive pill boxes and some remnants of the piling put into the river to deter tanks should there be an invasion. The river was widened and deepened in parts and defensive positions constructed.

At least two eye witnesses recalled the times when "war games" were played on the outskirts of the village and the Germans attacked. Fortunately, these "Germans" were played by Canadian soldiers dressed in German uniforms who were trying to capture the pill boxes and various farm out buildings and cottages.

Tank traps were constructed in other areas, the Arun was widened and deepened in a number of places, near the Church, near the Worthing Road and along the banks of the "Red River."

At various times traffic was disrupted on the roads into Horsham when the Army were on "manoeuvres". At strategic points large concrete blocks were positioned to slow traffic down, particularly during the period when it was thought invasion was imminent.

Defences for the town consisted of a number of searchlight batteries and anti-aircraft batteries, but I am told no Barrage Balloons. Some gun emplacements were built by the Canadians but were never used.

MANNINGS HEATH: THE VILLAGE SCHOOL.

In 1939 the village still had its own school, a Church of England School, catering for juniors and infants. The school as such no longer exists, although The School House remains in the village. The children from the village now attend the C of E. School at Nuthurst and it was this school that I visited along with a former pupil Mr Don Bateman to look at the old school Log Book, courtesy of the Headteacher, Mr Hall. Many of the names were familiar to Don, and he was very pleased to read his own admittance entered in the Log Book.

At the outbreak of war, the Headmistress was Miss Howard and I began my search in September 1939.

The School opened for business on 12th of September, but it is probable that the start of term was delayed to sort out the problems of the evacuees. The morning session on that day comprised 31 younger children and in the afternoon 24 of the older children came in. A Mr Stuart from Sunnyhill Road School, Streatham, reported for duty, but only stayed one day before moving to Southwater. The Headmistress decided to work the local and evacuated children together. On 23rd. Sept. a Mrs Babister reported from Woods Road School. One young man who stayed in the Horsham area after being evacuated, was admitted as a private evacuee on 26th September, one Robert Dominy.

A report on 13th of November states "That the Air Raid Shelter was showing signs of caving in." This shelter had been dug by the parents and was really a slit trench and was covered with corrugated iron sheets. Due to the heavy rains the sides had begun to collapse. Like many schools in the villages it took some time for a shelter to be provided for the children.

On the 2nd July the following year it is recorded that the Rector came to discuss the possibility of a shelter being built.

By December the school hours had been amended, 9.30 to 12.00 and 1.00 to 3.00, due officially to the interruptions by air raids. It was then that Don pointed out that it was also due to a lack of Black-Outs in the School. Even then it was the May of the following year before anyone called to arrange any protection! Many of the entries are about the day to day problems of running a school, but there were other items that show the human face of the school. Some I would not dare to disclose but this one amused me. 26th May, 1941. "While the children were practising wearing their gasmasks, Andrew Ford sat down while the seat of his desk was raised. He bumped the back of his head on the desk and a large swelling came up. The accident will be reported to the Clerk of the County Council.".

In August 1941 the Blackout material arrived from Scadgells of Worthing and at the end of August Miss Howard resigned.

In October Miss M.E. Sharp took over as Headteacher and an entry by her on the 29th records that the shelter was still unsafe! The numbers on roll at that period were:-

West Sussex.   Juniors .... 15.

                  Infants .... ll.

                  Others .... 7.   Total......33.

I was delighted to read that the well respected village "bobby" PC Joe Lemm visited the School from time to time. On the 21st January, 1942, he gave a talk on Safety First, but later in June called to warn against the children accepting gifts of cartridges from Canadian Soldiers.

Opposite:

MANNINGS HEATH VILLAGE SCHOOL 1939/40.

Back Row: Miss Howard, John Sumner, Ruth Dale, George Gander.

Standing: Andrew Ford, Eileen Sheppard, Doug Sheppard, Bob Dale, Pat Brown, Daphne Topper, Jessie Thornes, June Sumner, Joyce Ford, George Still.

Seated: Don Bateman, Rosemary Sheppard, Peter Topper, Edna Thompson, Joy Godsmark, Peter Daniels, Jean Thompson.

Front Row: George King, Dorothy Thompson, Austin Mangles.

MANNINGS HEATH: THE SCHOOL.

In November the School was requisitioned for Fire Watching Duties. What that entailed I have no idea because it would have been normal practice for staff to do some Fire Watching in any case. Later the same month the Caretaker was asked not to make such big fires. The reason was that the coal allowance was only 4 tons for the entire winter and these large fires were making a fuel shortage problem. Don Bateman seemed to recall that they did indeed have lovely red hot fires in the stoves! At the end of that term, Miss Sharp left and in February 1943 a Miss E.M. Sanderson took over.

I then came across a long saga of entries about providing a wireless for the School. It began in April 1943 with a "Bring and Buy" sale which raised £2.0.0 towards the cost of a new wireless. An Engineer, would you believe, came from the BBC to inspect the School and brought with him a wireless for the School to try. He made a number of visits because the school found difficulties with reception and on some of his visits he would be accompanied by an official from "Auntie"!

Eventually the problems were solved and the local Education Authority helped to provide the School with a brand new radio, sorry, wireless!

The children did their bit for the war effort. An after hours knitting club was held, including some mums, providing socks for the troops.

In August 1944 at 3.35pm a Flying Bomb fell in a field along Winterpick Lane. According to the Log Book "The children hid under the desks. No casualties were reported but windows were blown in and one ceiling was damaged". By this time the Black-outs had been fitted by Scadgells!

At the end of hostilities in May 1945 the children were given a two day holiday.

Considering the activities going on around the School at the time, with troops all round the village, it is surprising that the school functioned at all, and to do so throughout the Battle of Britain and The Blitz says a great deal for the Staff, the children and their parents. More so when one considers the shortages of teaching materials available during those dark days.

Bits and Pieces...

"One of the aspects after the fall of Dunkirk was the various obstacles of defence installed around the town. In Greenway, which was only built as far as Vale Drive prior to the war, concrete blocks about 18 inches high were placed in between the houses and a fence of about five rolls of barbed wire (I think it was called "Dannet Wire") stretched right across the south, passing through our garden and onwards through the allotments and fields towards Broadbridge Heath. Great ditches were dug on the open land it passed through. It was rumoured that it was the second line of defence, but who knows! German Prisoners of War removed it after the war."

Bill Sampson.

THE GOLF COURSE CRASH.

Almost until the end of the war, Mannings Heath seemed to attract aeroplanes! After a quiet period, although a V1 had landed at 'Swallowfields', suddenly on a murky afternoon in February, 1945 a Halifax bomber with a full bomb load plunged onto the golf course.

The story of the Halifax has been covered in depth in other booklets and by the County Times A short account of the event nevertheless is not out of place in our story of a village. By any stretch of the imagination it was a very lucky escape for the village, and the surrounding area.

The war in Germany was coming to its end and it was decided to attack some of the towns close to the German border, and it was to Wesel that the fully loaded Halifax was bound. It took off at about twelve with a crew of seven from Snaith in Yorkshire and somewhere over Oxford one of the engines caught fire. The Pilot tried a number of manoeuvres to quench the flames but all were in vain. The aircraft had come down to two thousand feet and was then over Sussex when the order to 'Bail Out' was given. Five of the crew managed to get out safely, but two perished in the crash. It is thought that the Pilot Flt. Lt.Winning did get out, but he was found later entangled in his parachute on the golf course. The other young man Flt. Sgt. Jack Webb must have been still on board at the impact for very little of his remains were found. The irony of the story is that the raid had already been abandoned and they had recalled all the aircraft.

One of the survivors, Bob Heseltine related how he was well tended by Mrs and Miss Wills at Plummers Plain and that he along with other crew members were taken to The Base Hospital where they stayed until they had recovered. He also told me that the Flight Engineer Vic Gilbert came from near Cranleigh and that they visited his parents for tea before they rejoined the squadron.

There were a number of eyewitnesses to the crash. Don Bateman and Peter Dawes were waiting on the village cricket pitch when it happened and like others ran across to where this large pall of smoke hung, only to be turned away by the adults. John Christian had the job of pulling the engines out of the crater so that they could go to Farnborough for inspection. Strangely, the village policeman, PC Joe Lemm does not remember the crash, "I must have been on leave" he said!

The two who perished are commemorated now on a plaque near the spot on the golf course. Gerry Winning, the Pilot came from the Birmingham area and Jack Webb, the Bomb Aimer came from a small village called Bickershaw, near Wigan.

Today at the spot there is still an enormous crater, and many of the trees are still showing signs of the event. In some places bits of the wreckage are embedded in the trees and the trees have grown round them.

The aircraft was operated from No 51 Squadron, coded MZ765 and was a Mark III.

In October Bob and his wife visited the village and met some of those who had tended them over forty years before. This incident was the final act for the people of the area. It seemed sad that it had to be a British aircraft!

MANNINGS HEATH

Almost fifty years ago, Don Bateman had been waiting with his pal Peter Dawes when he witnessed the Halifax bomber as it plunged to earth. Don is pictured on the cricket pitch in December 1991.

Don standing beside the crater, frozen over in 1991.
The wreath can be seen fixed to a tree.

MANNINGS HEATH: The Mystery of the Wreath.

Having asked and received permission to visit the site of the crash, it was a surprise to find hung on an adjacent tree a plaque and a wreath. The inscription on the plaque named the pilot Gerry Winning and Flt. Lt. Russell. Although Flt. Lt. Russell was on the crew list that day, he was not reported killed or injured. The other crew member who lost his life that day was Sgt. Webb.

Why, I ask, the plaque and who was responsible for placing it? It was in reasonable condition: in my estimation perhaps two or three years old.

VILLAGE LIFE

*After the horses, Aubrey Charman of Southwater
chats to Fred Hider, now on a tractor.*

*Harry Warman from Mannings
Heath.*

*Harry had joined the Royal Air
Force before the War as a pilot.
He was killed during the
evacuation from Dunkirk.
His Blenheim bomber was shot
down and crashed in the
Channel.
His body was not recovered.*

Photo - David Parker

A SAD SOUTHWATER STORY.

The West Sussex County Times carried a very sad story in October 1939, the war barely six weeks old when it announced the death of a young lad from the village, the first casualty of the war from the area.

HORSHAM'S FIRST WAR CASUALTY.
17 YEAR OLD "BOY" VICTIM OF ROYAL OAK DISASTER.

"The death is reported of young Harry Jones from Southwater who was serving on HMS Royal Oak, which was attacked at anchor in the so called safe haven of Scapa Flow.

Harry Jones died a few days before his 17th birthday. He had been at school in Horsham at Victory Road and then at St. John's. He left school at 14 but was too young to go straight into the Royal Navy so he worked for a while in a local shop, entering the Navy on February 8th, joining St. Vincent's Training Establishment at Gosport. Harry appears to have been hard working and diligent, being promoted to Leading Boy and then to P/O Instructor Boy, the highest rank possible at the time. Because of this he had to remain in barracks, but in June of that year joined the Royal Oak. Harry enjoyed sport, he was the Sussex Schools' High Jump Champion in 1936, clearing four feet seven inches. He enjoyed drawing and sketching and was nicknamed 'Popeye' after that well known character."

One of his contemporaries at the time was young Arthur Merritt from Slinfold. He joined HMS St. Vincent at the same time and recalled that the last time he saw Harry they met on the sea front at Southsea just before Harry was due to go north to join the Royal Oak. They chatted awhile and arranged to meet up in Scapa, Arthur also being due to go up to join a ship sometime later.

There has always been some controversy over the claim made by the German 'U' boat commander that he sank the Royal Oak. Arthur told me that he in fact did believe the story, because strangely Arthur sailed out of Scapa Flow that same day and as there were no 'Block Ships' in place at the time the account given by Lt. Gunther Prien does appear

---

to be accurate. The story of 'The Watchmaker of Kirkwall' which was talked about after the event was nonsense. Arthur told me that in his opinion up in Scapa "even a Scotsman was a foreigner"!

According to reports and books on the sinking fewer that thirty "boys" escaped that night and many of them had been sleeping not in the mess deck, but in the forward casemates of the starboard battery. So few "boys" survived that any eye-witness accounts are fragmentary.

FARMING & VILLAGE LIFE: SOUTHWATER.

To find out a little more about farming during the period I went over to Southwater to meet Mr Aubrey Charman. The Charman family have farmed in the village for over a hundred years and Great House Farm spans the centuries. Sitting in Aubrey's front room we talked about those days. "I left the farm early in the war to go as a Drainage Officer in Surrey, but I came back every weekend. In Surrey we dug hundreds of miles of tank traps, and in some areas erected posts in the fields to stop gliders landing, but in this area the fields are quite small, so the possibility of gliders landing was small."

"Everyone on the farm was speculating who would be "called up" – the cowman, the carter, who was going to volunteer, that sort of thing."

"We were told that because of the shipping losses to the submarines we would have to grow corn. The Government gave the orders that the South Downs had to be ploughed. The Downs, which are only 600 ft. high, were lovely and green in those days, all green sloping fields with sheep until 1942, then nearly every acre was ploughed up."

"Every farmer with over 30 acres had to grow corn whether he liked it or not. The South Downs actually grew very good corn, and in places is still ploughed ever since."

"Ploughing wasn't as easy, tractors had only just come in. This farm had 7 cart horses, and in our Sussex clay they said that you could plough one acre a day with a horse and you walked anything from 15 to 17 miles to plough an acre. If the farmer didn't have the equipment the Ministry of War Agriculture would send in a fleet of 30 tractors to do the ploughing and drill the corn".

"We didn't keep sheep in Southwater. Nobody kept sheep here because of the heavy clay soil, it tends to produce Footrot in the sheep. Corn was considered economic, more so than sheep, you could get more corn off an acre. We kept pigs; if you had one you had to sell half to the local butcher, if you had two then one had to be sold to the butcher. We killed our own – a lot of people in the village had a stye in the back garden. Mother kept chickens and sold the eggs in Horsham and we had a milk round which didn't finish until 1960. Milking was of course done mainly by hand. We had 8 chaps on the farm and they all came in to do the milking before going off to do their other jobs. There was plenty of labour. My father used to take 2 or 3 Pupils, he used to charge them £3 a week to teach them farming, they would stay here 2 or 3 years, we fed them and they had to do all the jobs around the farm, but by the time they had finished they knew how to farm. We had Land Girls as well, 2 at a time, the farmers requested them, if you lost a man you could have someone to replace him, and the only people available were Land Girls. They were very good, there were certain jobs that they could do as well as a man, they could milk, make the butter and drive a tractor, they fed the animals. They lived in, father paid them but the rate was half that of the men, There was no real problem with them, I think in total we had six, we had the usual flirting, but that's all!"

"We grew the first crop of flax for 50 years here in Southwater during the war. Father planted it; he had orders to grow it, in fact grandfather used to grow it. I came in for pulling it. You don't cut flax, you have to pull it. It has a very small root and when they get it to the factory they only nip off an inch or two off the bottom; ours went down to Five Ashes in East Sussex There they made it into linen I presume; we grew several wagon loads, a ten acre field of it!"

"Village life went on much as usual. We had the Home Guard, they used to meet in the School, my father was artful enough to "guard" the corn ricks in case they dropped any incendiary bombs. Most farmers did the same, others patrolled the village, the brickyard and the railway."

"There were few air raids on the village or damage to the farm, but about 11 one night a plane came over low and there was a terrific 'boom'.

SOUTHWATER SCENES.

Southwater School in the Thirties.

In the fields, even the children lend a hand. At one stage, flax was grown.

It had dropped one on the railway, one on Chase Farm and some more on Southwater Woods, 5 in all. The railway was closed for a while and some damage to the church."

"In those days the railway was busy, the brickyards sent for 5 or 6 loaded trucks every day."

"The cart horse finally went at the end of the war, but they worked throughout the war. When I took over the farm I sold them for £25 each."

"The pubs haven't changed, they were open through the war. The Bax Castle is the newest, it came with the railway. There was no 'real' Lord of the Manor, but the Village Fete and the flower show, the scouts all went on but we did not have any 'guides' until after the war, but the village survived. We had the Canadians around but they weren't any real bother."

Terry Briscoe arrived in the village of Rusper and thought that after London it was 'primitive', even after being bombed out in Brixton and Carshalton. Eventually Terry and the family settled down just outside of Rusper in Friday Street, near the Royal Oak Public House, where according to Terry the customers were so scarce that beer was only delivered once a year and the landlady, Mrs Mitchell would only light the fire in the winter if there were 3 or more customers in the bar!

Terry smiled when he told me that at the best of times 4 was the maximum you could get in the bar anyway!

I asked about feeding the family. All my other contacts had been involved in farming, and had access to food. Terry's dad had worked at Langhurst. "The whole of Porter's Gate, our home, half an acre was turned over to producing food, we were almost self sufficient. We had a tremendous amount of potatoes, stored in 'clamps'. You dig the potatoes up, carefully remove the soil without doing any damage to them or bruise them, pile them up in a rectangular shape so that they had four sloping sides with a flat top, and then cover the whole thing with straw and earth."

"That would store your potatoes safe, then you could open one end and take them as you wished. All the vegetables were bottled up. We kept hens and all the eggs were bottled. They were put in a special liquid which kept them soft and made the shells soft. Then when you wanted one you took it out and washed it, left it for a while to harden, then you could eat it. You could do anything with them. Rabbits were plentiful – you wouldn't believe the numbers – of course there were no gamekeepers around!"

"I went with my brothers to Rusper School, Mr Miller was The Headmaster. I got on well with him, he started my modelmaking. I remember when Mr and Mrs Cyril Hurst came to visit the School, all the boys had to bow and the girls curtsy".

Bits and Pieces

"The 'doodle bug' did more damage to the town than the farm."

Ron Francis on the Chesworth Farm VI.

"Andrew was employed for a while teaching the Canadians woodwork on a Sunday morning. They used to bring their own canteen with them. They used to send some of their food for our two children; that was the first time that we ever tasted peanut butter sandwiches."

Laura Snaddon on the Canadians.

"It was an experimental establishment, few people knew of its existence, developing flame throwers. 'FIDO' was developed at Langhurst."

Leslie Laker on Langhurst.

"Fuller's Cottage was turned into a sick bay, I remember every room filled with bright red blanketed beds."

Bob Dominy on Mannings Heath.

"I think that on most nights we were drunk; someone used to put me to bed; I would sit in the aeroplane next morning with an oxygen mask over my mouth for half an hour."

Christopher Doll, DFC on combat flying.

"Glayshers was a wonderful shop, even then you could get the unusual!"

Chris Lawrence on shopping.

"In those days we had 'nose bags' if you didn't have meals. Also a two mile Pondtail Run every Wednesday, and Saturday morning 'Detentions' if you had three 'Black Marks' in The Merit."

Ken Lane on Collyers School days.

"One Sunday, Father piled us all into the car and drove us to Kent to see what was going on, we went almost as tourists".

John Buchanan on The Battle of Britain.

"There were all these jokes about pregnant mothers who had to wear a pink label, even if they didn't look pregnant!"

John Buchanan on the evacuees.

"The feeling I have about the war is that I lost all those wonderful years as a teenager."

Tony Smith on growing up.

"Carefree days, you had the complete freedom of the forest, no game keepers, it was a paradise for children."

Terry Briscoe on living in Rusper.

"I don't think it would have happened in the way it did without the war."

Mrs C. Leighton-Porter, "Jane" of The Daily Mirror.

WHAT THE PAPER SAID: 1944.

Jan. 7th.

Local man in action against the Scharnhorst. C.P.O. R. Mansbridge and Gnnr. W. Whitington on H.M.S. Belfast. Psychiatric Clinic opened at the Hospital. "Teachers more important than buildings." Mr H.L. Flecker speaks on the Education Bill at Christ's Hospital.

Jan. 14th.

Masked gun man foiled by Woman. Hold Up at Southwater Cafe. Lorna Doone Cafe. Soldier outwitted by Mrs Matthews, Proprietor. "I want £5". 20.090 inches of rain in 1943.

Jan. 21st.

Horsham plans "Salute The Soldier" campaign. New Savings campaign to be held in June.

Jan. 28th.

Big reforms needed in rural education. NO increase in pay for Council Employees. Their job is "Part of the War Effort".

Feb. 4th.

Pioneer Apprentices sign up at Crawley. First in the Country under the new National Scheme. A Building Trade Landmark. Air Gunner at Sixty! Veteran of three wars wins D.F.C. Acting W/Co. Lionel Cohen. D.S.O., M.C., R.A.F.V.R., has been awarded D.F.C. W/Co. Cohen who is over 60 has set a magnificent example to all by his untiring energy and efforts. He has 45 Operation Flights in Coastal Command and over 500 hours to his credit. This veteran of 68 has served in three wars, lives in Slinfold.

Feb. 11th.

6am queues for Pillow Cases and Sheets!

Feb. 18th.

A.T.C. start fourth year.

Feb. 25th.

Murder charge against Canadian soldier. Alleged to have shot comrade with Sten Gun after argument over bread and cheese.

March 3rd.

Start made on Horsham Maternity Home! (At last!) "Monty" inspects troops in Horsham. Previously he had made a surprise visit to a school where he spoke to the boys. (Christ's Hospital). West Sussex Rate lowest in the country. New infants school at Victory Road. Hand Grenades stolen by boys - broke into Home Guard ammunition dump.

Mar. 10th.

Photo of Monty at the Cricket Field. Earl Winterton in the House . Question :- "Are women Crooners necessary?" "All this wailing about lost babies!". Education article. Sex training in Schools.

Mar. 17th.

Private enterprise in Post War World! Stirring talk at Rotary's 21st Anniversary. Earl Winterton speaks at Crawley - "Give the small trader a fair deal".

Mar. 24th.

"County Times Cup" for Best Allotment. Income Tax is getting popular! Inspector describes P.A.Y.E. to Rotarians. Death of Mr W.H. Weston - Worked at Horsham's Last Windmill. He worked at The Star Windmill from 1882 until it was demolished in 1895. The Star Mill was the last of four mills in Horsham. The others in order of demolition were - Comptons Brow. - Champions (Kings Rd.) - Wimblehurst Rd.

Mar. 31st.

Horsham's Rate remains at 10s. 5d in the £. Cricket Club to continue under great difficulty!

Apr. 7th.

Three Horsham babies die in fire. Hindhead Maternity Home Destroyed. "Big Scale Battle For Horsham!". Exercise combines all Civil Defence Units. Home Guard fights off "paratroops!".

Apr. 7th.

Memorial unveiled to Sir Neville Henderson, P.C, G.C.M.G. Tablet unveiled at Nuthurst Church. Sir Neville was British Ambassador to Berlin from June 1937 to the outbreak of war in 1939. Sir Neville died at his home at Sedgwick Park, Horsham.

Apr. 14th.

> Maternity Unit terms agreed with Council, but will there be Private Wards?

Apr. 21st.

> Mr A.H. Saunders elected U.D.C. Chairman. Why the water was discoloured, Southern Rail takes 20,000 gallons.

Apr 28th.

> New Mobile canteen handed over to N.F.S. The canteen was a gift from Canadian School children.

May 5th.

> New School site mooted for Horsham. Hard Labour for stealing shoes. Irishman goes back to prison, "Optimists" first three act play.

May 12th.

> Shunter's death on railway lines. Crushed by strange Brake Van. Mr Cyril Napper.

May 19th.

> Practice shells kill Home Guard. Maplehurst victim of Steyning tragedy. Two injured by shrapnel, Private Leslie Wiley killed by shells. Home Guard, 3rd Sussex Battalion parade for Drumhead Service in Horsham. Music Circle buys Grand Piano.

May 26th.

> Rural Council to think again! £100,000 needed for new Water Scheme. Full Military Honours for Private Wiley. Trains collide at Horsham Station. Passengers unhurt in overturned coach. Fresh waters for Horsham Anglers - member catches record roach.

June 2nd.

> Lord and Lady Hawke robbed. Thief chased in Country House. Residents pestered by "buzzers and biters". Warnham Road infested with mosquitos!

May 9th.

"Classrooms are training for Community Life!" "Exams are only a means to an end". P.A. Tharp. Collyers Founders Day speech. Horsham's new crest awaits a motto. "W.S.C.T" invites readers suggestions, Mr Hilaire Belloc to edit them.

June 16th.

"Tomorrow is (£$) D.DAY!". Will Horsham exceed £350,000 target? Now a race against time." "Prefabrication", the answer to Housing shortage, "The new 20th Century Science".

June   "Salute The Soldier Week."

June 16th.

"DUCKS" in Horsham Park! Amphibious Army vehicles on display in Horsham.

July 7th.

Management of Hospital at crisis point! "Detonator went off in his hand." Horsham youth loses three fingers. Engineer flies Bomber home. Sergeant G.J. Steere wins medal for gallantry. Sgt. Steere of Rusper flew his aircraft home after his pilot had been mortally wounded. "Gone with the wind" returns for a further week at the Ritz.

July 14th.

"Women victim of "Flying Bomb". Baby found unhurt among debris. 2 women killed at Barns Green. "Industry not fit for boys to enter", Mr H.L.O. Flecker, Headmaster of Christ's Hospital. Drums presented to Sea Cadets.

July 28th.

"Proudly we serve" is Horsham's motto. First V.C. was a Causeway Schoolboy! Flt. Lt. Jackson was at school, Cup to Commemorate his name.

Aug 4th.

Lammastide Broadcast from Warnham. "Light fingered "pests". Allotments robbed of their crops. Horsham F.C. Ground used for a Bank Holiday Horse Show and Gymkhana.

Aug 18th.

Soldiers from France give evidence in manslaughter charge.

Aug 25th.

M.P's house damaged by "Flying Bomb". Countess of Bessborough opens Red Cross Gift Shop. Untimely end to County Cricket match at Horsham. Northants make 207 for 8 against Sussex. The first County Cricket match south or the Thames was played on the Horsham Ground, both sides were almost full strength but rain brought an early end to the game. "Carry on" order to Home Guard.

Sept 1st.

500 compete in Home Guard Weapons meeting. Scouts on holiday hike! Two week tour of Berks. and Wiltshire. "Shooting of foxes is spoiling sport!" Post-war prospects debated at Hunt A.G.M.

Sept 8th.

Horsham may have to wait for brighter streets, modified lighting from 17th, Sept. Rotary views on Post-War Germany – "Drastic action to prevent aggression."

Sept 15th.

Horsham salutes Girl Land workers. Radio Star opens Fete and Rally, Joyce Grenfell opens fete in the Park. Sour milk , more complaints.

Sept 22nd.

Fire Watching suspended. "Cossacks" to give display at Horsham F.C. Ground. Mr. R.D. Brook appointed Professional at Mannings Heath Golf Club.

Sept 29th.

Horsham (Australia) wants Horsham settlers, 6,000 people needed. Rates 2/6d in the pound. Horsham Orchestral Society needs more players.

Oct 6th.

Horsham District had 23 Flying Bombs in a three month period. Seven women died in worst incident at Crawley.

Oct 13th.

"Maple Leaf Canteen" closes for Canadian troops. Earl Winterton pleads for the "Little Man". "Preserve land for food production".

Oct 20th.

Sir Stafford and Lady Cripps visit Horsham and Patriot Engineers. "Magnificent record of care and quality" and make over £3,000 profit.

Oct 27th.

H.U.D.C. set aside Town Planning Officer's advice and decide that Queen Street land to be sold for Timber business. Warnham Home Guards' last dinner.

Nov 3rd.

No "Cardboard boxes" for the homeless, L.C.C. Chairman speaks for the Building Trade. Home Guard "Stand Down Parade". Miss Vera Fillery chosen as Horsham's "Cover Girl" at The Ritz.

Nov 10th.

Home Guard wants Old Comrades Association. "Remembrance Day Parade" in Horsham. Parents visit Junior Technical School.

Nov 17th.

Anniversary luncheon to Earl Winterton to celebrate 40 years continuous service as M.P.

Nov 24th.

Children saved from fire by N.F.S. in Millthorpe Road. "Tank traps, Dragon Teeth" removed. "Germany has suffered enough" speaker at Horsham.

Dec 1st.

> Staff and materials hinder road repairs. Gifts needed for Christmas Fair. Sea Cadets 90 strong.

Dec 8th.

> "Home Guard Spirit must endure in peace" Col. G. Hornung's farewell to Horsham Battalion. Crowds line the streets for Stand Down Parade.

Dec 15th.

> Film Stars Richard Greene and his wife Patricia Medina judge local talent contest. Plaques presented at Horsham for "Salute the Soldier" campaign.

Dec 22nd.

> Hospital supporters raise over £3,000. Thousands flock to two day Xmas Fair. Queen Street site sold for £2,400

Dec 29th.

> Christmas at the Hospital, Drs and Staff entertain patients. "Wanton Damage" to War Department property, Police and Military appeal to Horsham public.

And so 1944 came to a close, the Home Guard had been Stood Down and the talk was of Victory. In Horsham the main topic of debate had been the new Hospital, it was nearly ready. The building trade were still trying to repair the roads and the bomb damage, but the lack of materials was an obstacle.

A Rusper man had flown his damaged aircraft home after the pilot had been wounded mortally and the Flying Bomb had been visited upon the people of Horsham, but next year the war would be over, at least in Europe.

BITS AND PIECES.

"Every day I would fly over the village and my parents' home, do a few aerobatics to let them know that I was safe but it wasn't until a friend pointed out that on the days I didn't appear my parents worried and thought that I might have been shot down."

Christopher Doll, DFC on Slinfold.

"To take any photographs or travel you had to have a Ministry of Information Pass."

Tony Smith on working on the newspaper.

"I was apprenticed at Scott and Sargents at 7/6d a week, and I remember Nellie Laughton coming in and saying "It's marvellous you boys carrying on while the men were at the Front"! I suppose we were, but I didn't see it like that! It hadn't struck me."

Tony Wales on working as an apprentice.

"The only time I put the lights out was the night Orchard Road was bombed."

Frank Holmes working in the Signal Box at Horsham.

"They asked for volunteers who could swim, so I volunteered. We went out of sight of land and then they told us that we were going to crash dive and that we would be left stranded in the water. If you see the film, we weren't acting, the look on our faces is sheer panic!

Jim Rourke on filming Western Approaches, in UNA.

COOLHAM AIRFIELD.

Very little remains today of the wartime airfield that was built at the village of Coolham. To the casual observer there is nothing to warrant a second glance, but during a few months in 1944 it rang to the sound of Spitfires and Mustang aircraft.

The story I'm sure will be covered in detail by others more qualified than I in the future, so I do not intend to cover the activities in detail.

It was built as an Advanced Landing Ground ready for the proposed invasion of 'Fortress Europe' and opened in April 1944. It was one of a number in the county, Chailey and Bognor being others.

During its short but hectic life it played host to a number of squadrons, both British and Polish.

It opened on the 1st of April, 1944, having two runways of interlocking metal strip. A good deal of tree felling took place and some buildings were demolished to get the runways in! If you take the time the line of the runways can be discerned even today.

One interesting tale tells of two pilots over France. They were attacking tanks near Cherbourg when one was hit and forced down in some marshy ground. His wing man was the C/O who then landed in a nearby farm, borrowed a Jeep, sped off and rescued his colleague. Later amazed ground staff watched as the two pilots climbed out of a very cramped Mustang!

As the war in France progressed so the need for Coolham decreased and the site was returned to its original role.

Probably the last aeroplane to use the airstrip could well have been a Liberator which made an emergency landing in January, 1945, and I believe was partly dismantled before it could be flown out.

The airfield came to life again in June of 1994, when a local policeman, Paul Hamlin, recreated for one weekend the atmosphere of this little airstrip. A memorial to those who lost their lives was unveiled and many of those who had served on the site returned and recalled those events fifty years before.

Not much remains today of this Advanced Airfield but for the curious this Pill Box is a silent reminder.

No. 49 MAINTENANCE UNIT, FAYGATE.

One of the busiest R.A.F. units in the area was not an active airfield, but a Maintenance Unit in the village of Faygate. In a field alongside the railway a huge pile of aircraft scrap was amassed, huts and a hangar sprung up, hundreds of men and women sorted, cleaned and repaired a variety of aircraft. Crews were sent out to recover aircraft both British and German which had crashed, or repair crews went out to local airfields to service and repair aircraft in service wherever possible.

Maintenance Units were often the unsung heroes, often working in dreadful conditions to recover aircraft, working literally "in the field" for long periods to get the job done. The hazards were many, some of the wrecks often contained unexploded bombs and ammunition which had to be moved with great caution. Worse still were the wrecks which had buried themselves into the ground with the crew still on board. The Maintenance crews had by their nature to be self sufficient. They became expert in living off the land and were expected to use their initiative when out on a job. The task of recovering wrecks in wet sand or high ground called for a high degree of skill and initiative.

The working day at Faygate was similar to that of a factory, in two shifts, morning and afternoon. The personnel were transported in a special train from Horsham to Faygate twice a day. It seems incredible now that the normal Air Force routine was still in operation when aircraft were in such short supply. Obviously, those involved in the collection of crashed aircraft worked a different routine from those on the site.

One of the young men who came to R.A.F. Faygate was Mr Norman Abrahams of Comptons Lane in Horsham. Norman grew up in Guildford and had never visited Horsham although many will remember that there was a direct rail link with Guildford in those days. Norman like many young men of his generation joined the RAF in the hope of becoming a pilot and due to a slight eye problem was not accepted for flying duties. After his initial disappoinment he volunteered to become an aircraft electrician. On being informed after training that he had been posted to Horsham, he assumed that it was Horsham St Faith in Norfolk!

Norman thought that Horsham of 1944 was a lovely little market town and thoroughly enjoyed his stay in the town. He remembered that Faygate was like a factory, it was just like going to work. You had a morning shift, went home for dinner and had the evening to yourself unless you were on guard duty, in which case you slept on the camp.

Norman recalled for me his days at R.A.F. Faygate, "It was split into two sections, Repair and Salvage. The Repair boys didn't get the credit they deserved, we went out each day to some airfield and did whatever was required and returned back in the evening, but the Salvage groups came back with their "Queen Marys" with great lumps of aircraft. You could see what they had done."

We travelled long distances. Our section was: an electrician, armourer, aircraft fitter and engine fitter, under a Flight Sergeant, usually the four of us. We worked at Chailey, at Shoreham, Tangmere, Lasham, Ford, Blackbushe, and we often went to Gatwick. Of course it was much different from what it is now, it was a grass airfield and had a grass runway. I went over on one occasion to service a Mustang. I never went to Coolham."

"A typical job would be the one I remember at Dunsfold. I had to do a D.I, a daily inspection on a Mitchell, check out its electrics. It was passed O.K. and then it had to go on an air test. I went up in it, but did not wear a headset. The noise was terrible, absolutely terrible. I thought the sheet skinning was going to come off and that we would be left with just the airframe! In those days after you had done your inspection it was possible to get in quite a bit of flying experience, if it was a twin engined aircraft or a two seater. If you wanted there was plenty of opportunity to fly."

"I think we worked a five and a half day week, and then you had to do guard duties, in which case you slept on the camp. When I was there in 1944, they provided a train. You caught the train in the morning, came back to Horsham for lunch and then went back on the train, twice a day. It was run just like a factory. There was a little NAAFI provided, but no facilities for eating. I stayed in 3 "billets" in Horsham. The first was in Oakhill Road, then in Lime Avenue and the third in which I stayed longest was in Bostock Avenue with a Mrs Richardson.

It may sound strange to the younger generation today, but we had to be in our billets by 11 each evening. You couldn't stay out all night, the landladies made sure that you were back each evening. There had to be some sort of camp discipline and the billets were inspected from time to time. The only time that I was on a "Charge" was when the billet was inspected and I had left some radio spares on my bedside table.

I spent my 21st birthday with Mrs Richardson, and she kindly made me a cake. I was rather upset when in a recent newspaper article about the Forces in Horsham during the war, the R.AF. were not mentioned, just the Canadians and the Poles etc.

But what is forgotten is that the people of Horsham gave so much to the Royal Air Force, they really did us proud. We were so much a part of the life of the town, not to be mentioned I think was so wrong!"

"I spent a couple of months in the M.T. Section, and there I met the rather shady side of the camp. They were producing all sorts of bits and pieces, electric fires out of landing lamps, table mats out of Bakelite, the Chippies Shop and the Metal Bashers seemed to be able to provide you with what you wanted; there was no real check on it. I seem to remember that there was great activity spraying private cars at odd times. I don't know the full extent of it, but there was an awful lot of it seemed to be going on! Even clothing would disappear and then reappear on some young lady in Horsham. Of course I had little to do with all this" said Norman with a smile!

"We had a very successful concert party, which gave performances all over the district: Base Hospital, childrens' parties; I played accordion, it provided a lot of entertainment and was popular."

"They were quite happy times. I met my future wife while I was at Faygate. I eventually brought my bike over from Guildford and used to cycle to Faygate. It wasn't far from Roffey, a nice ride on a sunny day, a bit of fresh air. The discipline on the camp was good, but easy going,. It was self discipline really, although we had a Flight Sergeant Chambers in charge of that side, very aggressive, he would pick on you – we all kept out of his way."

"The camp closed down very quickly after V.E. Day, we were cleared out very quickly. It was very abrupt and there were piles of scrap, great piles of aircraft on top of each other. Sometimes you thought that they would not be able to get any more in, but they did. There were British and German aircraft piled high and towards the end of the war bits of flying bombs and the remains of the V2 Rockets."

"If you go today they still have the large hangar where they used to wire up Spitfire wings, the M.T.Section, Sick Bay and the N.A.A.F.I., but there is little sign of the great piles of scrap and aircraft. Now it is a wood yard".

Faygate.

49 M.U. FAYGATE in 1992

Mr. Norman Abraham remembers: still the same gates which he drove through on his way to service aircraft on various Sussex landing grounds.

Faygate today. A timber yard: once this area was piled high with aircraft wreckage; a few of the old buildings remain.

A SLINFOLD STORY.

Whilst I was researching into the Spitfire story I came across a picture of a young pilot sitting in a Spitfire in a book which I had purchased in the sixties . The caption said," Flt Lt. J.C.S. Doll of Horsham sitting in Bexley's Spitfire".

I did my homework and tracked down Christopher Doll, still at that time living in the village. His story was fascinating, he had flown for most of his operational career from the airfields in Sussex! Tangmere, Westhampnett and Merston. His mother organised a Hurricane Fund, perhaps the only one of it's kind anywhere. He flew on the Dieppe Raid, which was one of the busiest days of air fighting ever recorded, and finished the war as a Squadron Leader with a D.F.C. to his name.

Photo: Imperial War Museum

During the course of conversation Christopher remembered that he had a habit of coming back over Slinfold in his Hurricane sweeping in over the garden of his parents' house dipping his wings before returning to the airfield. On one occasion he was talking to some friends in the village and they suggested that perhaps it was not a good idea, because on the days that he didn't fly over his parents were very concerned, lest he had been shot down. He said that it had never occurred to him, but he did not continue the practice. We talked generally of those days in wartime Sussex. He seemed to think that on most nights he was mostly drunk and that quite often someone put him to bed, and that next morning they used to sit in their cockpits for half an hour with their oxygen masks over their faces!

AIR GUNNER AT SIXTY.

Photo: Imperial War Museum

VETERAN OF THREE WARS WINS THE D.F.C.
COUNTRY HOME AT SLINFOLD.

Acting Wing Commander Lionel Cohen, D.S.O. M.C. R.A.F.V.R., a veteran of three wars who has been awarded the D.F.C. for "gallantry and devotion to duty in air operations" has a country home at Clapgate Cottages, Slinfold.

Since 1940 Acting W/C Cohen who was born in 1875 has been an air liaison officer to the Royal Navy and has taken an active part in Coastal Command operations. This was how the County Times recorded the events on Friday, February 4th, 1944.

It went on to tell how the Wing Commander had made some 45 operational flights totalling over 500 hours with Coastal Command, including the attacks on the Scharnhorst and the Gneisenau when they were lying at Brest in 1941. This veteran of 68 has behind him a military career of outstanding achievement.

In 1893 he served as a trooper in Matabeleland and during the Boer War was attached to the Portugese field intelligence. In February 1917 he was commissioned with the South African Light Horse and employed in intelligence. On February 1st, 1917 he was awarded the M.C. and in 1918, 1919, 1920, 1941 and 1943 he was mentioned in despathes. He won the D.S.O. in July 1918.

He was born in Newcastle on Tyne, was married with two daughters, both serving officers in the Forces.

"COVER GIRL": HORSHAM'S "COVER GIRL" CHOSEN.
500 QUEUE TO SEE HORSHAM'S COVER GIRL.
MISS FILLARY CHOSEN AT THE RITZ.

With every seat in the theatre filled over five hundred people queued outside the Ritz Cinema on Friday evening when Miss Vera Fillary of 36, Park Street was chosen as Horsham's "Cover Girl."

The majority of those waiting outside did not see the judging but they were nearly all admitted to see the film. Hundreds more, seeing the great crowd turned away without attempting to obtain seats. It was the biggest crowd Horsham had seen for a long time and was just like a "first night" at a West End theatre. The management received eighty three entries and the total number of votes placed in the ballot box was 2,566.

The winners, chosen by four Canadian soldiers in hospital blue judged by the volume of applause from the audience, were: 1, Miss Fillary; 2, Miss M.R. Richards; 3, Miss P. Burton. The other three contestants were Mrs M.Lawrence, Miss B. Miles and Miss M. Collinson.

From The County Times report of November 1944.)

Vera recalled for me that it was all over very quickly. Each contestant was interviewed on stage by Mr Macdonald the Manager. They were asked about hobbies and interests and as her prize she was given a large box of Max Factor Makeup. The following week a similar contest took place at Crawley.

The contestants after the competition pose for the County Times photographer. On the extreme right front row is Miss M.R. Richards, centre Vera Fillary and on the left Miss P. Burton. The four young men at the rear are Canadian soldiers from The Base Hospital.

"COVER GIRL"

Each contestant was asked to submit a photograph and from these six finalists were selected. The above photograph was the one that Vera had specially taken by E.W. Copnall of Horsham and submitted for the competition.

"THE DIARY OF A BRIGHT YOUNG THING",
or how a strip cartoon helped to win the War.

NEXT WEEK. Grand Variety Attraction

JANE COMES TO TOWN
featuring

JANE

The Original Model for the
DAILY MIRROR CARTOON
A Strip Round the World. ☆ Twelve Months of the Year

MACEY & MAYNE	TREVOR	ED ROYALE
Clean Crazy	MORETON	Singing Cartoonist
Del Monico Dancers	Welsh Comedian	Little Fritzi

RINGLE BROTHERS and RENE
Fun in a Restaurant

DUMP HARRIS	JOE	Always Jo-King
and STAN England's reply to Laurel & Hardy	KING	

Box Office open daily 10-0 till 7-0. You can book for this Attraction during the Interval

Commencing Boxing Day, December 26th. 2-0 Twice Daily 7-30
MR. and MRS. WILFRED SIMPSON
present their Annual Spectacular Christmas Pantomime

"RED RIDING HOOD"

PRICES OF ADMISSION (including Tax)

ORCHESTRA STALLS and DRESS CIRCLE **7/6** PIT STALLS **5/6** UPPER CIRCLE **4/-** BALCONY **2/6**

SEATS IN BOXES **7/6** Each. One Box holds Six ● Half-Price for CHILDREN under 12 at MATINEES ONLY Except Saturdays and Boxing Day (Excluding Balcony)

Booking Office now open for Postal Bookings Only. All applications will be taken in strict rotation, Please enclose Stamped Addressed Envelope otherwise Tickets will be Retained at Box Office to Await Collection, and in order to Save Delay Kindly Quote Alternative Dates.
The Booking Office will be open for Personal Applications from Monday, December 10th.
The Management regrets that Seats can no longer be booked by Telephone.

ALL SEATS BOOKABLE. ALL CHILDREN MUST BE PAID FOR
YOUR GREATEST GIFT TO THE CHILDREN IS A VISIT TO THE PANTOMIME
DON'T DISAPPOINT THEM !

HORSHAM'S OWN PIN-UP:
"Jane" of the Daily Mirror.

Although I have tried hard to ignore the stories outside Horsham and District, there are one or two which it would be foolish to ignore completely. Slinfold provided two such stories of interest which I felt I had to cover, for who could ignore the impact of the daily happenings of the strip cartoon character Jane in the Daily Mirror, not only on Horsham, but in the nation as a whole?

*Model and artist at work,
photographed in Norman Pett's studio at Crawley.*

"Jane" and the Daily Mirror.

I can't remember exactly when it was, but at some period in the war, my father had started reading The Mirror. He was a great fan of some of the cartoon characters and always said that his favourite was "Just Jake". Being only a young lad still at junior school, of course I believed him! When a few years later I became a young apprentice, I became aware that my workmates became quite excited when a certain young lady came to the Palace Theatre. I was quite surprised when these normally well behaved men produced photographs which they had taken surreptitiously of the young lady they had been to see with their wives! It only dawned on me later that the reason my father took The Mirror, and the reason for all the excitement amongst my workmates, was this young lady!

I think we are all now well aware of the effect the cartoon strip had on the Nation and the troops during the war, but I'm sure my father never for one moment considered that there was a real lady behind the cartoon. What would those former workmates in Grimsby say if they had known that some years later it would be the young apprentice who would be privileged to interview the lady who created such excitement.

I thought for quite some time about the questions I should ask her. It had all been said before on the radio, press and the television, so I thought that I ought to ask the same of her as I had of the others that I had seen.

So the first question that I asked "JANE", or Mrs Leighton-Porter, when I visited her in her home in Horsham was "What were you doing the day war broke out?"

"Actually, I was with my sister in Wimbledon. We were tied to the radio listening to what was going to happen, and I had a very vivid imagination, and I imagined the minute war was declared that gas bombs were going to fall on us. My sister, who was married, wasn't very much better either! We had another sister who lived near Devizes, so I gave her a ring and asked what should we do? She said that we should all go to her. My sister in Wimbledon had a little car so we piled into it for the journey. There was my sister, and her little girl, her husband and a man who was going to drive us over, a Red Setter, which had just produced 11 pups and myself in this little car, and to make matters worse my sister was pregnant!"

"The top of the car was piled high with everything you could think of, there was extra bedding, clothes we were just like refugees! That was on the Sunday. It was crowded on the roads, there was a mass exodus from London, it was nose to tail all the way down."

"When we got down to Devizes it was heaven, you wouldn't know there was a war on. Fortunately they had land and some stables so we were able to put the animals into the stables. We hadn't been down there long and my sister began to pine for London. There had only been a few false alarms, so after about six weeks she went back. I stayed a little longer, then I went back, but life in the country was lovely."

"The war didn't take me by surprise; for a while everything stopped but gradually life got back to some sort of normality.

"As far as I was concerned I was terrified, I didn't think for one minute that we would live for more than 2 or 3 days. I was panic stricken. Nobody knew what was going to happen – we could have had everything thrown at us that first day, we didn't know."

"I only knew what I had heard and read. We had been given our Ration Books and our Gas Masks. You didn't go anywhere without them at all. It is amazing, that after that I didn't give it a thought at all, it became mundane very quickly. In the end I think we took it all in our stride. You can't believe that, can you!"

"I think the war caught up with me really when I used to get used to being cold. Because of the lack of heating and now and again the electricity would be cut off, we didn't have much coal not unless someone was ill, then you got a certificate to allow you extra. Food was poor. I think the war really caught up with me when the raids started."

"I don't know how it was, but the Germans seemed to time it. My sister would be trying to get a meal on about 5.30 to 6pm - and as soon as she got it on, the raids would start, and by then we had a shelter in the garden, but by now I wasn't scared. I was the one that went backwards and forwards from the shelter to the house, making tea and coffee, but we did have some heavy raids in Wimbledon."

"Actually, my modelling started in Wimbledon. When I lived at Eastleigh, one of my sisters used to go to the Art School in Southampton and I used to model for her, and I had been to the Art School and modelled, but only head and shoulders, portraits and costumes. When I went up to my sisters in London I had come straight from school. Actually I should have gone to school in Wimbledon, but I didn't."

"I decided myself, that I ought to get a job. I didn't know quite what to do, so I thought I would look for some work in the Art Schools. So I went up myself to The Slade School of Art and asked if I could see the Life Master and asked if he wanted a model? Well they leapt on me because normally the models they got were big and old. They did have some lovely models, they do need all types, but to get someone who was pretty fit meant that I could do awkward poses and not many of them could stand for eight hours. It was an eight hour stint in those days. From the Slade I was put onto Chelsea Art School, St Martins and Westminster and worked in most of the Art Schools. It was while I was at The Slade that I was asked if I would go up to the Birmingham Central School of Art, to pose for an examination class. It was there that I met Norman Pett."

"Originally, Mary his wife had been his model, for a little cartoon called "Jane, or The Diary of a Bright Young Thing". The Mirror liked it and it was in once a week and then because it was popular every day. Norman had left his job at Birmingham because he was so busy but he came in one day to see the new man and I was on the Modelling Rostrum and he saw me and said "That's Jane". He came over and asked me if I would model for him? At first I was a little apprehensive. When you do that job you do get all sorts of suggestions and offers. When I did start his wife used to come over and collect me, so everything was fine."

"I stopped the Art School modelling and came back to London and it wasn't long before Christmas. I didn't want to be travelling up and down to Birmingham and decided I would like to do some dancing. There was a dancing school in Wimbledon and I went along and joined, I had of course done some dancing as a child. Funnily, this dancing school was run by a lady from Horsham; later she came back and ran a big dancing school here.

"Anyway, I went to her, had a few lessons and she said to me, "There's a Pantomime on, would you like me to put you forward for the Corps

The Author's Choice

There are hundreds of photographs of "Jane" to choose from and everyone has a favourite.

These two are mine; I make no apologies: I just like them!

de Ballet? It didn't mean that I had to be a ballet dancer, that was just the name that they gave to the chorus in the pantomime".

"I went up for the audition and got in, and for the next three days I went to rehearsal, doing the usual chorus things. I was in the ballet in the very back row of Cinderella."

"I don't know how it happened but I opened the Daily Mirror the next morning, there it was a full page spread "Perfect, and just right for Pantomime!" It went on, our "Jane" is in pantomime at Wimbledon, and there were all these bathing costume pictures which Norman Pett had let them have. I was called in next day by the Mulhollands who owned the Theatre, and they told me they could not now let me be just a dancer, because I was going to attract so much attention and that all the theatrical agents would be coming round, and people would be bound to come round to see me. They had to give me a part in the Pantomime; it was specially written in for me, and I was taken out of the Chorus Room".

"I behaved myself in the pantomime. I was out of my depth; even the chorus girls were sophisticated and beautifully dressed and of course knew their way around. At the end of the run, everyone got cards and flowers, and on mine was written "To Britain's Perfect Girl with perfect manners! The reason was that I had won a contest at the London Palladium called "Britain's Perfect Girl", and my mother was so pleased with the card, because it reflected on the way she had brought me up, that she kept it and had it framed!" I was in the Panto and at the weekend modelled for Norman.

"It was a period of great austerity, clothes were difficult to find, so was make-up. Everyone in the theatre had to give a list of their tour and you could claim extra coupons. If you were a stand-up comedian you could only claim for a suit and a pair of shoes, but you got extra. I got extra material; I would get so many coupons for 30 yards of material to make a crinoline dress; also I had four sisters who used to let me have theirs, and like my mother would go without to let me have coupons. Second-hand clothes were not on coupons. My first 4 or 5 Finale Dresses were made from second hand material and almost everyone used blackout material, and sewed sequins on it – times were tough!"

"Strangely, I never had a contract with The Daily Mirror. I worked for Norman Pett and he paid me, but I had a letter from The Daily Mirror giving me permission to use their publicity and the title "Jane of The Daily Mirror" for myself and the shows. I had to be careful and not do anything that would bring any adverse publicity on the paper or myself. Apart from the Pantomime my family didn't know much about my work. I would have liked to have been a Fashion Model but I was not tall enough, but I did model swimsuits for Jaeger. I spent the wartime in the theatre or modelling; because I was in a show, I had to be "on call" for E.N.S.A., but they never called me; I was a bit disappointed, I suppose they thought the show was a bit too naughty to show to the boys! Everything had to be passed by The Censor and the Lord Chamberlain's Office, then each town had its Watch Committee and all of them had different ideas!"

"It changed my life, because I became the character. A lot of the stories were based on incidents which had happened to me. I never uncovered purposely, always by accident! The first time Jane appeared in the nude, it was suggested that because it was a drawing it was O.K. In the cartoon I was having a bath with a screen round me and of course the screen gets knocked over, and there I was full frontal!"

"Arthur and I did get married during the war, but because I belonged to "the Boys" it was hushed up. We kept it quiet."

"There was a period when Norman was not meeting his deadlines and he was told that they would take the strip out if he couldn't improve. He did for a while but then slipped back, so it was taken out. The outcry was so big that they had to bring it back."

"I never appeared in Horsham; the only time I came I kicked a ball into the scrum at Crawley Rugby Club. I appeared in Brighton, I did a film in Brighton as well. I appeared in Portsmouth, Aldershot, Reading, but the people of Horsham never saw the show."

I asked Jane about the period when she had to make the transition from modelling in costume to being a nude life model, and had it been difficult?

"It was when I was up in Birmingham, I stayed on as Norman's model. The transition from head and shoulders to life model wasn't easy, no it wasn't! I remember my first nude in the Art School, I'd seen drawings of the other girls and nobody took any notice of them at all. It was difficult for the first ten minutes, that's all. they were so intent on what they were drawing, they didn't seem to notice me at all. They were so intent on what they were doing that nobody bothered whether I was nude or whether I wasn't. I might just as well have been a flower vase and very quickly I didn't take any notice of it whatsoever. I think that if I had not been in the theatre and only a model I would have certainly been "called up" for some sort of work, factory or land, and would have to have done my modelling at the weekends. I don't think I would have been excused."

WHAT THE PAPER SAID: 1945.

Jan. 5th.

100 children at N.F.S. party. Dr. E.C. Bradford retires after 24 years' service. A week of skids and slides after severe frosts.

Jan. 12th.

Earl Winterton remains as Horsham M.P. Horsham and Worthing Constituency to become Horsham, Shoreham and Southwick Constituency. Snow causes skids, many spills on roads and pavements.

Jan. 19th.

Exhibition of plans and models of new Council Houses. "Plough Sunday" revived.

Jan. 26th.

Crawley Bomb Damage. 1,100 houses affected since last June.

Feb. 2nd.

Coldest spell for many years, Horsham has 19 degrees of frost! Coal delivered by Taxi!

Feb. 9th.

Horsham British Legion opposes admission of Home Guard. Fewer cases of drunkenness this year. Thanks for sports gear from crew of H.M.S. UNA. Miss E. Bachmann wins Horsham "Bathing Beauty" contest.

Feb. 16th.

Boy shoots brother, "Serious accident with rabbit gun."

Feb. 23rd.

£5,000 cheque handed to Hospital Chairman. NO Artificial Insemination Centre for Horsham.

March 2nd.

Red Tape and Control holding up housing progress.

March 9th.

> Ten Wards in new Maternity Unit.

March 16th.

> How will Horsham celebrate Victory? Will Council be caught napping?

March 23rd.

> Cricket Club's good position after 6 years of war. Museum will get more support.

March 30th.

> Conservatives form new Association.

April 6th. Home Guards form Old Comrades Association. W.I Market has good year. Fewer visitors for Easter this year, but trains and buses are crowded.

April 13th.

> Council has no "V.Day" plans!

April 20th.

> Council will not sponsor "V. Day" Celebrations. Councillors opposed to "Jollifications and Festivities' First baby born in new Maternity Unit, a boy!

April 27th.

> Horsham men home from Germany, freed after years of captivity. Part - Time Firemen Stood Down".

May 4th.

> Council calls for water economy. Council's V.E. Day arrangements. Public buildings to be floodlit.

MAY 11th Edition 1945.

> Horsham celebrates end of war in Europe. Rejoicing crowds pour into floodlit Carfax. Victory Beacons lit in the villages. Victory Bells ring out!!!!! "Astoria Band" play in the Carfax. Park Service of Thanksgiving. "Dragon" has been slain but prayers for peace must continue.

Amongst all this was the news that L/Cpl Hodges of Stanley Street had been reported killed in action on The Western Front.

May 18th.

"Victory Parade" and V.E. parties for the children.

So in May 1945, the war came to an end in Europe. Horsham had survived. It had been bombed, machined gunned, its men and women had fought, died and suffered not only at home but in all the theatres of war. Not all the stories are told. The paper had been at the mercy of the censor so the stories had to be "tailored" for home consumption. I have read all the copies that are available and my overall impression is of how life seemed to go on as normally as possible. I was surprised by the amount of crime that took place in the town, mostly petty crime, but we did have a number of nasty murders and killings. Today they would have made the headlines on the television. My only complaint is that photographs of the period do not seem to have survived, likewise the Police Incident Records. Thank goodness the A.R.P. Logs survived!

Horsham, The Birth Rate.

Having spent some time looking at those who lost their lives, I thought it would be remiss of me not to look at the other side of the coin, how many births took place during those eventful years. The Office of Population Censuses and Surveys very kindly provided me with the following statistics relating to Live births for those years.

	HORSHAM URBAN DISTRICT.	HORSHAM RURAL DISTRICT.
1939.	202.	320.
1940.	208.	309.
1941.	225.	364.
1942.	256.	368.
1943.	280.	413.
1944.	305.	422.
1945.	248.	362.

Whether anything can be read into these figures, I'm not sure. I will leave that to other people. There was a slight increase each year, but to me there didn't seem to be a very dramatic increase, even when the Canadians were in the area!

THE BATTLE HONOURS.

A great many local men and women were decorated for their efforts and heroism during the period and perhaps someone may possibly try to compile such a list at some future date. I have scanned the papers and made a few notes but not in any kind of order.

Just a few that I have come across include:-

Captain Robert St Vincent Sherbrooke DSO, won the Victoria Cross in 1942 in a naval action round the tip of Norway, on those convoys to Russia. It was stated that the family lived at Strood Park, Broadbridge Heath.

We did have in our midst a young man who is commemorated on the Roll of Honour for The Battle of Britain. Flying Officer J.B.W. Humpherson won the DFC during the battle, but was later tragically killed.

Others who won the DFC, included Mr Algy Fry, flying Wellington bombers early in the war, John King of King and Barnes, John Lane from another well known local family, 'Nanny' White the George Medal for her efforts at Colgate. Gilbert Steere from Rusper the Conspicuous Gallantry Medal and perhaps belatedly for his efforts the B.E.M to Stan Parsons!

THE A.R.P. REPORTS.

The Incidents which are recorded in the County A.R.P. Control Officers' Minute Books, which are held at the West Sussex Records Office at Chichester, make fascinating reading and were a wonderful source of reference for me. Without the help of the County Archivist and the Staff and Mr Alan Readman in particular, I would not have been able to compile such detail. It is unfortunate from my point that the records do not start until September 9th, 1940. This is itself quite interesting, because it was one of the busiest days of the war in the Horsham area.

I have compiled a few of the entries that were made in 1940, to show the amount of activity that was taking place and which the reader might find of interest. I have omitted some of the incidents which can be found elsewhere in the book such as Orchard Road.

Let's start on September 9th, 1940.

9th. Sept.

> Spitfire down. West Grinstead. 18.57. Pilot O.K. Me.109 at Cootham. 18.41. Pilot P.O.W. Me.109 down at Roman Gate, Slinfold. 19.45. Pilot baled out. Enemy Bomber down at Nuthurst, Horsham. 19.45. 2 Germans wounded, 2 unhurt. Wounded taken to Horsham Base Hospital. Spitfire down at Loxwood. 19.55. Plane a complete wreck.

19/20 Sept.

> Shelley Farm, Lower Beeding. 3 H.E's dropped. No cas. No damage. 00.10.

20/21 Sept.

> H.E bomb craters at Smoke House Farm, Shipley.

21 Sept.

> Horsham Control report 3 bombs dropped at 11.32 at Adversane. Horsham Control report road still blocked at Shipley. UXBs' Chivers Farm, Brooks Green 18.59. 1 bomb.

23 Sept.

> Incendiary bombs east of Rusper House, Rusper. No damage. About 100 bombs.

25/26 Sept.

> Herons Copse, Coolhurst. 130 Incendiary bombs. 00.45. Kerves Lane. UXB. search abandoned. St Hugh's Charterhouse, Cowfold. 2 H.E. craters. 1 UXB. No casualties. Building destroyed, valuable library buried and another library endangered, living quarters evacuated. H.E. bombs damaged cloisters on South side.

26/27 Sept.

Lower Beeding. 16 H.E. bombs. 00.02. Damage to water main and telephone wires. 28 Sept. UXB at Bashurst, West Chiltington Lane. Itchingfield. 'Red Alert' 10.06 to 10.55.

29 Sept.

Slinfold. Dean Farm. 4 Petrol Incendiary bombs at 01.21. '459 Battery' at Broadbridge Heath reported UXB's. Bourne Hill, Horsham. Two H.E. bombs. Some damage to windows and ceilings. 12.43. Faygate, Rusper Road. 23.59. 2 H.E. bomb craters in fields.

30 Sept.

Lower Beeding. H.E. bombs in field at Prongers Corner. Some cottages damaged. 1 SHEEP KILLED. (P/c Joe Lemm's account!)

1 Oct.

Chennells Brook, Horsham. 4 H.E. bombs. 22.51. Little Haven Crossing. 23.53. 3 H.E. bombs. Damage to bungalow. Henfield. Hurricane crashed at 14.55.

2 Oct.

Hammer Hill, Plummers Plain. 1 H.E 01.55.

3 Oct.

Horsham. Stanley Street Laundry. Inc. bombs. 04.00. 4 Oct.

Mannings Heath, Hawkins Pond. 2 H.E's 2 Oil at 15.50. 6 Oct. Horsham, railway crossing in Worthing Road.Train wrecked, line blocked. 05.40.

11 Oct.

Bombs at Sedgwick Park, craters at Southwater. 4 H.E's at Southwater at 21.30. Line blocked.

13 Oct.

Horsham, line opened, service resumed.

18 Oct.

Lower Beeding. 2 H.E and 1 Oil bomb at 14.32. Slight damage to 2 cottages. Shipley. 6 H.E's and 2 Oil bombs. No cas. damage. Cowfold. 2 H.E's at 23.00. No cas. "GAS ALERT".

22 Oct.

Shipley. 2 H.E's. Lower Beeding. 2 H.E's at 23.15 on 21st!

26 Oct.

Southwater. 1 H.E at 20.35. No cas. Railway line blocked.

27 Oct.

Lower Beeding. 2 H.E's bombs at 04.20 today. No cas. Slight damage to 7 dwelling houses, Convent and farm buildings.

29 Oct.

B.B.Heath. 3 bombs (H.E.) in fields. Some damage.

31 Oct.

Mannings Heath. 2 H.E's at 20.50. No damage or cas.

The town had 'lived' through The Battle of Britain, but for many months the raids went on. Bombs were dropped in November at Slinfold, Coolhurst, Warnham, at Warnham Brickyard, eleven were dropped at Farthings Hill in Horsham and of course Orchard Road was attacked.

WE SHALL REMEMBER THEM ... EVENTUALLY!!!

It came as quite a surprise to many people when it was realised that those who fell in The Second World War were not commemorated on the Horsham War Memorial. Under the guiding hand of Mrs Jean Goodyear the names have been steadily collected and have now fifty years later been inscribed alongside those who fell in 1914/18. The list below does not include the men and women from the villages.

Adams-Acton. M.	Heath. T.J.	Richards. J.D.
Archer. C.W.	Haynes. A.E.R.	Rose. D.H.
Ansell. D.	Harris. R.T	Richardson. C.R.
Ansell. D.R.	Hodges. C.	Rudkin. P.A.J.
Bailey. R.F.G.	Hyde. L.	Richardson. C.S.M.
Burgess. W.F.	Holder. J.	Rowlands. D.M.
Baker. S.W.	Hewett. G.H.	Routledge. F.
Bone. A.V.	Horne. C.B.	Saunders. R.S.

Barnes. C.F.
Burchell. F.T.G.
Boyce. P.A.W.
Church. R.
Clark. A.
Cox. C.E.R.
Champion. K.W.
Codd. P.W.
Corydon. J.
Charman. F.R.
Dawson. C.H.
Dale. R.
Dade. F.W.
Denyer. R.G.
Daubney. R.P.
Drinkwater. H.
Dinnage. H.E.
Durrant. A.B.
Denham. C.C.
Dinnage .C.E.
Dennis. F.
Davies. N.G.
Dinnage, A.J.
Erridge R.M.
Fradley. W.
Francis. C.F.
Garman. L.
Greary. L.
Garman. J.H.
Grice. W.H.
Gardner. D.D
Griffiths. W.
Hampshire. C.F.W.
Hamilton. E.A.

Humpherson. J.B.W.
(DFC)
Jones. H.
Jupp. W,S.
Knight. F.H.
Kefford. L.W.J.
Kenward. C.
Kirkby. C.G.
Lawrence. D.R.
Leadbeater. C.E.
Lee. J.F.
Lowe. H. (DFC)
Lawson.
Laker. W.J.
Lloyd. V.W.
Luxford. L.
Lipscomb. C.A.
May. F.V.
Mitchell. C.F.M.
Musgrave. R.S.
Nightingale. D.A.J.
Newcombe. S.S.
Nickolay. G.
Ogg. E.C.
Olley. H.
Overington. C.
Pugh. C.E.B.
(M.B.E.)
Peach. L.J.
Pearson. W.C.R.
Peel. D. (D.F.C.)
Philcox. E.C.

Roberts. S.

Simmons. K.
Shore. J.
Smith. H.A.F.
Stanford. E.A.
Samuels. P.W.
Smith. J.M.
Standing. R.C.
Steer. A.M.
Scott. J.
Terry. K.V.F.
Thomas. J.C.
Turk. H.G.
J.M.Taylor. J.W.J.
Tugwell. A.E.
Thompson. E.
Ward. A.R.
Winch. F.
Whitehead. G.
Wilson. F.H.
Wholey. P.
Waters. R.S.
Woolven. R.H.

The above names were those on the list kindly given to me by Jean Goodyear on January 12th, 1993. It is possible that other names may well be added at a later date.

The people of Horsham raised a sum of money which in 1991 had reached £26,600 with interest, but it had not been spent. It had originally been intended to provide a Memorial Hall, but not enough money had been raised for the project.

ACKNOWLEDGEMENTS.

This is the section that I have found most difficult to write. How can you possibly say thank you and acknowledge almost an entire community without offending someone? During the time I have been researching the material wherever I have gone in and around the town, clubs, pubs, schools, shops, in the street people have told me stories or passed on material to me. To everyone I have to say thank you and if I have inadvertently forgotten anyone, I do apologise. To all those who invited me into their homes and gave me interviews or loaned me photographs my sincere thanks.

Where to start, perhaps with the organisations who so kindly gave me so much help and encouragement.

West Sussex Record Office and Staff.
West Sussex Library Service and Staff especially the Durrington and Horsham Libraries and Staff.
Horsham Museum and Curator.
Horsham Rotary Club.
Mannings Heath Golf Club.
Imperial War Museum. Lambeth.
The Royal Air Force Museum. Hendon.
The Submarine Museum. Gosport.
The Tank Museum. Bovington.
Tangmere Aviation Museum. Tangmere.
Yorkshire Air Museum. Elvington, York.
Ministry of Defence, Air Historical Branch. London.
Commonwealth War Graves Commission.

611 Squadron Association.

Royal Air Force Careers Service.

Brighton. Army Recruiting Office, Horsham.

Submariners Old Comrades Association.

West Sussex County Times, Editor and Staff, Horsham.

B.B.C. Radio Sussex. Brighton.

Radio Mercury. Crawley.

Royal Air Force Association, Horsham.

Apertures, Photographers, Arundel, (Copying originals)

The Royal British Legion. Horsham.

Office of Population and Censuses, London.

The Registrar, Hills' Cemetery, Horsham.

The Royal Observer Corps, Horsham.

Forest Community School and Staff.

Headmasters at Warnham, Colgate and Oxford Road Schools for the loan of Log Books and material. Oxford Road is now Clarence Road Infants. (Head teachers')

Thomas Keatings. Billingshurst.

Former Lintotts' employees.

King and Barnes Brewery, Horsham.

The Daily Mirror. London.

C.I.B.A. Horsham, now C.I.B.A. Geigy.

Agates, Timber Yard, Faygate.

Horsham Society.

Wigan Leisure Dpt. and Wigan Observer.

77 Squadron Association.

Librarian, Solihull Metropolitan Libraries and Arts Dept.

Battle of Britain Fighter Association.

The Mass Observation Unit, Brighton University.

AND WE ALL HAD A PARTY!

One of the everlasting memories for me are those street parties that were organised. Someone had one almost every day, or so it seemed. Looking back we must have had one for V.E. Day and another for V.J Day. The one above was attended by Marion Charman as she is now, and is quite typical of those that I attended. One other memory: it never seemed to rain!

RECORDS TAKEN BY THE MASS OBSERVATION UNIT.

Another source of local information is held by The Mass Observation Unit now housed at Brighton University.

This unit was set up to look at the social attitudes of the nation and kept information collected from diaries and questionnaires. It was set up before the war, but was in operation throughout the period.

I was surprised and delighted to discover that they held a number of items collected from Horsham and district inhabitants, so arranged a visit to read them.

There are two distinct types of material, the diaries and a Directive. The latter was a set of questions on a variety of subjects, and these were answered and returned. One question in 1940 was, "When did you last check your Gas Mask?" A sensible enough question, but another was "Have your dreams changed?"

They were asked how the war had affected their everyday life, and particularly during The Blitz, the sleeping habits?

One local returnee commented that they now slept downstairs and that they had placed mattresses around the walls, also before they went to bed each evening they filled the bath with water and had two buckets alongside, in case of an incendiary attack.

One question enquired about the use of radio. One answered that they now only used it for news broadcasts, they just listened between seven and nine in the evening.

Some of those questioned had been moved from other areas into the town, and found that apart from overcrowding in their offices, life had gone on as far as was possible.

The arrival of the evacuees was noted. One comment was "That Cockney language seems to be on every street corner".

These questionnaires where sent out each month, but not all were answered by the same people monthly, so they are rather haphazard, but nevertheless make interesting reading!

KEEP MUM.

Yes I know, it was a well worn wartime saying but we did our best not to spread rumour and gossip. But what did the Germans know about us?

I was intrigued when John Buchanan related the problems with the wartime censorship rules and only being allowed to take 'non-war' type pictures, so only flower shows and social events mainly featured.

As John said "We didn't know in Southwater what was going on in Mannings Heath. People were remarkably good at not talking and kept quiet. Even the most innocent photographs were withheld by the censor's office for fear that they could assist the enemy.

By chance a colleague at Forest had a copy of a wartime German Army Gazetteer covering all of Great Britain, so what did the German soldier know about Horsham in 1941?

According to the gazetteer Horsham had a population of 13,600 – quite close! It was a country town, with a railway station. It was an old town south of London. It was 32 kilometres south of 'Lewers', not spelt Lewes! 'Mit ein Lateinschule' a Grammar School. They knew about Collyers because of the exchanges which Andrew Henderson had been organising. It had a Hospital, but they didn't know about The Base Hospital. An Electricity Works, under 130kvs output. Cereal crops and poultry were produced. We had an ironmongers and a saddlers. The town had, according to the report 3 garages and a brickworks. That was the extent of the coverage in a booklet entitled:

MILITARGEOGRAPHISCHE ANGABEN UBER ENGLAND.

HOTELS AND PUBLIC HOUSES.

I mentioned earlier that there seemed to be a greater choice of public houses than we now enjoy, and of course beer was cheaper, but perhaps stronger! I wouldn't know of course being under age. A "Shandy Gaff" at Christmas was my only alcoholic drink allowed by my father. Let's have a look then at the choice, although many people have quite correctly named them all, I took the opportunity to browse through The Kelly's Directory of 1939/40.

HOTELS:

Bedford, in Station Road, Mrs E.F. Webber.

Black Horse, in West Street.

Bridge House, in East Street, Mr A. Barker.

Carfax, in The Carfax, Mr R.S. Ansell.

Chase, E.J. (private), London Road.

Crown Inn in The Carfax, Mr J.M. Kennedy.

Dog and Bacon, North Parade, Mr C.T. Boulting.

Green Acres, North Parade, Mr H.E.G. Dawson.

Heathfield in Hurst Road, Miss M.J. Matthews.

Nelson, Trafalgar Road, Mr R.T. Roots.

Park Temperance, Park Street, Mrs. C.E.J. Henrey.

Station in North Street, Mr G.A. Harley.

Swan in West Street (now Swan Walk), Mr S.H. Walker.

Ye Olde Kings Head Hotel in The Carfax.

PUBLIC HOUSES.:

Alexander, Queens St., Mr E.T. Powell.

Anchor, East St., Mr A.E. Potter.

Bear Inn, Market Sq., Mr E. Blunden.

Foresters Arms, St Leonards Rd. Mr T.V. Lacey.

Fountain Inn, Rusper Road. Mr W.C. Seymour.

Fox and Hounds, Worthing Rd. Mr T.W. Edwards.

Gardeners Arms, New St. Mr A. Inkpen.

Green Dragon, Bishopric. Mr J. Lovegrove.

Hornbrook Inn, Brighton Rd. Mr C. Green.

Horse and Groom, East St. Mr A. Turnbull.

Hurst Arms, North St. Mr A.Bryce.

Kings Arms, Bishopric. Mr J. Scott.

Lamb Inn, Carfax. Mr G. Napper.

Michell Arms, Springfield Rd. Mr A. Downs.

Prince of Wales Tavern, West St. Mr H.B. Sunderland.

Queens Head, Queen St. Mr F. May.

Rising Sun, Pondtail Lane, Mr J. Pearce.

St Leonards Hotel, Brighton Rd, Mr C.G. Season.

Star Inn, Crawley Rd, Miss E. Bailey.

Stout House, Carfax, Mr A. Grinsted.

Tanners Arms, Brighton Rd, Mr H. Pannell.

White Hart Inn, North Parade. Mr M. Parrott.

White Horse, Crawley Rd, Mr W.C. Scott.

It goes without saying that the village pubs we know today were all involved throughout the wartime period, The Dun Horse entertaining the Canadians. Both Southwater pubs were open, the Norfolk Arms being then considered outside the district!

King and Barnes were obviously brewing, but sugar became a problem , the premises being machine gunned on at least one occasion.

THE TOWN DOESN'T SMELL THE SAME.

I remember them well!! Just a little list of memory joggers.

In the Carfax.

Camplins. Phelps. Hedges. (Estate Agents!) Days. (fried fish) Wickershams. Chart & Lawrence. Coole & Haddock. G.P.O. Horstmanns. Freemans. Trevor Cale. Buddens. Durrants. The Milk Bar. Oldershaws. The Carfax Cake Shop. W S Parsons. Pages. Streetes. Westminster Bank.

West Street

Hunt Bros. Jury Cramp. Camplins. Boots. Midland Bank. Lloyds Bank. Boots. Wakefields. Foster Bros. Lanes. Dewhursts. Humphreys. Dolcis. David Greigs. Hepworths. International Stores. Home and Colonial, Walkers Stores. Lovibonds (wines). Dixeys. Singer Sewing Machines, Co-Op. Currys. Apedailes. Stephens. Tylers (wines). Dolands. Lakers. Josephs. Goughs. lyles. Hawkins. Jacksons. Jupps. Woolworths. Maypole. Alberys. Farleys. Quicks. Sayers. Liptons. Hulls. Burtons the butchers. Lewis. Chart and Lawrence. Timothy Whites.

East Street

Freeman, Hardy and Willis. Trelfers. Pearces. Blackistons. Ellmans. Scott and Sargents. Agates, Starks. Sweetapple. Y.M.C.A. Horsham Gas Co.

South Street

Evershed and Cripps. Red Lion Bookshop. Churchmans. Atteees (hairdressers).

Middle Street.

Tanner and Chart. Dendys. Elliotts. Glayshers. Lee (tailor)

Queen Street

Haffendens. Parkers. Horlocks. Knights (oil merchants). Fabians (Confectioners). Edwards. Sayers. Baker. Wheelers.

I'm sure you could add to the list, but these are a few taken at random. I hope that they bring back a few memories or perhaps stir up a little curiosity.

The end of the story? I doubt it!

Although I have collected a great deal of information on the wartime story, it is still 'living history' for many of the Horsham people and many may well read the book and say why didn't he mention so and so?

I have to confess that there were a number of areas where I would have liked some help, with photographs in particular, but not those taken by 'official photographers' but like those from Tony Wales by the average person in the street. Pictures that lurk away in family photo albums, of parties, soldiers, the street parties after the war. There were areas that I would have liked to cover in more detail, work at Lintotts Foundry and King and Barnes brewery spring to mind, the brickyards. I spent many hours searching the town for signs of old air raid shelters, we had them at Oxford Road for years. We kept the furniture in them, but there aren't many of them left.

Did the young German airmen get a Military Funeral? Is there still a copy of the film of the Patriot Engineers in existence; if so where? It would be nice to show it to the Rotary Club.

Chatting to John Elphick he produced a sheet out of the West Sussex County Times dated January 1st, 1943, and in a summary of the year's events, right at the bottom a small item caught my eye. It read, 'In view of the outstanding effort made during the "Tanks for Attack" campaign two tanks were allocated to the district". Tanks – I knew about the Spitfire and H.M.S. Una, but tanks?

So I duly wrote to The Tank Museum at Bovington. I had a letter in reply. It appears that they did not know much about the Tanks for Attack campaign, but they were able to tell me that Guildford had a tank named after the town/city. It does appear that tanks were named after towns, so the question is who can tell me where our two served. It has been suggested that The Guards' Museum may be able to help. Just one of the open ended questions left.

Another which has bothered me for some time concerns the young Horsham "Spitfire" Pilot from 611 Squadron. Despite numerous letters and appeals I have not yet found any of his relatives or his Obituary. I am still not able 50 years after his death to be given any details about his service career or his home and family.

Did Benson's Fair run through the war in the Durrants market in the Carfax, some people think it did? Did someone hit Sir Oswald Mosley on the head with a beer bottle in 1938 outside The Drill Hall?

I could go on and on, there are so many stories which are unanswered and I'm sure that in the fullness of time some of them may get answered, whether by me or someone else is of little consequence! It isn't my story, it is the story of the people of a little market town who through no fault of their own were thrust into the forefront of action and activity for 6 years and came through not unscathed, but unbowed! As Una Penny said you can't force them "They won't be druv!" I wonder if that ever dawned on those who were going to invade?

Back to Normal!

Horsham Football Club: October 13th, 1945
Resplendent in their green and gold strip, the team pose for the camera, both old and new players.
BACK ROW: D. Holden; P. Wilkins; M. Cope; G. Power; F. Carter; F. Nichols.
FRONT ROW: F. Alderton; J. Dixon; F. Meyer; R. Myerscoffe; T. Rook; Trainer G. Worcester.
The football enthusiasts in Horsham will note that the stand opposite the pavilion had not yet been built.
Unfortunately Horsham lost 4-2 to Eastbourne on this occasion.

"Der Englanders – you are being watched!"

This is an enlarged section of an aerial photograph taken over the Horsham area by the Luftwaffe on Thursday 15th August at 4.30 in the afternoon. The original shows an area from Capel in the north to Southwater and Mannings Heath across to Rudgwick. On this day the Luftwaffe lost 75 aircraft and it became known as 'Black Thursday'.

THE INDIVIDUALS.

The debt that I owe to individuals throughout this research is quite enormous, below I have listed many who have given their time and sat through interviews and have loaned me photographs. To those whom I may have omitted my sincere apologies. The omissions are not intentional.

Mr W.S. Parsons. B.E.M., Mr F. Holmes. JP., Mr & Mrs G. Menezes, Mr & Mrs J. Scrase, Mr & Mrs P. Spriggs, Mr & Mrs K. Lane, Mr & Mrs D. Gill, Mr & Mrs D. Bateman, Mr J. Christian, Mr & Mrs J, Buchanan, Mr R. Dominy, Mr T. Smith, Mrs G. Blye, Mr T. Jupp, Mr & Mrs R. Woolven, Mr & Mrs R. Taylor, Mr K. Parfitt, Mr G. Coomber, Mr G. Newberry, Mr A. Willson, Mr J. Lemm, Mr & Mrs A. Merritt, Mr T. Briscoe, Mr & Mrs R. Heseltine, Mr K. Reeves, Mrs U. Penny, Mr & Mrs N. Abrahams, Mr & Mrs L. Laker, Mr & Mrs W. Sampson, Mr J. Sampson, Mr J. Elphick, Mrs J. Evans, Mr & Mrs M. Payne, Mr & Mrs T. Wales, Mr P. Cox, Mr K. Nethercote-Bryant, Mr T. Perrin, Mr A. Charman, Mrs D. Compton, Mr P. Wilkins, Mr A. V. Murrell, Mr P. Lansberry, Mr C.J.S. Doll, DFC., Mr C. Lawrence, Mr C. Brown, Mr T. Holt, Mr John King. DFC, Mr Jim King, Mr T. Potter, Mr & Mrs P. Baxter, Mr A. Readman, Dr. F. Newby, OBE, Mr J. Fadden, Mr D. Vallance, Mr D. Childs, Mr J. Rourke, Mr J. Reeves, Mrs J. Boone, Group Captain Sir Leonard Cheshire, VC, Mr S. Weller, Mr & Mrs A. Leighton Porter, Mrs P. Chanter. Mr H. Champion, Mrs A. Harwood, Mr S. Bird, Mr P. Hamlin, Mr H. Day, Mr T. Hardy, Mr A. Saunders, Mrs L. Snaddon, Mrs E.D. Vincent, Mr S. Parry, Herr Marc Dahloff, Mr T.P. Belton, Mr Max Bygraves, Mrs H. Rose, Mrs S. Reynolds, Mr J. White, Mr J. Trott, Mr R. Childs, Mr Tom Greenhough, Mr T. Waters. Mr G. Head, Mrs V. Thompson, Mrs M. Bowyer, Mrs B. Lampard. Mr & Mrs Ted Tester, Mr B. Dendy, Mrs M. Charman, Mr & Mrs J. Goodyear, Mr E. Wilson, Mr D. Parker, Mr B. Barratt, Mrs S. Elphick.

I would also like to express my sincere and grateful thanks to my dear friend, colleague and former Deputy Headmaster at Forest Community School in Horsham, Mr. R.E.F. (Bob) James for his patience in reading and correcting the manuscript.

THE PHOTOGRAPHS.

Many of the photographs have come from private sources and I would like to express my sincere thanks to all those who have loaned photographs to me. To the following I would like to express my thanks in particular. Every effort has been made to obtain any copyright that may exist and every effort has been made to establish copyright. Some may be from agencies that no longer exist, and the publication of any picture for which clearance has not been given is unintentional.

The sources:-

Mr Stan Parsons, BEM, Mr K. Parfitt, Mr & Mrs J. Buchanan, Mr J. Scrase, Mr & Mrs R. Taylor, Mr. T. Greenhough, Mrs E. Farley, Mrs E.D. Vincent, Mr T. Wales, Mr J. Trott, Mr. A. Woolven, Mr & Mrs R. Woolven, Mr P. Wilkins, Mr & Mrs W. Sampson, Mr J. Elphick, Mr G. Head, Mr. S. Weller, Mrs M. Bowyer, Mrs B. Lampard. Dr. R. Wylde, Mr J. White, Mr K. Harris. Mrs N. Gill. Mrs B. Payne, Mrs. H. Rose, Mr A. Saunders, Mr B. Dendy, The Late Mr C. Lawrence, Mr F. Holmes JP, Mr D. Parker, Mr R. Childs, Mr G. Ritchie (Canada), Mr J. Leigh, DFC, Mr K. Nethercote Bryant, Mr J. Lemm, Mr & Mrs D. Bateman, Mr R. Heseltine, Mr J. Boone, Mrs V. Thompson, Mrs C. Leighton Porter, Mrs M. Charman.

To the Imperial War Museum for allowing me to use a number of photographs, which are available from the Museum.

H.M.S. Una. Returning from the Mediterranean, flying the 'skull and crossbones' (A 15489)

Wing Commander Lionel Cohen, DSO, MC. (CH 19522)

Flight Lieutenant J.C.S. Doll of Horsham on named aircraft "Bexley". (CH 5885)

Members of No. 35 Squadron, R.A.F. 1941 (CH 6373)